THE RENAISSANCE

J. H. Plumb

HORIZON • NEW WORD CITY

Published by New Word City, Inc.

For more information about New Word City, visit our Web site at NewWordCity.com

Copyright © 2016 by American Heritage Publishing.
All rights reserved.

American Heritage Publishing
Edwin S. Grosvenor, President
P.O. Box 1488
Rockville, MD 20851

American Heritage and the eagle logo are registered trademarks of American Heritage Publishing, and used pursuant to a license agreement.

No part of this book may be reproduced, stored in a retrieval system, or transmitted in any form or by any means, electronic, mechanical, photocopying, recording, scanning, or otherwise except as permitted under Section 107 or 108 of the 1976 United States Copyright Act, without the prior written permission of American Heritage Publishing.

Requests for permission should be addressed to the Permissions Department, American Heritage Publishing, Box 1488, Rockville, MD 20849 (email: licenses@americanheritage.com).

Permission for certain uses of this book can also be obtained at Copyright.com, or by mail or phone to Copyright Clearance Center, 222 Rosewood Drive, Danvers, MA 01923, (978) 750-8400.

INTRODUCTION 5
1
THE DAWN OF THE RENAISSANCE 11
PROFILE: PETRARCH 29
2
THE PRINCE AND THE STATE 51
PROFILE: MACHIAVELLI 73
3
THE ARTS 95
PROFILE: YOUNG MICHELANGELO 117
4
FLORENCE CRADLE OF HUMANISM 139
PROFILE: LORENZO DE' MEDICI 159
5
MILAN CITY OF STRIFE 185
PROFILE: LEONARDO DA VINCI 209
6
ROME SPLENDOR AND THE PAPACY 233
PROFILE: POPE PIUS II 255
7
VENICE THE GOLDEN YEARS 283
PROFILE: THE DOGE OF VENICE 305
PROFILE: FEDERIGO DA MONTEFELTRO 329
PROFILE: BEATRICE AND ISABELLA D'ESTE 353
8
THE SPREAD OF THE RENAISSANCE 379

INTRODUCTION

We have a habit of wanting to know where we have been and what we have done. This is our way of assessing the present and reassuring ourselves about the future, for we are heir to our past – and, just possibly, history may repeat itself. There are few ages that make us as proud of our humanity as the one called the Renaissance.

Curiously, scholars don't agree what the Renaissance was or when it took place. Some historians date the Renaissance from the twelfth or thirteenth centuries, while others say the Middle Ages lasted until the seventeenth; others argue that the Renaissance began with the fall of Constantinople in 1453 or with the introduction of the Gutenberg press in 1451. As for what it was – some call it the birth of modernity, others a rebirth of interest in the classics, still others an emancipation from darkness, a transition from medieval to modern times, or simply an era of unsurpassed creativity. There are even those who claim it did not happen at all.

This last opinion is, of course, an exaggeration. So many novel forces and ideas came to life in Western Europe in the fifteenth and sixteenth centuries – and so many old forms and thoughts were abandoned - that it is impossible not to view these years as a period of spiritual revolution. Before 1400, no one thought of building a permanent theater and staging a secular play in it; by 1600, theaters were springing up in cities everywhere, and accomplished playwrights were writing dramas for them. Before 1400, few artists would have dared paint a picture of a naked woman; by 1500, Sandro Botticelli had not only painted one of the most beautiful nudes in the world, but she represented Venus, a pagan deity. In 1350, no one in Western Europe could read a page of Greek; by 1500, thousands were studying the Greek classics, lost for a millennium. During the Middle Ages, Aristotle was considered the ultimate authority in many fields of thought; in 1536, Petrus Ramus took his doctorate with the daring thesis, "Everything said by Aristotle is wrong." Changes as potent as these influenced almost every area of intellectual and social life, and many felt they were living in a world born anew.

Yet, if the word Renaissance has any widely accepting meaning, it indicates a time of artistic achievement that conjures the names Michelangelo and Leonardo da Vinci, Raphael and Botticelli, Donatello, Titian, and Benvenuto Cellini and images of their magnificent works of art. Renaissance painting and sculpture, music, architecture, literature; fabrics, metalwork, jewelry, and furniture – all came impressively to life.

In the nineteenth century, Jacob Burckhardt proclaimed that the Renaissance was nothing short of the discovery of the world and of humankind itself, and his view of the period as a unique, self-generating epoch held for decades. Since that time, scholars have demonstrated that the Renaissance did not explode into the world full-blown, out of some medieval desert. Instead, the beginnings of ideas and institutions had taken root and developed through the centuries. The appreciation of arts and letters and the understanding of their relation to life – known as humanism - existed during the Middle Ages; a body of literature had been recognized since classical times. The Renaissance was just part of a continuing, ever-widening stream.

What made this an extraordinary century and a half in Italy was a coincidence of genius and circumstance. The times in which men and women are born affect how they use their talents and energies. For arts to develop fully, there must be patrons willing to use their wealth to induce artists to create. It is not enough for genius or creativity simply to exist; they need care and nurturing.

By 1400, the foundation of the Italian Renaissance had been laid. There was burgeoning trade and industry, new wealth for individuals and cities, and increased political freedom and energy throughout the land. The prevailing mood was one of change and improvement; old moral restraints and medieval dogmas were crumbling, and in their place was a zeal for building on the classics of ancient Greece and Rome to create a better civilization. And finally, there was rivalry: between cities, merchant princes, artists, all vying to do better than anyone else. It was the wealthiest and most menacing age Europe had ever known; Italy possessed the greatest concentration of gifted individuals that the Western world had seen for 1,000 years, and the conjunction of men and the times produced an explosion of energy.

Although the Renaissance was not exclusively Italian, it began there and developed there, and nowhere else was the scale so large, nor the roots so wide or deep. The Italians were pioneers on a frontier which would be explored by Dutch, English, French, Spanish, and other Europeans during the sixteenth and seventeenth centuries. They opened the windows on a new world that we have been exploring ever since.

1
THE DAWN OF THE RENAISSANCE

The face of medieval Europe was scarred with the ruins of its past. In Rome, the Colosseum housed the barbarous Frangipani family and their greedy, lawless, destructive retainers; the Forum provided rough pasture for the cattle market, and beneath the broken columns of the temple of Castor and Pollux, young bulls awaited slaughter. The countryside was littered with the ruins of aqueducts; the pavements of once splendid Roman roads were encroached by the returning wilderness. Elsewhere, scraps of walls, the ruins of the arena, temples, and triumphal arches constantly reminded citizens of the fleeting and erratic nature of life. The past was dead, and its crumbling relics were a warning.

The wealth wrung from the soil and the tenuous trade of those dark centuries was poured into splendid churches that soared to heaven in violation of the harmony of ancient art. From them grew towering fortresses and walled cities necessary in a society where the clang of armor was as common as the church bell.

Yet the relics miraculously survived the ravages of violence. The barbarian hordes had swept away the thin veneer of Roman culture and broken the powerful web of trade, law, and government that had bound the Mediterranean world together. This breach was widened by the surge of Islam, which swept across not only Northern Africa, Sicily, and Sardinia, but also the peninsula of Spain, and onto the plains of France. Under the hammer blows of Vikings, Europe and its culture had nearly bled to death. Yet, even in the worst of times, groups of peasants spread through the wastes and forests, colonizing vast tracts of Europe the Romans had dominated but never occupied.

Their lives were controlled by warriors who protected them and grew wealthy on their labors, or by priests and monks who controlled their existence and taught them that life was as fleeting as the crops they harvested. People of this isolated world lived simple, primitive lives in which pestilence, famine, and war marked the passage of time.

Yet the past was never quite destroyed, nor was

the structure of society ever utterly broken. Trade with Byzantium brought some wealth and new ideas but also lured warriors to battle. The wars of the Muslim world called to the knights of Europe, offering them riches in life or glory in death.

This society of peasant, priest, and warrior drew its strength from individuals rather than from nations and was held together by the Catholic Church and feudal law. The secular ideal was of an ordered, unchangeable society, full of obligations and rights fixed by law. The majority of men accepted the rarely attained social ideal of religious life: worship of God and contemplation of the spirit to overcome desires of the flesh. Churches were everywhere, but frequently they served mundane purposes as most found it sufficient to atone for their sins only in their old age or defeat. Those who genuinely sought the ideal in the most ascetic monasteries were still compelled to draw, paint, and sing for the glory of God.

Even in the darkest decades, trade was an integral part of primitive life, drawing together Christian, Muslim, and Jew. Trade fattened towns and sometimes bred them. The personalities of kings and popes could lead to strong government or to social anarchy; peace and good harvests could bring rapid prosperity or war; disease and famine could destroy that prosperity for a generation or more. At times, it seemed Europe would rise to a higher level of civility; at others that it would descend into barbarism. In the eleventh century, towns, trade, and craftsmanship grew rapidly, along with an interest in ancient learning, particularly in Aristotle. The success of the Crusades promised new power and prosperity, but the prospect faded and disaster followed. Western Christians savaged the Byzantine Empire; the Muslim world revived under the powerful leadership of the Ottoman Turks; the Black Death reduced Europe's population by at least a third. Instead of a rebirth, a new death seemed Europe's prospect. Yet, in the middle of the fourteenth century, forces were working in the economy and the spirit of Italy that would change life throughout the Western world.

During the Middle Ages, Italy never belonged wholly to Europe. The Romans had created an urban life that neither Goth nor Lombard nor Saracen ever totally destroyed. Feudalism was planted in Italy but never rooted deeply there. Gothic art never dominated the Italian imagination. Despite waves of invasion, when it seemed that Italian society might be destroyed or transformed, Italy was never a breeding ground for warriors. War weakened Italy, emptied her towns, diminished her trade, and enfeebled all institutions save the Church of Rome, which was endowed with some of the authority, if little of the strength, of the Caesars, but there was always trade and urban life.

Venice had been laying the foundations of its future greatness for centuries by exploiting Italy's advantage as the natural trade link between the primitive world of the North and the sophisticated East. Its most valuable trade was probably men, women, and children, who were shipped to the slave markets in Alexandria. Paid in coin, the Venetians then bought luxuries - silks, silver, and papyrus. And Venice was not the only mercantile community among Italian cities. Ships from Amalfi, Genoa, and Pisa ventured to the eastern Mediterranean as well, carrying pilgrims to the Holy Land, trading with the Greeks, Jews, or Muslims, and creating a web of commerce. But progress was neither steady nor constant. Pirates infested the seas, war was endemic, and risks, like profits, were huge.

Trade, however, was not the only catalyst at work in Italy and medieval Europe. Armed knights were not cheap; the courts of kings did not tolerate poverty, and though princes of the Church might preach self-denial, they rarely practiced it. As war became more technical, it also became more costly, and strong kingdoms required strong finances. As the network of churches and monasteries honeycombed Europe, the wealth and expenses of the Church became vaster. The result was that merchants, finding themselves in fresh and lush pastures, became financiers. As with trade, the seeding ground for the rest of Europe was Italy. The great banking street of London was, and still is, called Lombard Street after the Italian moneylenders who settled there in the thirteenth century. Of course, this high finance of popes, emperors, and kings could be as dangerous as trade. The Venetians rarely made any loans to a prince - the risk was too great and default too common. But in the handling of taxes, loans for war, and purchased rights of justice, families amassed fortunes. By the High Middle Ages – the eleventh to thirteenth centuries - the structure of international finance was as advanced as that of the ancient world, making Italian life more complex and secular.

The burgeoning trade and finance rested primarily on the growth of Europe's population. Britain, Gaul, and Germany absorbed generations of men and women struggling to conquer the forests, the marshes, and the wastelands, and few were spared from the toil of the land except through prayer or war. Italy's thick peasant population possessed remarkable powers of recuperation from famine, pestilence, and war. Wealth and commerce aided their growth, and the old walled Roman cities gave them protection. Cities, not states or kings or princes, dominated the land. The sole exception was the Pope, whose superiority in the hierarchy of Western power was universally acknowledged. The popes intended to protect the Patrimony of St. Peter and prevent any secular ruler from dominating Italy. To achieve this aim, they often called on the warriors of France - an ominous precedent for the future. To check the Pope's territorial ambitions, some cities occasionally asked for military help from the Holy Roman Emperor, to whom they owed a certain allegiance, but more often than not, the powers and rights of the Holy Roman Empire were ignored. The emperors claimed universal secular authority just as the popes claimed universal spiritual power, but in practice, the emperors' strength was based on the lands they possessed in Germany, their estates in Italy, and a vast, ill-defined collection of rents, dues, and legal powers over the cities and states of Italy, the Netherlands, and parts of Burgundy. Any threat to the riches of Italy brought the imperial armies across the Alps. Invasion and war, desperate and bloody, threaded the history of Italy for a millennium, making her poets and philosophers dream of freedom, of unity, of peace. No great power ever succeeded for long, and the absence of national law or secular jurisdiction, bred an openness to political experimentation in Italy toward the end of the fourteenth century.

Trade, high finance, a large and partially urbanized population, quickening industry, the absence of a powerful political structure - all factored into the dawn of the new age. There also were less measurable forces needed to change the whole of Italy. In the Middle Ages, ideas traveled along the lines of trade, and even in the most barbarous times, cultivated Italians never forgot the great traditions of their past or achievements in literature. Throughout the Middle Ages, the classics had been copied, studied, and enjoyed. Monks appreciated Horace as well as Seneca, and even Ovid was not unknown to the cloister. There were high points of excitement and discovery. The recovery of many of Aristotle's works from Arab sources in the twelfth and early thirteenth centuries created an intellectual ferment in scholastic circles. As secular life grew more stable and complex, Justinian law was thoroughly researched, and long before the Renaissance, Roman ideas of law, order, and government permeated Italian city life. This complex society idealized individuals of intellectual stature and literary gifts. Saint Thomas Aquinas had provided a philosophic argument for dogma that was to dominate for centuries. Dante, the Florentine, produced the first great poem in Italian - a poem that is medieval in spirit but modern in technique - and Petrarch showed that Dante's achievement was not likely to remain unique.

Europe during the Middle Ages was not a closed world. The Crusades had ripped open the Near East and given hordes of warriors a taste of sophisticated, cultured society. Italy was the door through which the Crusaders passed. Marco Polo had reached China, and links had been made with the long-lost Nestorian Christians of India and China. At one time, it seemed as if the Great Khan himself might turn Christian and link Europe with the East. The glimpse of the wider world proved brief - the Khan remained a Buddhist, the Chinese threw off Mongol control, and Ottomans swept the Christian powers out of Asia Minor and threatened Italy itself – yet this ebb and flow of European power interlocked the Christian and Muslim worlds. At the Sicilian court of Frederick II, it was an Arab who taught geography and presented the Emperor with a silver sphere on which the map of the world was drawn. Indeed, the Renaissance itself seemed at hand. Frederick, ruthless, amoral, violent, a realist in politics as in philosophy, might have been an uncle of Cesare Borgia. Although he was the Holy Roman Emperor, possessing vast lands beyond the Alps, the core of Frederick s strength and power lay in his kingdom of Sicily, which contained most of southern Italy as well as the island itself. Here he introduced laws based on Justinian's code, fostered city life, and favored the bourgeoisie. He patronized the arts and encouraged literature, poetry, science; kept an astrologer; dabbled in alchemy; brought together a menagerie of rare animals and an exotic collection of mistresses. The delight of his court in literature and in philosophic inquiry, the efficiency of his administration, the energy of his diplomacy, and above all the openness of his mind to all ideas, whether Muslim, Christian, or pagan, struck a rare chord in thirteenth-century Europe. Yet surrounding him was still an air of barbarism, a lack of sophistication, even of experience, that made his world closer to that of Charlemagne or Otto I than that of Lorenzo de' Medici or Ludovico Sforza.

By the time of Lorenzo and Ludovico, Italy had fundamentally changed, and this change is rightly called the Renaissance. In Rome, broad streets had been driven through the chaotic ancient slums that crouched amid the rubbish. A new city had arisen around the Vatican, and the plans for the Basilica of St. Peter were taking shape. The palaces of the cardinals proclaimed the tastes and the sophistications of this new age in Rome as well as Florence. Great towers had been razed, and in their place stood the opulent homes of the Strozzi, Medici, Rucellai, and other patrician families. These houses were designed according to the classical harmonies that the great architect of the Renaissance – Filippo Brunelleschi - had made fashionable. Out in the Tuscan countryside, the first villas of modern times rivaled those of Augustan Rome. Historians, concerned with origins and remote influences, stress how interlocked the Renaissance was with the medieval world, but the creative strength and originality of fifteenth-century Italy, which stretched far beyond architecture, cannot be underestimated. In sculpture and painting, the change was more profound. In both these arts there had been precursors - Giotto, the famed Florentine painter,

Duccio di Buoninsegna, the Sienese, and Andrea Pisano, the sculptor - and the break with the past was neither as sharp nor as vivid as in building. The achievement, however, was far greater. For the next four centuries, the themes, traditions, techniques, and preoccupations of the artists of fifteenth-century Italy dominated Western Europe. Their names - Fra Angelico, Giovanni Bellini, Botticelli, Donatello, Lorenzo Ghiberti, Leonardo da Vinci, Filippo Lippi, Andrea Mantegna, Michelangelo, Antonio del Pollaiuolo, Luca Signorelli, and Andrea del Verrocchio speak for themselves: A constellation of artistic genius, spread over a mere century and a half, would alone make the Renaissance a great epoch of human achievement.

Art was only one aspect of Renaissance Italy, which created a vision of human excellence that still lies at the heart of Western tradition. The Italians, particularly the Florentines, revered antiquity - its wisdom, grace, philosophy, and literature. Yet such knowledge had largely been part of the private world of scholars. At the time of the Renaissance, these humanistic studies spread through the upper and middle ranks of society and became part of the education of those who would wield power and authority. The timely invention of the printing press not only made the classics readily available to hundreds of thousands of men and women, it also helped to create a public for their study. What had been private became public, and familiarity with the classics became the hallmark of civility. A man might still be a warrior, a priest, or a merchant, but if he wished to be regarded as the complete man, l'uomo universal, he needed to be well-bred. The Italians of the Renaissance insisted on a refinement of taste, an ease of manner, combined with a capacity for manly pursuits, a knowledge of the classics, an acquaintance with history and philosophy, an appreciation of music, painting, architecture, and sculpture, and a connoisseurship of the rare and the beautiful, whether they be books, jewels, coins, or scraps of antiquity.

To acquire, let alone indulge, such sophisticated tastes required money, for education in so many disciplines and interests took time, and no one could patronize the arts without wealth. As patronage grew competitive, the arts became more costly. Renaissance society was designed for rich men, rich cities, and rich popes. To maintain such a costly pastime required an active and profitable commerce; to indulge it a concentration of expensive talent was necessary. Italian cities possessed both. Florence, Milan, Rome, and Venice were full of exceedingly rich men, and money, the base of all Renaissance achievement, nurtured genius. The transmutation of gold into works of art was the result of the marriage between aristocratic extravagance and bourgeois ambition. The aristocrats of medieval Europe did not vanish overnight; they lived on, maintaining their sense of separateness toward which wealthy merchants could direct their social ambition. The patricians of Florence, Milan, or Venice might be merchants, but they wished to live like nobles. In Italy of the Renaissance, aristocratic and bourgeois attitudes fused to create a pattern of life, a social expression adopted by societies of the West as the riches of the New World and the Indies poured into their cities. Commercial capitalism, struggling in the framework of feudalism, learned, through Italy, to express itself and make an art of life.

The great Italian achievements, in almost every sphere of intellectual and artistic activity, took place in a world of violence and war. Cities were torn by feud and vendetta. Alliances were forged and broken, the countryside was scarred by pillage, rapine, and battle, and in this maelstrom, the old bonds of society were transformed. After a brief period of peace in the second half of the fifteenth century, the confusion and carnage grew worse through the French invasions of Charles VIII, Louis XII, and Francis I, a time of agony that did not end until the sack of Rome in 1527 by the Holy Roman Emperor, Charles V. This violence influenced the way Italians regarded problems of power and government for hundreds of years. They ceased to look for answers in the dogmas of the Church and instead searched antiquity for precedents that might guide them to the truth. They sought to explain, as Niccolò Machiavelli did, the world in which they lived by what they knew to be the nature of human beings. Many came to feel that truth was elusive, a mood strengthened by the discovery of the world beyond Europe. The old dogmatic certainties did not vanish at once, and the habit of trying to nail truth down by argument from fundamental principles was not lightly cast aside. Some of the most original minds, however, particularly Machiavelli and Leonardo da Vinci, sought truth not in argument but in observation. Machiavelli brooded on people and events, on political action and the consequence of chance; Leonardo was preoccupied with the flow of water, the flight of birds, the formation of rocks. People of the Renaissance, through their fresh skepticism, and keen observation, promoted the search for truth on earth instead of in heaven.

Artistic expression, intellectual inquiry, social standing - the Renaissance enriched all these things. Its influence spread throughout Europe and continued for centuries. Hundreds of gifted individuals and a score of remarkable cities all made their contributions. Although each had its artists, philosophers, poets, and craftsmen, the full force of the Renaissance flowed most strongly from four cities - Florence, Milan, Rome, and Venice. Florence, a small city by modern standards, produced an astonishing array of genius which Rome and Milan, both far richer than Florence, patronized. The full tide of the Renaissance reached Venice late, but it lingered there longer, even as the Reformation broke Europe asunder. Neither Reformation nor Counter Reformation, nor the economic decline of Italy, brought on by the discovery of the New World, could check the spread of the Renaissance.

Profile: PETRARCH

Morris Bishop

"I was born to this world," says Petrarch, "in the Via dell' Orto of the city of Arezzo, just at dawn on Monday, July 20, in the thirteen hundred and fourth year of this latest age which takes its name from Jesus Christ, fountain and author of all my hope." The house of his birth still stands at the town's top, across from the cathedral.

He was christened Francesco Petracco, a slightly inelegant name which he Latinized to Petrarca, which we have Anglicized to Petrarch.

He was an Aretine only by circumstance. His father, Ser Petracco, was an attorney in Florence, living on the edge of poverty. In the revolution of 1302, he was banished, together with Dante and many others, and took refuge in Arezzo, some sixty miles away. But as Arezzo gave a chilly welcome to plotting Florentine exiles, Ser Petracco had to seek his fortune elsewhere. His wife, Eletta, and their baby were permitted to return to the family house in Incisa, on Florentine territory.

In 1307, Francesco's brother Gherardo was born, and in 1310 or 1311, the family reunited for a year in Pisa, and there, or possibly in Genoa, Ser Petracco was visited by his old friend and fellow exile Dante. By this time, Ser Petracco found a post in the papal court, which had moved from Rome to Avignon, and in 1312, his wife and sons joined him.

Avignon, a small town in southern France, had some 5,000 inhabitants, and the arrival of the papal court caused major changes. Cardinals' trains were quartered in citizens' homes; petitioners and office seekers camped in the streets, on the walls, and in cemeteries. Signora Petracco and the boys found lodgings in Carpentras, fifteen miles away, and there they spent four happy years. Writing years later to Guido Sette, a schoolmate and lifelong friend, Petrarch remembered the joy, security, peace, freedom, and silence he enjoyed in Carpentras. He recalled how the boys talked all night on the eternal subjects. He remembered also that while his companions were studying their Latin, "I was noting down the substance of thought - the pettiness of this life, its brevity, haste, tumbling course, its hidden cheats, time's irrecoverability, the flower of life soon wasted, the fugitive beauty of a blooming face, the flight of youth, the trickeries of age, the wrinkles, illnesses, sadness, and pain, and the implacable cruelty of indomitable death."

One day, his father came to Carpentras with Guido Sette's uncle. Despite Signora Petracco's fears, they visited the famous Fontaine de Vaucluse, fourteen miles away. Francesco was enchanted with the lovely rocky gorge and with the fountain itself, a mysterious swirling pool where underground waters emerged under limestone cliffs. This was the place, he said, he would most wish to live, rather than in any great city.

Francesco, Gherardo, and Guido Sette were sent to the University of Montpellier and then to Bologna, to study law. Seven wasted years, Francesco called them, but although he detested the law - the art of selling justice - he had time to read the classics, to perfect his Latin, and to correct his Italian. He loved Bologna; he also loved to escape for long country walks, returning after dark to climb the crumbling walls.

In 1326, when their parents died, Francesco and Gherardo returned to Avignon. Francesco always maintained that his guardians robbed him of his small property, which reinforced his dislike of the law. He refused to practice – "I couldn't face making a merchandise of my mind," he said - but he must have had some employment at the papal court, for he and his brother led the life of elegant young men.

Francesco was tall and active, with dark eyes and reddish-brown hair, which turned prematurely gray, to his great grief. He later recalled to Gherardo how the two of them would work all night on their coiffures, sometimes burning their brows with curling irons; how they would compose their gowns, terrified that the wind would dishevel them and the horses would splash them with mud; and he recalled his long, tight boots, which would have crippled him if he had not revolted in time. He remembered their stylish talk, with dislocated words and dropped syllables, and their popularity, their swarms of visitors, and the lewd songs they sang. He wrote poetry, which he later destroyed, and he had more than his share of success with the women who followed the papal court.

On April 6, 1327, when he was not yet twenty-three, he attended the early morning office at the church of St. Clare. There, for the first time, he saw Laura and fell in love.

To rid himself of Laura's obsessing image, he says, he traveled far. But the real reason was a longing to see new sights. He went to Paris, Flanders, Germany, and Rome; he would have liked to push on to the farthest Indies, to Taprobane. Even in old age, he loved to travel, if only through books and his imagination. He has been called the first tourist, journeying for pleasure alone; it is hard to think of a predecessor, for even Herodotus wandered with a book in view.

For pleasure, he climbed Mont Ventoux, which rises to more than 6,000 feet. Stirred by the view of the Alps, the mountains around Lyons, the Rhone, and the Bay of Marseilles, he took St. Augustine's Confessions from his pocket and reflected that his climb was merely an allegory of aspiration toward a better life.

To qualify for church benefices, he shaved his head in the clerical fashion, which committed him to nothing much. Aided, no doubt, by wealthy patrons, he bought a small house in the picturesque gorge of Vaucluse, a retreat only twenty miles from Avignon. When he went to town, he tried to make himself invisible, but he was already well known as a poet and scholar, and, of course, Laura was there.

If he did not exactly discover the love of wild nature, he established it as a literary convention for later times. His beautiful descriptions of country sights and sounds, of the little river Sorgue, with its crystal waters and the emerald luster of its bed, still move the poetic imagination of the Western world. But his solitude was laborious. "I rise at midnight, leave the house at dawn; and in the fields I study, think, write, and read. I fight off sleep as long as I can, and keep dainties from the body, pleasures from the soul, sloth from my behavior. All day I wander on bare mountains, dewy valleys, and in mossy caves, alone with my thoughts." He lived simply. A servant once asked him, "What do you eat?" "Polenta, toasted turnips, greens, vegetables, sometimes delicious cows' milk." "No meat?" "I'm not a wolf that feeds on flesh."

He worked fruitfully, producing, in Italian, poems of love's longing and despair, which were passed hand to hand and diffused throughout Italy, sung to the lute in various gatherings. In Latin, he wrote giant compendiums of ancient learning, an epic poem to rival Virgil's, and endless enchanting letters. His retreat was not a rejection of the world; it was a roundabout means of attaining fame.

And fame he gained. For him, Rome revived its ancient custom of crowning a poet with symbolic laurel. On April 8, 1341, on the holy ground of Rome's Capitol, he became the first laureate of modern times. His celebrity spread far: An old blind poet from near Genoa was carried by his son to Naples to hear and feel the presence of his idol. Missing Petrarch there, they pursued him to Parma, and for three days, thanked God for their fellowship with the poet.

Petrarch's vanity and depression increased; he went through a period of crisis. His brother Gherardo, shocked by the death of the woman he loved, entered a monastery to spend a six-year novitiate in virtual silence. Was this not the better way? In his self-questioning mood, Petrarch wrote a beautiful series of penitential psalms and also his extraordinary Secretum. This book, which he kept to himself during his life, is a dialogue with Saint Augustine, in which the saint explores Petrarch's character and faults and brings to light his subconscious motives. He berates Petrarch for his sensuality, his love of fame, his longing for the unattainable Laura, and his fits of unreasoning gloom. "Give yourself back to yourself!" says the saint. The book, stemming from Augustine's own Confessions, is the first example of introspective self-analysis of modern times.

His sensuality bore fruit. He had a son, Giovanni, born in 1337, and a daughter, Francesca, born in 1343. Whether there was one mother or two we do not know. Petrarch did his best for his children. He legitimized them, gave his son the best education obtainable, and procured for him an ecclesiastical living, but the boy was a disgrace, at least in his father's eyes. He died at the age of twenty-four, in the Plague of 1361. His daughter, on the other hand, was the consolation of Petrarch's later years.

From 1343 onward, Petrarch spent more and more time in Italy. In Parma, during the Great Plague of 1348, he learned that his Laura had died on April 6, twenty-one years to the hour from the moment he had first seen her in the church of St. Clare.

He lived for a time in Padua; he visited Florence and was grandly received. The city restored his family property to him, but because he did not immediately make his residence there, it took the property back again. After he returned to Vaucluse, his house was robbed of everything except his books. He settled in Milan, city of the Visconti tyrants, hateful to all Florentines. He served the Visconti as envoy to Venice and to the Emperor Charles IV, and he made an official trip to Paris to placate the bloodthirsty King John the Good of France on his release from an English prison.

In Milan in 1359, he received a visit from poet Giovanni Boccaccio, nine years his junior. The two became friends; their correspondence is a literary treasure.

Restless, he left Milan in 1361 for varying stays in Pavia, Padua, and Venice. The city of Venice gave him a palazzo on the Riva degli Schiavoni, where he could watch the ships sailing for the Black Sea, Egypt, and the Holy Land. In return, he offered his books to the city, expecting them to be the core of the first public library since ancient times. But after his death, they were not delivered.

Venice did not satisfy him; nothing satisfied him. Four young Aristotelians visited him and made clear that they thought him old. He was shocked by a cleric who called Paul and Augustine and the rest a bunch of gabblers. He was inspired to write the treatise, On His Own Ignorance and That of Many Others. He was tired and feeling his age and conscious of being out of date. He moved to Padua and bought a country house in the hills of Arquà that still stands, among its olive groves and vineyards. His daughter Francesca joined him. She had married well; her son Francesco was the image of his grandfather. The child's death at the age of two nearly broke the old man's heart. "I never loved anything on earth as I loved him," he grieved, but he came to love his winsome granddaughter Eletta, named for his mother, just as much.

Illnesses plagued him: fevers, fainting spells, foot trouble. He was so thin that he was afraid of vanishing. Boccaccio urged him to rest, to stop writing. "No," he said, "nothing weighs less than a pen, and nothing gives more pleasure; it is useful not only to the writer but to others far away, perhaps even to those who will be born a thousand years from now."

In the morning of July 19, 1374, he was found dead at his writing desk, the pen dropped from his hand on his Life of Julius Caesar. He lacked a day of reaching his seventieth birthday.

"What am I?" he had asked a few years before. "A scholar? No, hardly that; a lover of woodlands, a solitary, in the habit of uttering disjointed words in the shadow of beech trees, and used to scribbling presumptuously under an immature laurel tree;

fervent in toil, but not happy with the results; a lover of letters, but not fully versed in them; an adherent of no sect, but very eager for truth; and because that is hard to find, and because I am a clumsy searcher, often, out of self-distrust, I flee error and fall into doubt, which I hold in lieu of truth. Thus I have finally joined that humble band that knows nothing, holds nothing as certain, doubts everything - outside of the things that it is sacrilege to doubt."

Petrarch is important to us in three ways - as a poet, a humanist scholar, and a human being.

The interruption of Laura - or love's reality - into Petrarch's life turned him into a great poet.

Who was Laura, his muse? Some doubt she ever existed. They point to the Provençal convention that a poet must forever dream of an unattainable lady, to Petrarch's desire to outdo Dante's mystical love for Beatrice in his Vita Nuova, to the discord between Petrarch's proclaimed devotion for Laura and his simultaneous amours, and to the convenient triple meanings of the word Laura; Il lauro, the laurel; l'auro, the zephyr; l'auro, gold. Laura, they say, is merely an allegory, a useful fiction.

No, Laura was a real woman. Many efforts have been made to track her down. The identification with Laure de Sade, nee Laure de Noves, is old, and while it presents difficulties, it is not unlikely. An identification is not important, but readers always want to know how much is true in any fiction, as writers are usually reluctant to tell.

His Rime in Vita e Morte di Madonna Laura, 366 poems, give us plenty of specific facts. Laura was young, golden-haired, noble, rich; she came from the hill country near Vaucluse, and she was married and settled in Avignon. She was one of a group of young matrons who went bathing and boating together. Many of the poems take their rise from an incident - the poet's attempt to steal a glove; an eye affliction of Laura's; a new dress, purple with pink spots, blue-bordered, reminding the poet of phoenix feathers.

We have other evidence of her reality. In Petrarch's Secretum, his private, undivulged self-examination, Saint Augustine sneers that Laura's body, worn out by illness and frequent childbirths, has lost its old beauty. Petrarch admits the fact, but protests that she cleansed his youthful soul of all filth and taught him to look upwards. "Nonsense!" says Augustine, a hardheaded confessor. "She has ruined your life! She turned you from the love of the Creator to the love of the creature!" Augustine makes his charge admit that Laura's youthful beauty, and her significant name, lured the poet, and that he besieged her with his sensual desires. "But she never yielded!" protests Petrarch. "I could never love anything else! My soul is so used to adoring her, my eyes so used to gazing on her, that all that is not she looks dark and ugly!"

What exactly did he want? He is always pleading in his poems for "pity," for "yielding," for the gift of mercy forever sought by the Provençal poets. It is amusing to imagine that one day she might have decided to "yield." How he would have fled! She would have ruined his whole book.

Long, hopeless fidelity is the poet's best theme. But it has to be sincere. Then it has to be converted into beautiful poetic form. Every reader of Petrarch's poems must feel their truth and recognize their beauty.

His common device was to take an incident of the endless courtship and develop it in sonnet form into a "conceit," or a coherent rounded thought. Some of the conceits are very thin-spun, elaborate, on the edge of absurdity. The form was enthusiastically adopted by the poets of Italy, France, and England, and the Petrarchan sonnet gained a universal vogue which eventually brought it nearly universal scorn. The fading of the Petrarchan tradition has left in many minds an aversion to Petrarch, wholly undeserved, for much of his poetry is simple, straightforward, expressing a deep emotion in everyday words that turn into lovely harmonies.

Laura died of the plague, and Petrarch commemorated her in his Triumphs, an exhausting parade of ancient heroes and heroines. Though he was not with her at the time, there are few sweeter poetic passages than his description of Laura's death.

Petrarch was the first modern scholar, the first modern literary man. He loved to write, rising often at midnight to get to his desk. When a friend tried to force a vacation on him and locked up his books and papers, Petrarch fell into headaches, and the friend, alarmed, gave him back the key.

He wrote, as he read, with passion. He said: "I write to please myself; and while I write I converse eagerly with our elders, in the one way I can. And I gladly forget those among whom I was forced by evil fate to live; I employ all my power of mind to escape them and seek out the ancients. As the very sight of my contemporaries offends me, the remembrance, the splendid deeds, even the bright names of men of old allure me and fill me with inestimable joy; so that many would be shocked to learn how much more I find my delight among the dead than with the living."

His reading was a communion with ancient spirits, alive in books. He wrote them personal letters; he called Cicero his father, Virgil his brother. A great volume of Cicero, disturbed on his shelves, fell and wounded his ankle, making him wonder what he had done to make Cicero angry. He called books "welcome, assiduous companions, always ready to appear in public or go back in their box at your order, always disposed to speak or be silent, to stay at home or make a visit to the woods, to travel or abide in the country, to gossip, joke, encourage you, comfort you, advise you, reprove you, and take care of you, to teach you the world's secrets, the records of great deeds, the rules of life and the scorn of death, moderation in good fortune, fortitude in ill, calmness and constancy in behavior. These are learned, gay, useful, and ready-spoken companions, who will never bring you tedium, expense, lamentation, jealous murmurs, or deception."

He served his ancient friends well. He discovered several lost works of Cicero and gave them to the world. With Boccaccio, he engaged an Eastern scholar to translate Homer into Latin. He loved to examine and caress Greek books, although he was unable to understand them, and he tried in vain to learn the language.

"I have got rid of most of my passions," he wrote a friend, "but I have one insatiable thirst - book-buying." Yet in the end, his library numbered only 200 volumes, partly because he was always giving books away.

We call him the chief reviver of ancient learning. His example stimulated others to collect the classics and to copy them or have them copied. He aroused an interest in the critical study of ancient texts, which abounded with copyists' errors. He said that if Cicero or Livy should read current examples of their writing, they would disavow them as the work of barbarians. He developed principles of stylistic analysis, rejecting, on the basis of style alone, works ascribed to Cicero and Virgil.

His own formal Latin style was, and is, recognized as a modern model. It is thoroughly Ciceronian - exact, subtle, and sensitive. When a Pope wanted to make him apostolic secretary, he escaped the unwanted task by submitting an essay couched in such high style that the Pope rejected it as unpapal. In his letters, he employed a lower, familiar manner, easy and flowing, and individual. "The style is the man," he said. "We all have naturally, as in our person and movements, so in our voice and speech, something singular and our own." He advised a friend not to cling slavishly to the ancients but to graft the new on the old, for the first inventors were men, too. "Don't believe the common statement that there's nothing new under the sun, and nothing new can be said. True, Solomon and Terence said that; but since their time how much is new!"

His critical sense was keen. He called a treasured document of Julius Caesar a fake; he read an absurd, ill-written life of Saint Simplicianus and said outright that he did not believe a word of it. He opposed supernatural explanations, preferring to rest on reason. He was anti-Aristotle, he said, whenever Aristotle was anti-commonsense. He rejected astrology because it denied human liberty. "Can celestial bodies deviate from their courses, break all their laws, run in irregular orbits, to give warnings to men? Ridiculous!" He was skeptical even of miracles, since so often lies, follies, and frauds hide under the veil of religion and sanctity.

Essentially, he taught the blending of faith and love with exact, rational, critical method, as he blended in himself the poet and the scholar. One must approach knowledge with emotional desire and examine it with cool distrust. "Theology is a poem, with God for subject," he said. But theology is also a rational science, susceptible to reason.

This union of love and reason is called humanism. Properly, Petrarch is the first humanist.

With all his modernism, he retained much of the medieval. The word medieval would have surprised him; he thought medieval times were modem times, and he thought they were bad times. He took for granted their social, political, and religious structure, the antithesis of human and divine, the contempt of this world, which is a mere proving ground for the next. But he had no interest in scholastic philosophy or in medieval literature in general. He pinned his faith to Plato, not to Aristotle, the medieval master. While he knew his immediate poetic predecessors in France and Italy, he never mentions most of the great medieval classics, barely even Dante, and did not own a copy of the Divine Comedy until late in life when he received one from Boccaccio.

He loathed the world that he saw, for it was filled with wars, plagues, tyranny, cruelty, ignorance, and political and religious cynicism. He turned to the Roman classics and the Bible to escape the present; he dimly realized that his backward-turning was at the same time a forward-turning.

In his time, he was recognized as an intellectual leader. His fame was great, first as a poet, then as a moral philosopher. He was the counselor of princes and the Emperor, the public critic of popes. He brought to his age a new concept, or an old, forgotten concept, of the possibilities of human existence on earth.

Petrarch was the first man since Saint Augustine, 1,000 years before, to give himself to us entirely. His Letter to Posterity is the first modern autobiography. His intense self-consciousness prompted him to self-analysis, and since he was a literary man, his self-analysis took shape in self-expression.

He was a great introspective. Introspection was hardly a new discovery. Every religious practiced it, especially the mystics. However, they were concerned only with the soul's welfare, with sin and salvation, whereas Petrarch sought self-knowledge. "What use is it to know things if you don't know yourself?" inquired his mentor, Saint

Augustine, in the Secretum. Most of Petrarch's work is an effort to know himself and to display himself completely, with his shortcomings and faults, and also his virtues. He never tired of exploring his inner world. We may know him better than any other man since antiquity.

We know that his self-consciousness proceeded from a profound youthful self-distrust. To gain confidence, he surrendered to passion and ambition. But passion and ambition led him far from self-mastery; he had to subdue them. Finally, he learned to scorn the world, to gain possession of himself, and to at last find peace and happiness.

His introspection did not prevent him from looking at the world with delighted, observant eyes. His appreciation of scenic beauty and country charm has no parallel in medieval literature. His description of the beauty of mountains was not to reappear in recorded words until the end of the seventeenth century. When asked his profession, he liked to reply, "gardener." On the other hand, he ignored medieval architecture and had little taste for art, although Simone Martini did paint a small, portable portrait of Laura for him. Music, however, he loved; a good concert made him envy the gods their privilege of listening to the music of the ages.

His sense of beauty occasionally awakens corresponding chords within us. Frequently in his poems, a phrase or set of phrases will leap out as a personal communication across the years.

One stormy night in Venice as he sat writing late, in his study overlooking the Riva degli Schiavoni, he heard shouting below and ran to look down from his window, where a number of ships were casting off from the marble quay below. "Their masts considerably overtopped the two corner towers of my palazzo. And at this moment, with all the stars hidden by clouds, as my walls and roofs were shaken by the wind, as the sea roared hellishly below, the ships cast loose from the quay and set forth on their journey. One, perhaps, was bound for the river Don, with passengers for the Ganges, the Caucasus, the Indies, and the Eastern Ocean. My heart bled for these unhappy men. And when I could no longer follow the ships with my eyes, moved and stirred I picked up my pen again, exclaiming: 'Oh, how dear to men is life, and how little account they take of it!'"

Again, he writes: "I had got thus far, and was thinking of what to say next, and as my habit is, I was pricking the paper idly with my pen. And I thought how, between one dip of the pen and the next, time goes on, and I hurry, drive myself, and speed toward death. We are always dying. I while I write, you while you read, and others while they listen or stop their ears, they are all dying."

These are expressions of modern sensibility, with awareness of the mystery and marvel of common experience. Petrarch helped to form and define the modern sensibility, which is, indeed, an eternal one. Petrarch is frequently called the first modern man; he is also the eternal men.

2
THE PRINCE AND THE STATE

"Horror waits on princes," wrote John Webster, the Elizabethan dramatist for whom the bloodstained annals of Italy had a compulsive fascination. Certainly, the way to power was strewn with corpses: Men murdered their wives, wives poisoned their husbands, brother slaughtered brother, family raged against family, city sacked city. In 1402, the members of the ruling house in Lodi were burned alive on the public square; at Bologna in 1445, the people, enraged by the slaughter of their favorite family, the Bentivoglio, hunted down their enemies and nailed their steaming hearts to the doors of the Bentivoglio's palace, as a token of their love.

But Bologna was a tranquil city compared to many, even bloodless when matched with Foligno, where a noble - Pietro Rasiglia – betrayed by his prince, took his vengeance by flinging his wife, with whom the prince was having an affair, from the turrets of his castle and killing two brothers of the prince. In retribution, the whole Rasiglia clan was butchered and chopped up, and their joints, hung like meat, were paraded through the streets. Of course, ghoulish chroniclers liked to exaggerate the horror, and their imaginations reveled in sadistic fantasy. Regardless, politics became a murderous game in which a peaceful death in bed came only to the skillful or the lucky. The savagery used by men in pursuit of power was due to the nature of society and the prizes it offered.

The city-states of Italy had won their independence by playing the two greatest powers of medieval Europe - the Papacy and the Empire – against each other. In theory, the Pope ruled men's souls, the Emperor their bodies, but the facts did not align with theory. The Church had acquired property which no emperors or kings could match; its real estate, its fiscal rights - first fruits, Peter's pence, and the like - made it rich enough to challenge the Empire and to claim spiritual supremacy over temporal power. Yet bishops were princes as well as bishops; abbots and their monasteries owed feudal obligations on their lands. The baronage of the Empire bred too many sons to view the

Church's dependence on Rome with equanimity. Who should or should not select or confirm the bishops became a vital matter for emperors. And although the struggle between the Empire and the Papacy expressed itself in the language of theology, its roots were land, money, and power. Behind the Papacy stood the clergy, formidable in size, in learning, and in authority. The Emperor's major strength was drawn from his lands and rights in Germany, Austria, and the Netherlands, but as King of Lombardy, he possessed important and valuable lands in Northern Italy. His presence was rare in these territories, and his enemies flourished at his expense. Chief among these was the Papacy, rendered strong and inflexible by the powerful reforming popes of the twelfth and thirteenth centuries.

The Papacy, conscious of its God-given role in the Christian community, had not hesitated to encourage the revolt of the Italian communes, any more than it had hesitated to call the ferocious Norman barons to help it in its conflict with the emperors. This struggle between the Pope's party, the parte Guelfa, and the Emperor's, the parte Ghibellina (Guelphs and Ghibellines), polarized the participants' passion and anger and rivalry, often to the point of absurdity, as when the Ghibellines of Milan tore down the Christ from the high altar in the Cathedral of Cremona because his face was turned to his shoulder in the manner of a Guelph.

The conflict between Pope and Emperor unleashed a chaos in which the strong devoured the weak and trivial wars alternated with struggles that involved thousands of lives. From 1350 to 1450, Italy scarcely knew a month, let alone a year, of peace. During this time, the great states - Florence, Milan, Naples, Venice - emerged as the arbiters of Italy's destiny. With none powerful enough to overthrow the others, they lived in an uneasy equilibrium of power that lasted for nearly fifty years until, in 1494, welcomed by Milan, the French king invaded Italy to assert his dynastic claims. Wars more terrible and more violent than Italy had ever known turned Lombardy into a cockpit in the struggle between the Hapsburg emperors and the French kings that lasted until the sack of Rome in 1527, when Charles V brutally reasserted Imperial power and tied the destiny of Italy to the house of Hapsburg.

In war or in peace, in freedom or in subjection, the towns grew from hopeful democracy into greedy oligarchy. They varied greatly in size and power - a few like Florence, nearly 100,000 strong, were a hive of trade and manufacture; many like Orvieto of about 20,000 were busy market towns of farmers, shopkeepers, and artisans. Yet, great or small, they had each undergone a novel political experience - the flowering of a democracy in the midst of feudalism. Within these cities the popolo - members of craft guilds - had taken over or devised their own institutions of government, and usually, without formal authority or a written constitution, they exercised power and solved their problems ad hoc. They represented not only the wealth and enterprise of the city, but also the oligarchy of families that held and maintained authority. Force, and the consent of their immediate supporters, was the basis of their government. There was rarely unity - feuds and rivalries raged even before the division between Guelph and Ghibelline gave hatreds a sharper edge. And although the artisans and merchants dominated city life, they frequently needed the skill and the training of the nobility both in diplomacy and in war. Furthermore, the lax nature of these city constitutions enabled men seeking power to manipulate the quasi-democratic methods of government, as the Medici were able to do in Florence. The relics of the nobility or the great merchant oligarchs had little difficulty in acquiring the leadership and control of seemingly popular movements. Consequently, there was a pronounced tendency for all communes to drift, either secretly or openly, to the despotism of a family or a clique. This was the groundswell that would lift the Renaissance prince to power.

Chance, however, in the shape of the great bubonic plague that ravished Italy in the middle of the fourteenth century, also took a hand. Men and women died in masses, and death ran through the cities more rapidly than the countryside. Chroniclers tell of the empty streets, the pillaged houses, the yawning pits of graveyards, and the resulting poverty from the decay of trade. In this blighted world, it was easier for tyranny to flourish.

Plague or no plague, tyranny probably would have thrived. From the earliest days of these tightly-knit communes, force and expediency had ruled. War stimulated growth. A small town such as Orvieto, perched on its impregnable fortress of rock, absorbed large tracts of countryside stretching south to the Lake of Bolsena, westward to the coast, eastward to the Tiber, and north almost to Lake Trasimeno. Siena and Perugia wanted the same territory that Orvieto coveted. Florence hated Siena and attacked or courted Perugia according to her need. War was endemic, and the citizens were constantly marching out to battle with their neighbors.

The further element of diplomacy, with its treachery, pressure, and secrecy, found its breeding ground in the rivalries and conflicts of these city-states, for what was true of Orvieto, Siena, Perugia, and Florence was equally true of the cities of the Lombard plain or the Patrimony of St. Peter. Only in the south, in the kingdoms of Naples and of Sicily, was the conflict of cities held in check by the hereditary monarchy. The Papacy, which might have given coherence to the Patrimony of St. Peter, had been transferred to Avignon in 1309, where it remained until 1378. From then until 1417, the Great Schism provided additional causes for division and strife throughout Italy. And it was not until 1421 that Martin V reestablished the Papacy firmly and securely at Rome. The Emperor lacked the power to influence, let alone control, Lombardy's political development. Hence the appetites of the city-states for their neighbors' lands went unchecked, and war – as well as treason, murder, and plotting - was constant. Some states lacked the constitutional formalization of economic and political power that was sanctioned by tradition or by law. Power was captured by groups, by inter-related families, depending on oligarchic or popular support, and occasionally with the help of other city-states and foreign invasion. Murder, trickery, and civil war were accepted elements of political activity. Gradually, as war diminished the localization of power, the city-states emerged. Florence battered Pisa and Pistoia; Venice absorbed Padua and Verona; Milan ate up Pavia and Lodi. Only by skillful alliances did a few smaller states - Ferrara, Mantua, and others - survive. War was becoming too technical for simple peasants and workers. The cities had the money to hire the professional soldiers - the condottieri - who roamed Italy to ravage a living from its people. As the wily Venetians realized, the condottieri prevented armed power from being placed in the hands of a citizen and his faction, so it became a fixed principle that no one born Venetian could command its army. At first, the condottieri were foreign, but soon the tyrants of petty states put themselves and their citizens out for hire. Some, like the Montefeltro of Urbino, kept their states, their heads, and their reputations; others, like Francesco Sforza, won a duchy. Most died violently, executed, murdered, or killed in battle. They lived for hire, but they could not be trusted, since bought troops meant treacherous troops. This the Venetians and the Florentines knew, and they peppered the camps of their condottieri with spies. The use of hired professional armies reduced violence even though it increased treachery, for no captain wished to waste his greatest asset - his fighting men. As a result, battles were rare, sieges infinitely prolonged. And increasingly, the deliberate exaggeration and the hidden subterfuges of diplomacy added to the rumors of war and conspiracy.

Diplomacy as we know it arose in Italy of the Renaissance and grew strong in the fifteenth century through the equilibrium of power created by the three great northern states – Florence, Milan, and Venice. The leaders of these mercantile societies enjoyed and believed in hard bargaining and were familiar with the merits of partnership for the destruction of rivals. The collection of intelligence and the assessment of personalities and contingencies was the stock in trade of bankers. Every Venetian abroad was expected to spy for his country. Nor was intelligence required solely for foreign affairs; it was equally important internally. The fear of tyrants intensified their suspicion as well as their cruelty; their citizens and followers were encouraged to spy and to betray. Elsewhere, fear took on more fantastic shapes, and friends, relations, and children of tyrants lived on a volcano of violence that erupted with the slightest suspicion. Naturally, such insecurity bred a desire to survive that overrode all other claims to loyalty or affection, and frequently poison or the dagger momentarily cleared a state of its bloodstained ruler. Yet such actions and attitudes were an accepted part of the political and military life.

The frequent assassinations, the perennial plots, and the constant changes encouraged superstition and a romantic view of fate. Men turned to astrologers and magicians to strengthen their hope, to alleviate despair, and to help them meet the uncertain future. The stars were studied as a guide to action, and superstitious dread threaded the daily course of men's lives. Even the popes felt more secure in their faith when the heavens were favorable. Julius II fixed the date of his coronation on the advice of his astrologers, and Paul III arranged his councils at the dictates of the stars.

The ever-present sense of death and danger heightened instinct as well as superstition. Power, naked and absolute, was sought at all costs. At the courts of the despots, sexual license was as common as treachery. And in the rampages of the flesh, as in the pursuit of power, the popes were second to none. The powerful princes of the Renaissance lived in a dangerous, excitable, and exciting world, where morality was not considered, only success. But only a few princes, nobles, and merchants were involved in any state. The mass of the people eschewed office, and the disasters of government troubled them only in military defeat.

It would be wrong to think the tyrants of Italy sought power only through cruel methods. Though all desired fame, many were intelligent, some even sensitive. Since fame involved outward expression - buildings, statuary, art, pageants, and even public sponsorships - patronage, in its widest aspects, was an illustration of social and political grandeur. Splendor added stature to the Doge as well as the Pope, and the Visconti with their Cathedral of Milan and their Certosa di Pavia glorified their state as well as their dynasty. Display became part of the art of government, and the wealth of Italy permitted an extravagance that would have befitted an ancient Roman emperor. Pageantry was also a part of the aristocratic tradition, but the riches of the Medici, the Sforza, the Gonzaga, or the Este, and the skill of their painters and sculptors, raised this art to a more intense level. The competitions that celebrated the wedding of Beatrice d'Este and Lodovico Sforza were prolonged, extravagant spectacles that took months to prepare and days to enact, directed by no less a genius than Leonardo da Vinci. The power of princes and the glory of cities were expressed in spectacular buildings, paintings, and sculptures. Leonardo da Vinci sought the patronage of Cesare Borgia as well as Ludovico Sforza; Raphael began his career in the most bloodstained and power-ravaged city of Italy - Perugia. The patronage of tyrants took delight in all that gratified the mind as well as the senses of men. Exquisite and extravagant food, sumptuous clothing, delicate and intricate jewelry, masterpieces of craftsmanship in silver and gold, lightened the strain and soothed the anxieties of princes. So did the memorials of antiquity: the broken torsos, the green, encrusted bronzes, the coins and medallions, which the earth yielded. Books were novel, not only in their contents but also in their new printed form, and it was not long before they became as worthy of collection as the illustrated manuscripts of the recent past. Popes and kings, cardinals and princes, outbid each other to persuade the most learned in art, letters, and science to join their entourage; rarely has such a premium been placed on creativity. These strange courts of princes - so close to violence, yet so alive to beauty, so transient in power, yet so permanent in expression, need a closer focus.

At Mantua, high above the Piazza Sordello, swings an iron cage that throughout the fourteenth and fifteenth century was usually occupied by a dead or dying man. The grim, embattled palaces of the Bonacolsi and the Gonzaga provided a fitting background to the sagas of their princes. The lords of Mantua had their quota of fratricide, treasonable sons and murderous uncles, of wives caught in adultery and killed for their crime. Its citizens, as well as its princes, had their times of horror, their years of tribulation. Like all city-states, it was born in feudal anarchy and nurtured by interurban strife. Gifted with a natural strength - on three sides, the Mincio swells out into large, wide lakes that proved difficult to cross - Mantua dominated the surrounding countryside and held it against the most formidable assaults of its combined enemies. Still, it is doubtful whether it could have survived if not for Venice. Though too strong and too remote for Venice to absorb, its powerful princes were a buffer against their common enemy, Milan. So the Venetians hired the Gonzaga as condottieri and paid them with Lombard towns that were too weak to maintain their independence and too poor for Venice to covet. The Gonzaga were too clever to become dependent on Venice, and from time to time, they sold their skills to the rulers of Milan. The balance of power kept Mantua independent, and the needs of Venice or Milan made it rich. Violent though its history was, it enjoyed more peace and greater security than most Italian cities. The unruly, battle-scarred Gonzaga were never simply condottieri; they governed as strongly as they fought. Under Ludovico Gonzaga, in spite of plague and pestilence and flood, trade in wool and silks flourished, and the population grew to 40,000 or more. Money from war and trade was spent not only to delight the eye, but also to train the mind. In 1459, Pius II called a council there to declare a Crusade against the Turks, and in 1474, the King of Denmark paid a state visit and found a royal welcome. Powerful neighbors - the Sforza from Milan, the Este from Ferrara - expected and received extravagant hospitality. The births and marriages and deaths of Gonzaga princes were celebrated with appropriate solemnity and expense, as were their triumphs: Few public occasions matched the reception of Francesco Gonzaga, the first cardinal of his house, a prince of the Church at seventeen and a symbol of his family's greatness.

As was expected of Renaissance princes, the Gonzaga sought a permanent expression for their wealth and power. Ludovico (1414-1478), perhaps the most gifted of his family, embodied the skill and decision of a man of action with the sensitivity of a scholar. He proved himself ruthless in war, adept in diplomacy, yet more generous toward his treacherous brother Carlo than was usual in a despot, a sign of that human warmth which infused his private life and his artistic sensibilities. By 1460, he had persuaded Andrea Mantegna to become his court painter. The result was a series of frescoes that remain one of the great achievements of the Renaissance. As with painting, so with architecture: He employed Leon Battista Alberti - a leading Florentine figure in the Classical revival - to design his churches, and urged Mantuans to give generously so that plans for Sant'Andrea could become a reality. Huge buildings, sumptuous palaces, brilliant paintings - these were the common extensions of a prince's greatness. Ludovico, however, a man of wider and deeper sympathies, encouraged philosophers and poets to stay at his court. Pico della Mirandola, Bartolomeo Platina, Poliziano, Guarino da Verona, and Francesco Filelfo all brought distinction to the Mantuan court. Ludovico himself took a delight in books and collected not only manuscripts of the classics, but also those of Dante, Petrarch, and Boccaccio, and employed the most gifted craftsmen to illustrate their books.

The width of Ludovico's interests was due partly to his inherent genius and partly to his education, for it was in the education of princes that Mantua made one of its most remarkable contributions to the Renaissance. Ludovico's father had established the great humanist Vittorino da Feltre at Mantua, whose ideas were to influence European education for centuries. Vittorino believed that education should concern itself with the body as well as the mind, with the senses as well as the spirit. Wrestling, fencing, swimming, and riding alternated with hours devoted to Virgil, Homer,

Cicero, and Demosthenes. Luxury was eschewed, and Vittorino educated the poor with the rich and the princesses with the princes. Above all, he believed individual greatness was a desirable part of the nature of people, one that was not opposed to the obligations people had to one another. To Vittorino, the virtues were human. Although a devout Christian and insistent on regular religious practices, he nevertheless cherished an optimistic view of man's capacities. In Ludovico, Vittorino found an apt pupil, and the traditions he helped create kept the Gonzaga from gross excesses and saved Mantua from the terrible sufferings that were frequently the lot of other Italian cities. And Ludovico was as lucky in his children and his grandchildren as Mantua was in its dynasty. His son Federigo proved himself as skillful a condottiere, as wily a diplomat, and as sensitive a patron as his father, but it was his grandson Francesco and his wife, Isabella d'Este, who lifted the court of Mantua to its highest fame.

There were few cities that enjoyed such serenity as Mantua or were led by such an able man. Ferrara under the Este, Bologna under the Bentivoglio, and Urbino under the Montefeltro were perhaps its nearest rivals, but the common lot of cities was usually more grievous and their tyrants more terrible. In little more than fifty years, Orvieto was sacked and ravaged eight times - and with a brutality that was exceptional even for those murderous times. Even in an age which had grown immune to violence, the thought of Perugia and its tyrants brought great fear.

The cities of the Papal States experienced the worst fate of all the Italian communes. The absence of the popes at Avignon gave princely anarchy a chance to flourish; the Great Schism encouraged lawlessness and rapine; the return of the popes to Rome merely led to punitive wars. Both by its geography and size, Perugia was regarded as one of the most important cities of the Patrimony. By the middle of the fifteenth century, its history was steeped in unequaled bloodshed. Even though chroniclers exaggerated the bloodcurdling deeds, the Perugian story is horrifying in its cruelty and disregard of human suffering. The great families, who raged and stormed and slaughtered in its streets and churches, failed to exterminate each other; some always seemed to escape to live to plot revenge. The cities that feared Perugia were ready to provide them with arms and money for their campaigns of revenge. And the oppression the Perugians suffered too often made them think that changing one master for another might be for the better.

In 1488, the Baglioni and their enemies the Oddi fought a pitched battle in the Piazza, and the governors of the city were helpless to stop it. In 1491, in the Palazzo dei Priori, the Baglioni strung up 130 Oddi supporters who had found their way into the city. Shortly after this, the Baglioni were saved by the bravery and skill of Simonetto Baglioni, only eighteen, who held a narrow street with a few followers until they were nearly hacked to pieces. Then four of the leading Baglioni were slaughtered in their beds - including Simonetto. Between 1520 and 1535, practically all the remaining Baglioni were either publicly executed or murdered by each other. But these fratricidal vendettas were not the only horror the Perugians had to suffer. War was waged with a ferocity unusual for the fifteenth century, for the Baglioni, as condottieri, did not believe in half measures. To add additional horror, the plague found Perugia a happy playground - between 1424 and 1486 there were eight severe epidemics.

Violence and sickness, suffering and death, made the Perugians susceptible to religious fervor. The slaughters by or of the Baglioni were usually followed by days of solemn ritual and purification. On one occasion, the cathedral was washed with wine and consecrated once more; on another, more than thirty altars were erected in the Piazza, and Mass was held continuously. It is not surprising then, that the vivid preaching of Fra Bernardino of Siena found fruitful soil in Perugia. He condemned the crimes of its citizens, called them to repentance, reconciled enemies, and made a large bonfire of worldly delights in a great act of public repentance. Although his results proved as fleeting as the reconciliations of the Baglioni and the Oddi later in the century, this religious revivalism was not unusual in city life of fifteenth-century Italy - it was a common response to the insecurities created by war and pestilence and crime.

Although the constant strife destroyed trade and reduced the population, these actions failed to kill the thriving artistic life of Perugia. In the midst of the turmoil, exceptional paintings were produced: Pietro Perugino and Raphael shared the city with the Baglioni and the Oddi. Perugino's frescoes and Bonfigli's charming and tender Madonna provided the background for fratricidal slaughter in a piazza reeking with blood and adorned with the grotesque shapes of butchered youths and men. At no other place were the dark and the light of Renaissance life brought to a stranger contrast.

Sensitive, thoughtful people realized that this was a world like none other. They searched the histories looking for the keys that would unlock the problems of princes and of cities. What made men succeed or fail? Why did some cities grow wealthy only to dissipate in war and rebellion? Why did free citizens become the prey of professional thugs? What caused tyranny? Was tyranny bad? Did cities have a natural life like people - youth, maturity, age? And were learning, art, and the practice of humanism bound up with institutions? Did philosophers make the best citizens? They read again Aristotle and Plato and, above all, Cicero, who demonstrated the virtues of a philosopher in civic life. What they did not turn to was theology, to Saint Thomas Aquinas, to Saint Ambrose, or to Saint Jerome. The theological way of thinking was alien to them. The key to their problems was rooted in the lives and actions of individuals, not in universal mysteries or the attributes of God. Consequently, there is an astonishing freshness about the historians and the political philosophers of the Renaissance, and, as with painters and sculptors, the greatest were the Florentines, and the greatest of the Florentines was Machiavelli. However, Machiavelli is not an isolated phenomenon - from Coluccio Salutati to Francesco Guicciardini, people were asking the same questions. What general rules can be derived from political experience? In the Middle Ages, political philosophers were theologians, in the Renaissance they were historians. This change was brought about by the conflict of cities, despotism, and the crisis of liberty.

Profile: MACHIAVELLI

Garrett Mattingly

Renaissance statesmanship is typified by a single man, Niccolò Machiavelli. Though few people have any clear recollection of the life and character of the man, to everyone the name signifies deviltry, hypocrisy, intrigue, and treachery. More than 150 years ago, Frenchman René de Maulde la Clavière identified the Renaissance - the last decades of the fifteenth century and the first ones of the sixteenth - as the Age of Machiavelli. It came as naturally as saying the Age of Augustus, or of Louis le Grand, or of Napoleon, and it carried, like those labels, its own sinister connotations.

In a way, it was appropriate that Machiavelli should have become the interpreter of Renaissance politics to future ages. He was the Florentine of Florentines;

the citizens of his city were the embodiment of the new spirit then stirring in Italy. Not at first, of course: In the years after the popes had broken the power of the Empire in Italy, Florence was only one of the vigorous, turbulent city republics in northern and central Italy. Some of these paid a token allegiance to the Papacy, although the popes knew how little that really meant. Some professed loyalty to the Holy Roman Emperor, since no Emperor could endanger their liberties anymore, but they had all torn away from the hierarchical system in which the rest of Christendom was enmeshed and were engaged in an external struggle against their neighbors and an internal one of faction against faction for control.

At first, most of these new states were republics, but as the bigger fish devoured the smaller ones, there were fewer independent cities, and fewer of the survivors were republics. Soon only one republic was left on the Italian mainland - or only one that mattered. By force or guile, the Duke of Milan, Gian Galeazzo Visconti, was building himself a kingdom. All Lombardy yielded to him - from Piedmont to the Adriatic, then Genoa and Pisa, Perugia and Siena, and finally proud Bologna. Only Florence still held out.

Florence had as checkered a political past as any of her neighbors. In the century since she had exiled her greatest poet, the bitter factional strife Dante had lamented so pathetically had never ceased and only occasionally diminished. In the moment of crisis, some said it would be madness for Florence to pit herself against the wave of the future and that it would be better for Florentines to live as the subjects of a tyrant than to die as his victims. But the Florentines chose to resist. Willing to risk death as free men rather than embrace life as slaves, Florentines saved not just their own liberty but the liberties of Italy.

In a series of studies, German-American historian Hans Baron has shown how the outcome of this crisis altered the whole tone of Florentine thought; with this change, Florence became the center from which a new humanism spread, a new appreciation of political liberty and civic virtue, and a new attitude toward a person's place in society. This attitude insured the independence of the major Italian states and led to that vigor and diversity of Italian artistic and cultural development that characterized the Renaissance. But even without Baron's insight, Florentine civic humanism has long been recognized as a characteristic of the Italian Renaissance. Although he was no humanist, if we make that term include a mastery of Greek and Latin letters, Niccolò Machiavelli was soaked in the spirit of Florentine humanism.

He was soaked, too, in the Florentine obsession with politics. Machiavelli came from a family that had played a great role in the city's political life for more than two centuries. His ancestors had been honored with the republic's highest offices, and his father saw to it that Niccolò was thoroughly imbued not only with the history of ancient republican Rome, but also with the great traditions of his own city. When he was forty-four, Niccolò wrote that politics was the passion of his life, and he could think and talk of nothing else.

When the French invaded Italy in 1494, the Florentines, who had begun to be restive under the scarcely disguised rule of Lorenzo the Magnificent and even more so under Lorenzo's incompetent son, rose up and drove the Medici out of Florence. Niccolò was then twenty-five. We do not know if he held any position in the first years of the re-established republic, but when the revolutionary fanatics swayed by Girolamo Savonarola's eloquence gave place to a more solid, less hysterical government in 1498, Niccolò Machiavelli, just turned twenty-nine, was appointed second chancellor of the republic. Shortly afterward, he was given the additional job of secretary to the influential committee known as the Diece di Balia, or the Ten of War.

War was the restored republic's chief preoccupation. Foreign armies were tramping back and forth across Italy. Spaniards slowly tightened their grip on Naples; Frenchmen periodically invaded and were chased out of Milan; the Germans and Swiss were fighting, sometimes for foreign paymasters, sometimes for their own lands; around Rome, first the bastard son of the Borgia Pope and then Julius II were trying to unify the anarchic Papal States; and once, all the warring powers put aside their quarrels to combine against the powerful, independent Venetian republic. In the midst of these big wars, Florence was busy trying to reconquer Pisa, which, in the confusion of the first French invasion, had slipped from under its yoke. Since his nominal chief, the first chancellor, was more interested in Greek poetry than Italian politics, Machiavelli took a large part in these affairs. Deep in the business of war and the diplomatic haggling that accompanied it, most of the correspondence of the republic passed through his hands. He informed and advised his masters on a variety of subjects, and the Signory sent him on numerous diplomatic missions in Italy, Germany, and France.

Early in his diplomatic career, he crossed paths with the man who typifies the Machiavellian prince - the leading figure of Machiavelli's famous little book. Actually, Cesare Borgia was no more typical of the princes of Italy than Caligula was a typical Roman emperor, or Al Capone was a typical tax dodger, but there is no denying that Cesare attracted a lot of attention, even eclipsing his notorious father.

Throughout his papacy, the whole family of Rodrigo Borgia, who ascended the papal throne as

Alexander VI, was surrounded by a buzz of scandal. Gossiping about popes has always been a favorite Italian pastime, but no pope ever afforded so much occasion for juicy gossip. Other popes had kept mistresses in the Vatican, and immorality was no more common under the Borgia Pope than it had been under his predecessors and would be under his successors, but there was a childlike shamelessness about Alexander VI that invited comment. Other popes had auctioned off high ecclesiastical offices, doubled-crossed their associates and allies, and used their exalted position for the advancement of their families and for base personal ends, but usually they pretended they were doing something else. Rodrigo Borgia had either an honest scorn for hypocrisy or a naïve ignorance of the force of public opinion. Other popes had thrown wild parties at the Vatican, but none so flamboyant or so public. And no other pope had a portrait of his mistress, robed as the Virgin Mary, painted over the door of his bedchamber, while at the same time, given his mistress so many well-publicized rivals. Although he drank little wine and ate sparingly, Rodrigo Borgia was a great lover of women, and this alone was the source of innumerable stories that grew more outrageous with each retelling.

But neither his private conduct nor his carelessness can account for all the stories about the Borgia Pope. Although far from a saint, he was a first-rate administrator, with enormous energy and a driving will. He tried to police not only the streets of Rome, but even the Roman campagna and the disorderly Roman nobility and did his best to make sure the papal treasury received its cut of the money the swollen papal bureaucracy and its hangers-on extorted from suitors at his court. This made him extremely unpopular with the Romans. And because he tried to assert the rights of the Papacy and his jurisdiction over the Papal States wherever it was challenged, be it in Milan or the republics of Venice, Florence, or Naples or by the petty tyrants of Umbria and the Romagna, he was unpopular with the ruling classes throughout Italy as well. Worse, he was a Spaniard, and Italians have always resented a non-Italian pope. Hence, another cluster of stories, different and more sinister.

Two of Rodrigo Borgia's children, his eldest son, the Duke of Gandia, and his daughter Lucrezia, were less than ideal targets for malicious gossip. Gandia, although he inherited some of his father's disposition to run after women, was otherwise conventional and colorless. Lucrezia, although she had a checkered history of successive marriages before she was out of her teens - a foundation on which Roman scandalmongers readily erected a towering superstructure - was a bland creature. But the Pope's younger son Cesare was something else. Even at seventeen and a newly made cardinal, he was already a spectacular figure, a head taller than most tall men, with massive shoulders, a wasp waist, classic features, a leonine mane, and blazing blue eyes. It was said he could leap into the saddle without touching pommel or stirrups, bend a silver coin between his fingers, or straighten a horseshoe with a twist of his wrist. He dressed himself and his household with insolent magnificence and enjoyed organizing corridas in the Piazza Navona so the Romans could watch him behead a bull with a single stroke of his broadsword. Before long, his legend was gaudier and more lurid than that of his father.

Rumors said he was his father's rival for his sister's incestuous bed (almost certainly false) and that after the sack of Capua he seized forty highborn maidens and added them to his personal harem (highly unlikely). He supposedly seduced Astorre Manfredi, and when he tired of him, had him murdered. (Possible, but the motive was probably political.) It was even said that he murdered his brother, the Duke of Gandia (his father believed it) and that he had his brother-in-law, Lucrezia's second husband, murdered (certainly true). But it was a dull week when one of the embassies in Rome did not chalk up another murder to Cesare's credit, sometimes by poison, sometimes by the hands of hired assassins, sometimes by his own dagger, and he probably was responsible for a fair share of those bodies hauled out of the Tiber. Freed by his brother's death from his cardinalate, Cesare became Duke de Valentinois (the Italians called him

Valentino) and Gonfaloniere of the Church, cousin and ally of the King of France, and commander in chief of the papal army. As he marched through the anarchic Papal States, seizing one town after another, by bribery or trickery or sheer terror, his legend hung over him like a thundercloud.

When Machiavelli first encountered the Duke, the legend must have heightened by the manner in which Valentino received him and his chief, at night, by the light of a single candle that dimly showed the tall figure clad in black from head to foot without jewel or ornament, his still white features like those of a Greek statue. Perhaps the cold beauty of those marble features was beginning to be marred by the pustules that led Valentino later to wear a mask. Perhaps the eyes already held the look of a savage beast at bay. Perhaps a shrewd observer might have noticed the Duke endlessly repeating the same banalities about his eternal friendship for Florence and how wise the republic would be to employ his services, while his captains warned the Florentine envoys that the Duke's patience was growing short, that France would support him against Florence and the Venetians would not stir, that the army could be at the city's gates before the news of its coming. It was one of the cruder forms of blackmail, but something about the Duke's personality pulled it off, and the Florentine envoys carried away the image of a great prince - subtle, inscrutable, and dangerous.

Not long after, Machiavelli had the opportunity to observe Cesare Borgia at the time of his greatest triumph. Cesare was not much of a general: he never learned the rudiments of tactics or strategy, logistics or supply. He was not even a good combat leader, and though he has been praised as a disciplinarian, it is only because he once quelled a riot among his brawling soldiers by the terror of his presence. Similarly, there was never any proof of his ability as a statesman or ruler. But he was ruthless, and the revolt of some of his captains gave him an opportunity to display it. Machiavelli watched as Cesare lured his mutinous subordinates into a peace conference, lulled their fears, invited them to a banquet to celebrate their renewed friendship, and when they arrived unarmed and unescorted at a rendezvous where Cesare had hidden his bodyguards, had them murdered. Delighted at the virtuosity of his performance, Machiavelli set it all down in detail for posterity.

Machiavelli had a third opportunity to observe the Duke. He arrived in Rome on business some months after the death of Alexander VI, just as Cesare, with incredible stupidity, had helped swing the election of his most implacable enemy. It was plain to see that Cesare was finished. Everything depended on his father being Pope, and as soon as his father died, his allies deserted him, his people rose against him, and his army fell apart. Machiavelli assessed the emptiness of the man, avoided him when he could, wrote of him and looked upon him with contempt. But later, Machiavelli seems to have forgotten the cringing, whimpering, blustering creature his hero had become. Although the picture is spread out in some detail in his dispatches, Machiavelli never openly alluded to this aspect of Cesare again.

One thing Machiavelli admired about Cesare was that he employed soldiers from his own domain instead of hiring foreign mercenaries. He had been urging the Florentine government to adopt Cesare's methods for years, and when at last they did, they named him the republic's minister of defense. Instead of the cut-rate mercenaries who had prolonged the Pisan war for twelve years, Machiavelli persuaded the government to raise a militia in its own territory. Since the militia were not Florentine citizens, but wretched peasants without political rights or any material stake in the success of their bourgeois masters, the scheme had an obvious weakness, but did not work badly at first. When Pisa fell in 1509, Machiavelli's militia could claim a share in the long-delayed triumph. Three years later, however, when the veteran Spanish infantry attacked Prato, the militia ran like rabbits, and the Medici family returned behind a column of Spanish pikes to rule Florence once again. Though Machiavelli's career in politics was over, his interest in politics was not. He could think about nothing else, and until he died in 1527, only a few weeks after the Florentines had again expelled the Medici, most of his writings were concerned with the politics of state. He also wrote some verse and a not unamusing version of an old joke and comedies, but mostly he wrote about politics. Had he been asked to name his political writings in order of importance, the top three would surely have been his History of Florence, his Art of War, and his Discourses on the First Ten Books of Livy. Into these writings, and particularly the last, Machiavelli had poured all his practical experience of government and diplomacy and his wide reading of ancient and modern history. If the successful statesmen of his day would have been surprised to find him the political spokesman of their age, Machiavelli himself would have regarded the reputation as just compensation for the fame fate had denied him. He had often said he was the first modern man to look at politics with a clear and open eye, and he would certainly have taken the recognition as nothing more than what he was due.

Of course, when people speak of Machiavelli, they are not thinking of any of his books, but of one pamphlet dashed off in 1513 after the fall of the Florentine republic. *The Prince* bears only an ambiguous, tangential relationship to Machiavelli's big, serious works or to the actual history of the time and place over which its fame casts such a lurid and sinister light. The impression of Renaissance Italy gathered from *The Prince* and that given by the rest of Machiavelli's writings raises doubts about the appropriateness of letting *The Prince* describe the political atmosphere of the day.

Perhaps letting Machiavelli speak for the age that bears his name ought to be increased by knowledge of his private life. Among his contemporaries, Niccolò Machiavelli was one of the least Machiavellian. While he often professed a preference for drastic methods and sweeping all-or-nothing solutions, along with a contempt for delay and compromise, it does not seem to have affected his own behavior. Machiavelli often praised the efficacy of hypocrisy and smooth deceit, but in his dealings with both his own government and foreign potentates, he was usually inept at concealing his feelings, and, in negotiation, blunt to the point of tactlessness. He frequently spoke of the value of clear-eyed, dispassionate observation, but he was easily deceived and was not, in the things that really mattered, an acute, discriminating, or accurate observer. This judgment, suggested by comparing his dispatches with those of his contemporaries, is reinforced by the fact that his employers, the Florentine Signory, never gave him responsibility for any important mission.

Niccolò not only lacked the virtues he praised, he possessed others even more incompatible with our picture of Old Nick. Like most literate adult male Italians of the time, he was anticlerical, and in spite of his pious mother's teaching, was no more a zealously practicing Catholic than one would expect. But he had been baptized, confirmed, and married, so he died in the arms of the Church, having seen to it that his children followed the same conventional course. He was probably no more faithful to his wife than most middle-class husbands, but he seems to have been a kind, affectionate, considerate husband and father, a warm and true friend, a man of his word, and an admired and respected citizen.

One inappropriate virtue surprised even Machiavelli himself. The man who wrote that men are moved so predominantly by self-interest that princes need take account of no other motives, that "a man will resent the loss of his patrimony more than the murder of his father," was himself the devoted, unselfish servant of his ungrateful state. For fourteen years, in an age when the use of public office for private gain was customary, he had unrivaled opportunities to enrich himself at the expense of the condottieri and other contractors he dealt with as secretary to the Ten of War, yet he quitted the Florentine service as poor as the day he entered it. His entire public career was a testimony to the inaccuracy of his own cynical maxims. It is hard to reconcile it with the trend of his major works and impossible to square it with the lurid picture he has drawn in his one famous little book, *The Prince*.

Most people, whether they have read *The Prince* or not, retain the conviction that Machiavelli commends the actions of the poisonous Borgias and justifies the pagan debauchery Protestant countries have since associated with the Italian Renaissance.

Most of these false assertions harken back to a book called Anti-Machiavel, written by a Huguenot pamphleteer against Catherine de' Medici and her Italian entourage after the Massacre of St. Bartholomew's, in which as many as 30,000 died. But even after these errors have been eradicated, *The Prince* remains a shocking book, both for its message and the provocative way it is relayed, as well as the discord between its contents and the life and other writings of its author.

The major premise of *The Prince* is that men, in general, are selfish, treacherous, cowardly, greedy, and, above all, gullible and stupid. Because of this, a prince, particularly a new prince who hopes to destroy the liberties of those he rules, is advised to employ hypocrisy, cruelty, and deceit, to make himself feared even at the risk of making himself hated, to divide the people and destroy their natural leaders, and to keep faith with no one, since no one will keep faith with him. The world of politics is viewed as a jungle in which moral laws and standards of ethical conduct are merely snares for fools, where there is no reality but power, and power is the reward of ruthlessness, ferocity, and cunning. In such a jungle, it is not the actual Cesare Borgia, but the picture Cesare conveyed at the height of his fame, a savage beast - half lion and half fox – who would be the natural king. To a society that considered its relationships ruled by justice and equity and sanctified by religion, this was shocking.

It was shocking, too, to find a man of staunch republican principles and flawless republican antecedents, who had served the Florentine republic with selfless devotion and suffered greatly for that devotion, writing a handbook for tyrants, a book meant to teach the Medici, the enemies of his country, how to hold his fellow countrymen in thrall, and all for the purpose of helping himself wriggle back into some minor government post. If this was how Machiavelli behaved, he earned, for the only time in his life, the epithet Machiavellian. That his behavior seems to have been a momentary aberration makes his defection all the more puzzling.

There were at least two explanations of the puzzle. The first was that Machiavelli had been inspired by the Evil One to write a plausible book of advice for princes, meant to damn the souls and ruin the fortunes of those who followed it, and to destroy the prosperity of their subjects. This was the official view, shared by the cardinals and popes who banned *The Prince* and by Protestant pamphleteers who pointed to it as the manual of the Jesuits and the political inspiration of the Counter Reformation. A second view expressed by some of Machiavelli's countrymen (those in exile) and hinted at by some who remained in Italy, where the banned book continued clandestinely to circulate, was that *The Prince*, under the guise of giving advice to princes, was meant to warn free men of the dangers of tyranny. From this second view sprang the judgment, popular in the eighteenth century, that *The Prince* was, in fact, a satire on absolute monarchy, and that all its epigrams were deliberately double-edged. The nineteenth century solution to the puzzle was that, although he was an ardent republican, Machiavelli made up his mind that only a strong prince could liberate Italy from the barbarians, so he chose to sacrifice the freedom of his city to unite Italy. Just before World War I, this began to be questioned by those who said that Machiavelli was not a patriot but a detached, dispassionate political scientist who described political behavior as it actually was. After 1920, this view took a powerful lead over its competitors.

But none of these answers is entirely satisfactory. Though it is possible that Machiavelli was needy enough to sell out his republican ideals for some third-rate civil service post under a petty tyrant, to believe that a book like *The Prince* was the best way into Medici favor, and to let highly secret advice escape into general circulation seems much less credible. To say that *The Prince* was inspired by the devil or that it was the subtle weapon of republican idealism seems equally oversimplified. And the proposal that *The Prince* was conceived as a satire is the kind of anachronism only the eighteenth century could have perpetrated. As for the theory that Machiavelli was willing to accept a tyrant prince to effect the unification of Italy, there is no indication anywhere in his writings that he would have grasped the idea if anybody had put it to him. There is nothing about unifying Italy anywhere in *The Prince*, only about driving out the barbarians, common Italian rhetoric from Petrarch to Paul IV. But Machiavelli the Italian patriot is a little easier to swallow than Machiavelli the dispassionate scientist.

It is probably hopeless to try to explain the motives of a man more than 400 years in his grave who has left only the scantiest and most ambiguous clues to what they might be. How much of the distortion in *The Prince* was due to the faulty observation of a passionate man and how much to the deliberate irony he sometimes practiced? How did bitterness and the collapse of all his hopes affect his writing and which wild statements came from anger, which from despair, and which from a calculated will to undermine his enemies?

Like most insoluble problems about men of genius, this one has taken up more time and energy than it deserves. The real importance of Machiavelli is not in the points in which *The Prince* differs from his other writings, but in those in which it agrees. Here the transformation of his legendary figure from a diabolist or a rebel, a spirit who says "No," to a major culture hero, offers the clue. What had happened, in almost three centuries between the time when Machiavelli was praised as a daring rebel or denounced as an emissary of Satan and when he began to be acclaimed as a prophet, was that all Europe had become what Italy in Machiavelli's lifetime already was: an aggregation of autonomous, temporal sovereign states, without any common end to bind them into a single society or any interest higher than their own egotistical drives for survival and expansion.

To pretend that the relationships between such states were governed by Christian ethics seemed to Machiavelli a contemptible hypocrisy. Italians since Dante had lamented that the nearer one came to Rome, the wider the gap between Christian teaching and Christian practice, and charged that the Papacy had corrupted the morals of Italy. Indeed, the major assumption of the Counter Reformation was not much different. But Machiavelli went further. He compared his own embittered picture of the degeneracy of his countrymen with the virtues of republican Rome, and without asking how much exaggeration there might be in either, leaped to one of his drastic conclusions. Because Christianity, whatever its value as a guide in private life, was not a viable foundation for good society, he proposed to substitute the religion of patriotism. In politics, the Christian ethic was positively harmful. It might keep the masses more law-abiding in their private lives, but when it came to public actions, the only test of good or bad was what best served the safety and aggrandizement of the state. Since every state was autonomous, recognizing no interest higher than its own, no rules of ethics applied to relations between states - the only test was success. This was Machiavelli's consistent position. It appears in his earliest state papers and is as firmly held in his writings in praise of republics as it is in *The Prince*. In 1513, it was a desperate paradox. By 1813, it was an axiom of statecraft. By 1914, it was the tritest of platitudes. This was apparent in the behavior of the Italian states of Machiavelli's time and more or less openly acknowledged in the memoranda of statesmen and diplomats. But Niccolò Machiavelli gave this attitude a permanent literary form, and history compelled recognition of his insight. For that reason, perhaps his age should be called the Age of Machiavelli.

3
THE ARTS

In 1546, Giorgio Vasari, a young painter, attended a small supper party in Cardinal Alessandro Farnese's palace in Rome. The conversation turned to the extraordinary flowering of Italian art in the previous century and to the exceptional artists who had revolutionized painting and sculpture since the far-off days of Giotto and Pisano. Yet Vasari's presence was even more remarkable, for 100 years earlier it would have been unthinkable for a young painter to have been a guest at a cardinal's table. The social position of the artist had changed as much as art itself. To the men at that supper party, the age of heroes was passing; only the formidable genius of old Michelangelo could challenge the giants of the past. Encouraged by the others, Vasari determined to collect what information he could about these remarkable artists of the recent past and to immortalize the painters of Florence, which, for Vasari, was the cradle of the arts. Florence nurtured what Rome had used. Milan, with Leonardo da Vinci at the court of Ludovico Sforza, had once seemed on the verge of becoming the leading city of the Renaissance, but the great invasions cut that short. Venice, secure and wealthy, became the heir of Florence and the rival of Rome. But in these four cities - Florence, Milan, Rome, and Venice - the practice and patronage of art had become a civic virtue; these cities witnessed the triumphs of painting and sculpture and the emergence of the artist from the confines of his craft to the lonely pursuit of his genius.

In the early fifteenth century, the artists had been as certain as Vasari that they were heralding a new age; they acknowledged the genius of Giotto and Cimabue, but few others. The modern age began with them: painting with Masaccio, sculpture with Ghiberti, architecture with Brunelleschi. This was not idle boasting. Donatello's statues possess exceptional originality. In painting, the break is less vivid than in Donatello's freestanding statues, but it is remarkable enough. In architecture success came more slowly. In literature and music, people were equally confident of their own originality. Seen against the broad sweep of modern history, their claims seem justified. The language of

Renaissance art is the language of the modern world - at least until recent times - whereas the art of the Middle Ages possesses some of the same difficulties as the art of Islam or India or China. Its beauty can be recognized, but its impact is never, or rarely, immediate.

And yet, as soon as one examines individual works of Renaissance art, one is immediately aware how entangled the artists of fifteenth-century Italy were with Gothic art and the art of Byzantium. They were also indebted to the originality and technical skill of the Flemish and Burgundian schools of painting and illumination. This tradition and foreign influence added texture to Renaissance painters, but when all debts and obligations are acknowledged, what a fabulous achievement in painting and sculpture remains.

Certainly the social circumstances were favorable for artists and craftsmen. There was a deep-rooted tradition, dating back to the earliest days of Christian Europe, that men God had blessed should give thanks for their good fortune by enhancing the churches and monasteries in which they worshipped. Building for God and adorning God's buildings were part of the Christian life, sanctioned by time and anchored in belief. It was inevitable that as the wealthy and powerful flourished in Florence, Milan, Naples, and Venice, they should wish their status to be reflected in their parish churches, in the monasteries and nunneries they founded or patronized, and in the cathedrals of their cities. And in this artistic benevolence in the service of God, a Pope was their supreme mentor. At Avignon and Rome, the popes had fostered a splendor that was the envy of the kings of Europe as well as the princes of Italy. Pride in the visual expression of piety was universally permitted even by the most puritanical characters. To all men, even the most ascetic, these were a part of religion as old as the Church itself.

Furthermore, it was the custom of princes to adorn their palaces: to encourage metal-work and to delight in tapestries and frescoes that told them well-loved stories or reminded them of the pursuits - hunting or the art of love - in which they took delight. It gave them satisfaction to read their prayers from costly books, illuminated with exquisite skill. By 1400, however, there were hundreds of merchants in Italy and Burgundy who could afford the artistic elegance that had once been the sole prerogative of the country's aristocracy. These merchants were city-born; their families had risen to greatness with their towns, and their civic pride was as strong as chivalry, perhaps stronger than a knight's loyalty to his prince. They wanted their city to mirror their greatness, for their wealth to reflect in its buildings and their adornment. The state system of Renaissance Italy was not merely competing for power; it was fighting for supremacy in the arts. It added to the stature of kings to have a world-renowned artist attached to their courts, and the republics - particularly Florence and Venice - were jealous of their geniuses.

Consequently, enormous amounts of money and social energy were poured into the pursuit of art, and the effect was as dramatic as the investment of capital in technology and invention during the nineteenth century - and with similar results. Naturally, the need for artists drew some into a career which they might otherwise have ignored: Any poor peasant boy who showed some natural skill could find a sponsor among the neighboring gentry or local merchants, like Mantegna, who was a shepherd in the fields near Padua until he was discovered by Francesco Squarcione. Of course, the greatest source was craftsmen - the jewelers, goldsmiths, metalworkers, and decorative painters - where there was a tradition of design and the opportunity for early apprenticeship. Previously, only the religious life had drawn such a rich variety of human temperament. This, in itself, enriched artistic expression.

The rivalry among artists added to the overall competition. In early centuries, a craftsman could spend a lifetime beautifying one cathedral or monastery, adding a personal touch to the traditional themes and colors, unconcerned with public reputation or his fellow artists. By 1450, however, rivalry among artists was commonplace in Florence and Venice, which led men to exploit their techniques to the fullest and give their imagination free rein. It took a skilled eye to distinguish one Burgundian master of illumination from another; a child can tell the difference between a Botticelli and Paolo Uccello. This does not mean that attribution is easy or absolute. A successful painter of the Renaissance was the head of a workshop - often a large-scale family affair in which brothers, sons, and even daughters joined. Furthermore, apprentices abounded, as did journeymen who were skilled in hands or costumes or backgrounds. As ever, the works of the second rate emulated the genius of a few.

The circumstances of the Renaissance encouraged the cultivation of individual style, and the rewards of a successful personal creation were so large that artists took risks that earlier craftsmen would never have taken. Some men followed their demons wherever they led, and painters committed themselves to their artistic vision with the fervor of a saint. The stories Vasari tells may or may not be true, but they reveal what Italian society expected of the lives of its artists: Andrea del Castagno killing Domenico Veneziano in envy of his talent; Piero di Cosimo boiling the eggs that he lived on, fifty at a time, with his varnishes to save time; Paolo Uccello loving perspective much more than his wife. Common to all is dedication to their work and self-acceptance. This crowd of painters, sculptors, goldsmiths, decorators, and jewelers had widely differing gifts and varied temperaments: the profound curiosity of Leonardo, the soaring imagination of Michelangelo, the intellectual powers of Piero della Francesca, the sensitivity of Giorgione, and the technical accomplishment of Raphael.

The three great arts - painting, sculpture, architecture - changed profoundly between 1400 and 1500. Painting in the thirteenth century had been largely dominated by Greek or Byzantine influence - many of the artists were themselves Greek; the olive-skinned, slant-eyed, kinglike madonnas of Cimabue and Duccio di Buoninsegna are established traditions. In comparison, Giotto is naïve and primitive, even by fifteenth-century standards. His figures have, in art historian Bernard Berenson's words, "tactile values": You feel you could touch them, walk round them, and that they could walk around you. He used light, shade, color, and strongly featured men and women to create a sense of solid form and three-dimensional space. Yet for 100 years, there was little advance from his innovating skill. Florentine art was less imaginative, less technically dexterous than that of the great painters and illuminators of Burgundy, Flanders, and Avignon, whose skills steadily seeped through the Alps to enrich Italy. Florence lacked the achievement of Siena, where strong Byzantine and weaker Gothic influences blended to create an original school of landscape painters, including – Ambrogio Lorenzetti, Martini, and Duccio. Then, suddenly, as Italian art seemed to be drifting gently and skillfully into its own version of the Gothic, the promise of Giotto was fulfilled in Masaccio - one of the greatest of all Florentine painters. His frescoes in the Brancacci Chapel of the Carmine were revered by generations of artists, who studied them closely. From 1400 on, two artists of outstanding ability - Donatello and Brunelleschi - also helped to create a new attitude to art. Both were entranced by perspective, human nature, and reality as they saw it - not through symbol or myth, but clearly and directly. Donatello's David - a boy's naked body displayed frankly for the first time since antiquity – marked the birth of a new age. Brunelleschi contributed as much by his ardent proselytism of the rules of perspective as by the soaring dome he built for Florence's cathedral. And in addition to these three, there were others - Fra Angelico, Ghiberti, Uccello, Luca della Robbia - painters and sculptors of exceptional talent, who were deeply moved by the new technical triumphs the study of perspective had brought. Uccello rarely painted with any other intention than to demonstrate his skill in handling perspective. A preoccupation with the density of things, combined with a tragic view of life, became the dominant theme in Florentine art. A further preoccupation was a sense of movement, which infused the reliefs, the statues, the pictures of this extraordinary city, and culminated in the writhing nudes of Michelangelo, locked forever in their struggle with Fate. Intellect, solemnity, and a sense of time were expressed visually by these artists.

In addition to perspective, Donatello and Brunelleschi, who were devoted friends, were concerned with intellectual pursuits and searched deliberately and consciously for the antique. In Rome, Brunelleschi measured and sketched ruin after ruin while Donatello studied the few Roman and Greek bronzes and statues that were beginning to be collected at the time. Both men saw themselves as the heirs of Rome; they believed that between them and the fifth century existed a great gulf of barbarism.

And yet the art of the early fifteenth century was deeply entangled in its past. Painters were called to paint the traditional scenes of Christian mythology - nativities, circumcisions, crucifixions, the miracles of saints, the Stations of the Cross - and were expected to execute them on the walls of churches and monasteries and on altar panels. Skill in perspective, or even a delight in the antique, did not abolish the old symbols or traditional iconography: Four or five jagged rocks, realistically drawn, still represented mountains, as they had for centuries in Byzantine art. The egg, hanging in the apse in Piero della Francesca's great picture of the Madonna and Child with saints in Milan, represents the four elements of the universe - a purely medieval symbol - as well as being a perfect conic section and the central point of a complex composition, requiring superlative skill in perspective. And although Uccello might gently mock the traditions of chivalry in his Saint George and the Dragon, nevertheless they absorbed his imagination; and Benozzo Gozzoli's Journey of the Magi is as Gothic in feeling and intention as a fifteenth-century tapestry from Burgundy. The new art of Donatello and Masaccio had no easy victory except in technique, for the Gothic feeling from the North seeped like an estuary tide through the brushes and canvases of Italian artists of the fifteenth century.

The other great triumphs of Renaissance art - the painting of landscape, the exploration of space and light through color, the full acceptance of the nude, and the development of the portrait - came slowly.

And again, they were partly due to foreign influence. Landscape in early Renaissance art was mainly the landscape of symbol, such as the paradisal gardens derived probably from Persia, containing delicately observed flowers and plants and animals painted not to stir feeling, not to evoke mood deliberately, except in a formalized and quasi-theological sense, or the terrible mountains, rocks, and forests, which were the age-old symbols of hell and horror. But as individuality crept out from traditional expression, and as technique, became more certain, painters and illustrators could not resist the challenge of the outward-seeing eye. In the Très Riches Heures of the Duc de Berry, peasants cut the crops, children swim, and sheep feed on the mountain side. About the time that the Limbourg brothers painted this, a Flemish artist, Jan van Eyck, began to paint small background landscapes in his great altarpieces, which influenced Italian art as profoundly as his discovery of oil painting. Van Eyck took both his feeling for landscape and his knowledge of oils back to Italy, where Antonello da Messina was one of the first to employ the new technique. Color, light and shade, the intimate relation of people and nature became dominant themes in Venetian art. Florentine artists had not been indifferent to landscape; its study was involved in their preoccupation with perspective. Also, being inspired by nature was an integral part of their Neoplatonism. Brunelleschi made an optical device for viewing the city, and Leon Battista Alberti told how nature stirred him to tears and to joy. The intellectual problem of drawing figures against a distant background preoccupied Piero della Francesca, and he solved it about 1465, when he painted his Urbino diptych. Antonio del Pollaiuolo painted realistic landscapes, particularly of the Val d'Arno, shortly afterwards. But neither painter responded with such a deep sense of personal discovery as Giovanni Bellini, although his preoccupation may have come as much from della Francesca as from van Eyck. Bellini loved the first clear light of morning that touches the mountaintops and leaves the plain in shadow, and the golden light of the last hours of day, a time that gives depth to shadow and softness and glow to color. Even the harsh and brilliant light of midday did not repel Bellini. He drank in its heat and intensity, as his Saint Francis does with his arms raised, as much to the sun as to God. Although his delight in light and its effects on color passed into the Venetian tradition, his concern with the detail of landscape did not.

Landscape was used to reflect the emotion felt by the painter and to stimulate it in the beholder. In Giorgione and in the early works of Titian, landscape painting reached hallucinatory heights of feeling, reflecting mystery, horror, fear, tenderness, security, bliss, and love. As with perspective, landscape created a new world of artistic expression.

The Venetians were not the only artists in the early sixteenth century to delight in painting landscape. True, Michelangelo largely ignored it, and Botticelli used it merely as decoration or to emphasize his flowing, vibrant movement, but the Umbrian painters - Perugino and Pinturicchio - drew from the tradition of Piero della Francesca;

a tradition that was absorbed by Raphael. Nature stirred Leonardo da Vinci's sense of beauty as well as his avid curiosity. The geological structure of mountains caught his imagination, as did the turbulence of water and the mechanics of its flow; as did the flight of birds and the botany and beauty of flowers. As in so many other aspects of Renaissance art, the scientific spirit and the delight in the eye combined in one esthetic pleasure, for in Leonardo the creative imagination was as multidimensional as geometry.

Throughout the Renaissance, artists worked for a small, intimate public. They were well known in their cities, familiar to popes and princes, and their art served a civic as well as religious purpose. The Venetians realized early that narrative paintings about their heroic moments could impress both citizen and stranger with the republic's greatness. For that reason, artists were paid to paint vast pageants that gave drama and color and pomp to the Venetian year. In those pictures, citizens of Venice appeared, as recognizable as the Piazzetta itself. The princes, too, helped to domesticate art with their profiles cast on medals – sometimes their only claim to fame. They hungered for eternity and needed not only to patronize painting or construct huge palaces, but also to see themselves immortalized in bronze, gold, and silver. They appeared, as the Medici did, in the retinue of kings making their offerings to the infant Christ, or in symbolic pageant, as Federigo da Montefeltro and his wife, Battista, did in the Urbino diptych. And the preoccupation with human nature led to the attempt to interpret character through portraiture, and for this, a face in profile was insufficient. Although there were brilliant portraits elsewhere, Venice was the true home of the portrait, and the walls of private palaces were adorned with the portraits of their owners, many of them masterpieces by Titian.

Through perspective, through the introduction of oils, through the exploration of landscape and the human body, Renaissance Italy created the traditions of Western art, where it remained embedded for centuries. Sculpture and architecture likewise flourished. Donatello's David remained an isolated phenomenon only for a generation. Verrocchio, Leonardo, and, above all, Michelangelo created magnificent statues that equaled the best the ancient world had to offer; Michelangelo infused his statues with an emotional force that none have since equaled. The tragic nature of man - his immense loneliness and his inevitable end, his tension and suffering, generalized for humankind, passed into stone or paint. Social circumstance and technical change allowed such supreme artists to flourish. The distance traveled in a little over 100 years - from Lorenzo Monaco, Gentile da Fabriano, or Lorenzetti to Leonardo, Michelangelo, or Raphael - is stupendous. Such a leap was possible only because art had become the expression of complex social forces.

By the High Renaissance – the early 1490s to 1527 - art pervaded all aspects of life. From the arrangement of a dinner plate to the construction of fortifications - all were matters upon which an artist's opinion might be needed or offered. Most of the great artists, too, regarded themselves as Jacks-of-all-trades. Leonardo did not think it beneath his dignity to design the costumes for the masques his patrons loved or to fix the heating for a duchess's bath. Michelangelo was initially wholly dedicated to sculpture, yet he overcame his reluctance to paint the frescoes of the Sistine Chapel and even turned to architecture and poetry. The versatility of a Leonardo or a Michelangelo was far from unusual. Princes and patrons who wanted their lives to be richly, ostentatiously, and beautifully embellished were willing to pour out their ducats and florins on all the arts and crafts available to them. Their heightened sensibilities demanded color, richness, and wanton display. These aristocrats had no use for pewter dishes, sober costumes, modest feasts, or chaste jewelry. They reveled in bronze, gold, silver, silks, satins, and damasks, in cunningly wrought pearls, sapphires, rubies, and emeralds. The pageantry, masquerades, feasts, dancing, and music provided the background to their peacock world. This pride and ostentation found expression in the intellectual world as well as in the senses, and collections of antique bronzes, marble statues, illuminated manuscripts and beautifully bound books, ancient rings and seals, defined a prince as much as his palace or his pictures. The mania for collecting, as a reflection of social grandeur, emerged during the Renaissance. This desire to impress created a constant demand for the services of the great masters, even for the most trivial and ephemeral commissions - molding pastry, decorating a table, casting a candlestick, cutting an intaglio, designing a dagger - almost all of which have disappeared. The works of a few genius craftsmen - the terracottas of della Robbia, the metalwork of Cellini, the bronzes of Andrea Riccio - survive, but those belonging to nameless craftsmen who achieved high excellence are more plentiful. Their ornate cassoni, their haunting bronzes, their brightly patterned majolicas, and above all, their exquisite jewelry, scattered about the museums of America and Western Europe, give a glimpse of the sumptuous world for which they worked.

This was the way, they thought, the great Romans had lived. They loved to act the parts of classical mythology, to be Jupiter or Hebe or Apollo or Diana for a day. And although they never gave up their Christian roots, they were drawn increasingly closer to the pretense of a pagan world. It gave them what all aristocracies need: a sense of separateness, just as chivalry and feudalism had given a sense of caste to the warrior knights of the Middle Ages. Classical mythology, Neoplatonism, the mysteries of the pagan world, became chic. The education of a gentleman took on the strong classical bias it would not lose until modern times. The popular philosophers - Marsilio Ficino, Pico della Mirandola, friends of painters as well as their patrons - encouraged the revival of these ancient allegories - not to be shared with the vulgar, but to be linked with esoteric, almost private, knowledge. Poets, philosophers, painters, should speak in the language of riddles, of mysteries, which the intelligentsia alone could read. Such an attitude bred a sense of singularity and exclusiveness, which courts and courtiers found as seductive as sin. Even Leonardo jotted down the trivial riddles of the Sforza, and Pico boasted in a philosophical essay, "If I am not mistaken it will be intelligible only to a few, for it is filled with many mysteries from the secret philosophies of the ancients." The esoteric and the mysterious developed a fashionable following, and its cult opened the floodgates not only to much of the nonsense of late Neoplatonism, but also to astrology, to the language of emblems, and to the absurdities of late medieval bestiaries, and into the revival of learning was intermingled a great deal of hocus-pocus. Much of this is germane to the image that Renaissance man created of himself, but this delight in an exclusive world of myth and mystery also influenced artistic expression. A naked Mars and Venus, tired but happy from their wanton sport, might shock the uninitiated, but the cultivated knew better. Mars, of course, was War, and Venus Love, so Love could conquer War and bring forth Peace. And if by chance Venus was wearing a bit of the armor, the costume merely illustrated that Love itself involved Strife. These were simple allegories which even the fringe of the elite could read, but the theology, as well as the mythology of poetic virtue, grew ever more complex.

A great artist like Giorgione could give universality to a private and exclusive myth and deepen his genius by indulging in it, but many lesser artists could not. In their hands, the mysteries became hollow, the allegories obvious and banal. Also, this cult of a private language of art marked the drift of the tide. The great masterpieces of the Renaissance had been, and many of them, even in the first quarter of the sixteenth century, still were, great public performances, even if they were created for popes or princes. But increasingly the direction of art was toward private enjoyment, and its style was more aristocratic and more exclusive. This was bound to be, as the heroic age of the city-state waned; as power and wealth and the sense of opportunity passed to the sea-borne nations of the West. Yet the achievement was so great that the traditions created in four or five generations proved far too strong for the creative imagination to wither quickly, and for the next 400 years, the arts of Italy continued to entrance the mind of Europe.

Profile:
YOUNG MICHELANGELO
Arthur C. Clark

Our image of Michelangelo is of an old man, his face deeply marked by struggle. But as a young man, his force of character was equally apparent. The following episode, recorded by his biographer Ascanio Condivi, serves as an example. In 1506, Michelangelo left Rome in a huff because he had been barred from seeing his patron, Pope Julius II. Seven months later, when Michelangelo returned to Rome and was summoned by Julius, the pope asked him why he had left the city so abruptly. Michelangelo answered, "Not from ill will, but from disdain." A bishop nervously intervened: "Pay no attention to him, your holiness. He speaks out of ignorance. Artists are all like that." Before the bishop could finish his apology, he was hustled out of the room, and Michelangelo resumed his cordial relationship with the pope. Julius was then the most formidable figure in Christendom; Michelangelo was a powerless artist of thirty-two.

Michelangelo used his transcendent force to make over the physical perfection of antiquity. He appeared at the moment when Greco-Roman sculpture was a new and compelling discovery, accepted by artists and patrons alike as an ideal model. But the bland materialism of antique art alone could not have expressed the crisis of the human spirit that took place during the years between Martin Luther and Galileo Galilei. Michelangelo, by changing and twisting the forms of antique sculpture, created an instrument through which the spiritual turmoil of the sixteenth century could become visible.

He was born in Florentine territory on March 6, 1475, and was one of the few artists to come from aristocratic stock, although his family fortunes had declined. His father, who claimed to be descended from the counts of Canossa, objected to his son becoming an artist, which at that date meant an artisan, and even when Michelangelo was one of the most well-known men in Italy, his father still regarded his fame with incredulity. Michelangelo treated his father with patience and respect, asked for his prayers, sent him money, and often said that his sole aim in life had been to help the family regain its former status.

From the first, no one had any doubt that he was supremely gifted. After a short apprenticeship with Domenico Ghirlandaio, the most successful Florentine painter of the period, he joined the privileged youths sketching antiques in the Medici gardens under the direction of the sculptor Bertoldo di Giovanni, where he attracted the attention of Lorenzo de' Medici. Michelangelo's earliest carvings seem to confirm the story; they consist largely of imitations of a kind he would have only learned in this particular school. Bertoldo's own masterpiece was a bronze relief of a battle, mimicking an antique sarcophagus in Pisa; Michelangelo's earliest carving is also an imitation of a battle sarcophagus, the Rape of Deianira. This first carving foreshadows not only the classical style of his Florentine period, but the anticlassical expressiveness of his later works. In many respects, it is closer to the Last Judgment of the Sistine Chapel than to the cartoon of the Battle of Cascina. Michelangelo's heroic seriousness was perhaps a step back from the daintiness of the quattrocento to the passion and gravity of the first founders of Tuscan art. His earliest drawings were copies of Giotto di Bondone, and Dante's poems were his continual inspiration.

During his years in the Medici garden and for some time afterward, Michelangelo's conscious effort was directed toward imitating the classical style, and he succeeded so well that one of his works, a sleeping cupid, was sold as an antique. When the fraud was discovered, Michelangelo, received praise for his skill, and afterward, the cupid was purchased by one of the most celebrated women of the Renaissance, the art patron Isabella d'Este. It has now disappeared, and the Bacchus, which survives from about the same era, suggests that the loss is not a serious one: The Bacchus is an unattractive imitation of Hellenistic sculpture. The swaying movement of the body and the beauty of the head fail to compensate for the lack of tension in the modeling, and one wonders how Michelangelo, even in a technical exercise, suppressed his energetic hand.

The Bacchus was executed in Rome soon after Michelangelo's arrival there in 1496. After the death of Lorenzo de' Medici in 1492, he stayed two more years in Florence, and is thought to have studied anatomy under the protection of the prior of Santo Spirito. These were the years when the Dominican friar Girolamo Savonarola was the virtual ruler of Florence, and although Michelangelo was never a direct follower, he read Savonarola's books throughout his life and told Condivi that he could still hear the preacher's voice ringing in his ears. The two essential ingredients of Michelangelo's art, a passion for anatomy and a consciousness of sin, were poured into his mind at the same moment. But he was unhappy in the Florence of Lorenzo's son, Piero de' Medici; and in

October 1494, he embarked on the first of a series of panic flights that he experienced several times throughout his life. Psychologists have questioned why this man of immense moral courage, who was utterly indifferent to physical hardship, should have suffered from these bouts of irrational fear. Perhaps his continuous inner tension led to an occasional snapping of the spirit, which expressed itself in the sudden need to escape. Or perhaps he had a legitimate reason for running away and felt he must preserve his life at any cost. In 1494, he fled to Bologna, where his gifts were immediately recognized, and he was commissioned to work on the chief sculptural project of the town, the ark of St. Dominic. But fifteenth-century Bologna had little to offer to a youth of Michelangelo's genius, and he soon returned to Florence and then moved on to Rome.

He arrived in Rome in the summer of 1496 at the age of twenty-one, bearing a letter of introduction from banker and politician Lorenzo di Pierfrancesco de' Medici. A week after his arrival, he wrote Lorenzo, "There are many beautiful things here." Michelangelo's chief patron, Jacopo Galli, already had a considerable collection of antiquities, and Michelangelo's Bacchus was given a place of honor among them. However, his outstanding work during this first visit to Rome was the Pietà in St. Peter's Cathedral. It was commissioned by a French cardinal, Jean Bilheres, accounting for

Michelangelo's acceptance of a Gothic motif in which the full-grown Christ lies on his mother's knees. The Pietà was originally a wood carving, and adapting it to marble was a feat of technical skill. In this work, he shows the consummate mastery of his craft, which his contemporaries, both artists and patrons, valued so highly. It also required a stretch of the imagination, for he achieved what theorists tell us is impossible - a perfect fusion of Gothic and Classic art. The motif and sentiment are northern, the physical beauty of the nude Christ is Greek; and Michelangelo has given the Virgin's head, painfully distorted in Gothic Pietàs, a union of physical and spiritual beauty entirely his own. Since the Pietà was put in place, people have questioned how the grieving mother of a grown man could appear so young and beautiful. It expresses in vivid, colloquial form the doctrines of Neoplatonism, which he absorbed from the Medicean philosophers of his boyhood, and the physical perfection reflects a pure and noble spirit. Michelangelo's belief led his friend Lorenzo di Pierfrancesco to commission Botticelli's Venus, and we know from Michelangelo's sonnets that it justified his admiration of the naked beauty of young men. Our modern way of thinking may reject Neoplatonism as a compound of myth and self-deception, but there is no question that Michelangelo believed (in Spenser's words) that "soule is form, and doth the bodie make."

In 1501, Michelangelo returned to Florence. The Florentine republic had been able to assert some of the heroic virtues that had made it great a century before, and Michelangelo must have found the atmosphere of his native city a sharp contrast to the relaxed lifestyle of his youth or the parasitic, antiquarian character of Rome. It suited him perfectly, and he immediately was called upon by the city magistrates to carry out commissions that would express the pride, vigor, and austere idealism of their regime. The results were the David and the cartoon of the Battle of Cascina.

The David was carved out of a gigantic block of marble from which, seventy years earlier, the sculptor Agostino di Duccio had begun to carve the figure of a prophet. Agostino had completed little more than a knot of drapery, and when the block was given to Michelangelo, his first act was to cut this drapery away. In his austere and uncompromising nudity, the David exhibits the essence of Michelangelo's ideal. The torso is equal to the finest work of antiquity, both in science and vitality. Cut out the head and the hands, and you have one of the most perfect classical works of the Renaissance. Put them back, and you add the rough Tuscan accent that was part of his birthright. There is a certain lack of harmony between the two elements: the David is an imperfect work in many respects. The marble block was too thin, but apart from this fact, Michelangelo made a mistake common at the time: He took a motif from a relief as the basis for a figure in the round. Regardless, the David is a work of overwhelming power and magnificence, and it is Michelangelo's first heroic work. The heroic in life or art is based on the consciousness that life is a struggle, and in this struggle, it is courage, strength of will, and determination that matter, not intelligence nor sensibility. The heroic involves a contempt of convenience and a sacrifice of creature comforts that contribute to what we call a civilized life. It is the enemy of happiness. But we recognize it as humankind's supreme achievement. For the heroic is not merely a struggle with material obstacles, it is a struggle with Fate. It magnifies the individual in his conflict with destiny, and as such, it is the highest expression of a humanist ideal. But the heroic looks beyond the borders of humanism. To struggle with Fate, man must become more than man; he must aspire to be a god. If there is a single point at which the classical art of antiquity turns toward the Middle Ages, it is when the emperor is accepted as a god. The first great medieval work is the statue of Constantine at Barletta: Like the David, it is of heroic size. On the perfectly antique body of the David is a head that looks, with proud and conscious heroism, away from the happy, concrete world of the quattrocento. Like other great revolutions in history, we may wish that it had never happened, but once it has taken place, we must accept it.

The mere size of the David - the statue stands over sixteen feet high - impressed Michelangelo's contemporaries. As a technical achievement, it was a source of civic pride. Significantly, the committee of artists who considered its site removed it from the cathedral and placed it in front of the Palazzo della Signoria, the center of government. A few months later, in this building, Michelangelo began the other great composition of his heroic Florentine years, the Battle of Cascina. Michelangelo was competing with Leonardo da Vinci, but unlike Leonardo's Battle of Anghiari, the Battle of Cascina was never carried out as a painting, and the cartoon on which it was based proved so irresistible to artists that it was soon cut up and lost. Vasari called it "the school of all the world," and Benvenuto Cellini pronounced the professional verdict when he said that Michelangelo never did better. What gave it this immense authority? We can see from copies and from Michelangelo's original studies that it consisted of a number of nude men grouped in such a way as to show the human body in action. Each body was a perfect human specimen modeled with anatomic knowledge, posed completely and nobly. Such poses were the legacy of antique art, surviving almost like symbols, through 400 years of attrition; and in fact, some of Michelangelo's drawings for the Battle are not done from nature, but from wax models he had made from antiques. The Battle of Cascina was the foundation of the academic ideal that has dominated art education throughout the centuries, and the fact that Michelangelo transcended this ideal has always confused his more academic admirers.

Michelangelo's vision of antique art was not bound by the firm and finished outlines of the Cascina drawings. Throughout his life, he had two ideals of antiquity that, in a sense, complemented each other. One was the ideal of perfection, the belief that the durability of antique art was based on the unflinching firmness of every detail. This had inspired the Bacchus and the David and would be later seen in the drawings of cameos and gems Michelangelo executed for his friend Tommaso dei Cavalieri. But parallel with this admiration for completeness, Michelangelo was fascinated by the fragmentary character of ancient sculpture, and the appeal of these weather-worn survivors was stronger because they gave free play to the imagination. This attitude toward ruins and fragments became common in what we call the Romantic Movement. Michelangelo was not the first man to feel it - Mantegna had already made evocative use of ruins - but he was the first to let it influence his style. The rough and unfinished state of Michelangelo's sculpture has evoked endless speculation, and no doubt the cause lies deep in his temperament. It is likely that he was encouraged by the suggestive decay of antique sculpture. Proof of this dates from the time of the Battle cartoon, in the unfinished figure of St. Matthew, commissioned by the Duomo in 1503 and executed a year or two later, which mimics a battered Roman figure, the so-called Pasquino, that had already inspired Donatello. It's doubtful that this rather grotesque work would have appealed to the two great artists had it been better preserved. Only in decay were the large lines of movement perceptible, and gave the effect of a giant struggling to escape the mists of antiquity.

This titanic struggle was an aspect of Michelangelo's character that had already appeared in the Dejanira relief and came to dominate his art; the crumbling magnificence of antique sculpture showed him that he could express it by leaving much to the spectator's imagination. This presented him with two other advantages that appeal strongly to modern artistic principles: It allowed him to preserve the style and character of his material, and it allowed him to eliminate those parts of a figure that did not fit into the main rhythm of his design, as with the arms of the Torso Belvedere.

This struggle of form to emerge from matter reaches its climax in the marble figures destined for the tomb of Julius II. In March 1505, Michelangelo was summoned to Rome and commanded to design and execute the greatest tomb in Christendom. His new master was a formidable man of action, with a powerful mind and boundless ambition, as proud and willful as Michelangelo himself. It was a relationship for which posterity must be grateful, for without Julius II, Michelangelo might never have developed the full power of his imagination.

In the summer, he went to Carrara to oversee the quarrying of blocks of marble big enough for the tomb, and he remained there for eight months, inaccessible in that awe-inspiring landscape, surrounded by stone. These long sojourns in Carrara, repeated several times in his life, were like religious retreats to Michelangelo and were the prelude to his greatest activity. He returned to Rome in the winter of 1505-1506, ready to concentrate all his force on executing his ideas. Then a catastrophe occurred that all writers on Michelangelo have called the tragedy of the tomb. Pope Julius refused to see him. It was Michelangelo's first experience with court intrigue and the capriciousness of princes. Later in life, he would accept such intrigues with a firm and melancholy stoicism, but to the young man of thirty-one, his mind charged with colossal images, his spirit burning like a fire, this treachery was intolerable. In April 1506, he left Rome without a word and returned to Florence. For seven months, the Pope tried to lure him back to Rome, but Michelangelo was suspicious and the Florentine government protected him. Finally, when the Pope conquered Bologna in November, Michelangelo felt bound to go there and ask for forgiveness. Although Condivi says that this account came from Michelangelo, contemporary documents suggest that the artist was considerably more penitent.

A Quarrel With the Pope

A letter from Michelangelo to the papal architect Giuliano da Sangallo, sent from Florence in 1506:

I learn from a letter sent by you that the Pope was angry at my departure, that he is willing to place the money at my disposal and to carry out what was agreed upon between us; also, that I am to come back and fear nothing.

As far as my departure is concerned, the truth is that on Holy Saturday I heard the Pope, speaking at table with a jeweler and the Master of the Ceremonies, say that he did not want to spend another baiocco on stones whether small or large, which surprised me very much. However, before I set out, I asked him for some of the money required for the continuation of my work. His Holiness replied that I was to come back again on Monday, and I went on Monday, and on Tuesday, and on Wednesday, and on Thursday, - as His Holiness saw. At last, on the Friday morning, I was turned out, that is to say, I was driven away; and the person who turned me away said he knew who I was, but that such were his orders. Thereupon, having heard those words on Saturday and seeing them afterward put into execution, I lost all hope. But this alone was not the whole reason of my departure. There was also another cause but I do not wish to write about it; enough that it made me think that, if I were to remain in Rome, my own tomb would be prepared before that of the Pope. This is the reason for my sudden departure.

Now you write to me on behalf of the Pope, and in similar manner you will read this letter to the Pope. Give His Holiness to understand that I am more eager to proceed with the work than ever I was before, and that if he really wishes to have this tomb erected it would be well for him not to vex me as to where the work is to be done, provided that within the agreed period of five years it be erected in St. Peter's, on the site he shall choose, and it be a beautiful work, as I have promised: for I am persuaded that it be a work without an equal in all the world if it be carried out.

If His Holiness now wishes to proceed, let him deposit the said money here in Florence . . .

Almost as a penance, he was commissioned to make a gigantic bronze statue of the Pope to go over the door of San Petronio in Bologna. It cost him one of the most miserable and unproductive years of his life, and shortly after, it had been put in place, it was broken up and melted down for the bronze.

At the beginning of March 1508, he left Bologna

for Florence, intending to settle down in his native town and complete the commissions he had left unfinished there. He thought he was "free of Rome," but within two months, his old master had forced him to return. Worse, Julius did not allow him to finish the tomb, but gave him a new, and in many ways, unsuitable commission, to paint the ceiling of the papal chapel in the Vatican, known as the Sistine. Michelangelo's early biographers believed this project was suggested by his enemy, Donato Bramante, in order to discredit him, and it's true that Michelangelo protested the commission, complaining that painting was not his art. Documents show, however, that the proposal had been discussed two years earlier, and Michelangelo had undoubtedly practiced painting. The Holy Family, or Doni Tondo, in the Uffizi, dates from 1504, and as Ghirlandaio's apprentice, he probably had a hand in the frescoes of Santa Maria Novella.

The Sistine ceiling was more of an intellectual challenge than a technical one for Michelangelo. Prior to this assignment, his sculptures had been concerned with single figures or traditional themes, and in the Battle of Cascina, the subject was just a pretext to paint. Now he was charged with illustrating the first phase of human destiny. He was no longer concerned solely with problems of form, but with philosophic problems as well.

In most history paintings of the Renaissance, the artist was usually given a "program" by either his patron or some attendant poet or philosopher. But Michelangelo, in a well-known letter, explains that he was told to work out his subject for himself. Even he could not conceive the whole theme in a single flash of inspiration; the project developed both in subject and style as the work continued. Yet, at some early point, Michelangelo recognized that the story of the Creation could be transformed from a fanciful narrative into a profound philosophy. He compelled us to read his "histories" in reverse order. Entering the chapel, above our head, is the Drunkenness of Noah; at the far end, over the altar, is the Creation. In this manner, the ceiling illustrates the Neoplatonic doctrine, so dear to Michelangelo, and so often expressed in his sonnets, that life must be a progression from the servitude of the body to the liberation of the soul. It begins with the inert figure of Noah, where the body has taken possession, and ends with the figure of the Almighty dividing light from darkness, in which the body has been transformed into a symbol of the spirit, where even the head, with its too evident human associations, has become indistinct.

The same evolution of spirit and style can be seen in the athletes, those deeply personal creations which come to most people's minds at the mention of Michelangelo. They are not mere decoration, but symbolize the thoughts of the prophets and seers in the arches and link them to the histories. But because this subject is represented by a single naked youth, we are more conscious of changes in style. At first, they are classical: symmetrical, bound by a firm outline, forming a closed rhythm, and several are actually derived from antique gems. The athletes on the middle of the ceiling, beside the Creation of Eve, are less symmetrical, and the unity of planes has been abandoned. In the last pair of athletes, those beside the Creation of Light, a balanced and reciprocal movement is abandoned, and Michelangelo has created a continuous movement which twists around the central scene.

In this twisting rhythm, he is employing a technique he had visualized almost five years earlier, after seeing the famous antique group known as the Laocoön. It had been discovered in January 1506, and Michelangelo had been one of the first to admire it and recognize that it confirmed his own feelings about the potential expressiveness of the nude. But he had a long period of gestation, and it was not until 1510 that characteristics of the Laocoön are perceptible in his work. Then, in the Crucifixion of Hamar and the Brazen Serpent, he uses the tormented rhythms and violent foreshortening to express mental and physical agony pushed to their limits. By 1511, Michelangelo had established a style that would captivate artists for hundreds of years.

Two years before the ceiling was completed, rumblings of its magnificence began to surface. Raphael had been smuggled in by Bramante and immediately added a Michelangelesque figure to the already complete design of his fresco of the School of Athens.

When, on October 31, 1512, the frescoes were officially unveiled, artists and connoisseurs were prepared for something that would change the course of painting. In fact, it did just that - and not only painting, but the whole mode of feeling. The freshness and wonder of the early Renaissance, the delight in living creatures unburdened with a conscience - birds, children, flowers - all this was crushed by the oppressive awareness of human destiny. And instead of a natural ease of arrangement in which flower was set beside flower and face beside face, a new unity of struggle was born, of Hercules grappling with the lion.

On October 31, 1512, when the ceiling was finally unveiled, Michelangelo was thirty-seven. He lived to be eighty-nine. In his last half century, he executed some of his greatest works - the marble prisoners, the Medici tombs, the Last Judgment, the marvelous and tragic Pietàs of his old age. The mood becomes graver; the confidence in physical beauty diminishes and is finally rejected with a kind of horror. But there is an unwavering aim to use the human body as an instrument to reveal the ascent of the human soul. The body must perish, and the soul must be judged: Michelangelo became increasingly preoccupied with death and the consciousness of sin. But in his imagination, body and soul remain indivisible, fatally united in their struggle. Out of this involvement, he creates movement: gestures, limbs, proportions that allow us poor mortals, with our sordid material interests, to become, through the contemplation of form, momentarily capable of spiritual life.

4
FLORENCE
CRADLE OF HUMANISM

"In a few hours they were burnt, their legs and arms gradually dropping off; part of their bodies remaining hanging to the chains, a quantity of stones were thrown to make them fall, as there was a fear of the people getting hold of them; and then the hangman and those whose business it was, hacked down the post and burnt it on the ground, bringing a lot of brushwood, and stirring the fire up over the dead bodies, so that the very least piece was consumed. Then they fetched carts, and accompanied by the mace-bearers, carried the last bit of dust to the Arno, by the Ponte Vecchio, in order that no remains should be found."

So wrote the diarist Luca Landucci after watching the execution of Girolamo Savonarola and his disciples. So ended the life of the strange, doom-haunted Dominican monk from Ferrara, whose bitter tirades against luxury, greed, extortion, and tyranny had torn Florentine society apart.

The Piazza in which Savonarola met his end was adorned with some of the most profoundly moving works of Renaissance art. He had given the apocalyptic sermons for which he was condemned under the vaulting dome of the cathedral, a triumph of the new architecture. In his audience had sat the flower of Italian humanism - Pico della Mirandola, Angelo Poliziano, and Marsilio Ficino, the president of the Platonic Academy - and he told them roughly that an old woman knew more of faith than their Plato. Even Lorenzo de' Medici, the greatest of all Florentine patrons, had sought his friendship, only to be spurned. Savonarola rejected the Renaissance. He would have none of it, ignoring the fact that for 100 years Florence had led Italy in painting, sculpture, philosophy, and sophistication. Of all Italian cities, Florence had been the cradle of the Renaissance, but curiously, except in its earliest days, the spirit of Savonarola had always been abroad. Florence was a city of violent contrasts, a city of the light and the dark.

Physically, Florence deceives: The golden Tuscan landscape, rich, fertile, gentle in climate, suggests a pastoral, idyllic life in harmony with nature. Here is a countryside made for a Giorgione or a

Titian, yet Florence produced neither, nor indeed any painter who sought to immortalize the poetry of nature. Florentine life was brutal, not gentle. However rich and beautiful its situation might be, economically and strategically its position was always desperate. To the west, controlling its only outlet to the sea, lay prosperous and powerful Pisa, linked by its commerce with the four corners of the Mediterranean world. Across the route to Pisa, Florence had an unbeatable enemy in Lucca. To the north stood Milan, ravenous for land and rich in men and money. To the south, almost on Florence's doorstep, Siena controlled the road to Rome, and the Sienese were as fiercely proud and warlike as the Florentines. To the east were the wolves, the ravagers, the petty tyrants of the Papal Patrimony who lived by war and violence; for these despots, the rich lands of Tuscany were sweet to plunder. To survive, let alone expand, Florence required from its citizens both courage and resourcefulness, a willingness to practice diplomacy as well as war. Both required money, and in the end, wealth alone enabled Florence to survive and to triumph over the disadvantages of its geographical situation. The realities of Florentine life were the sword and the florin. The use of both was improved by skill in reading human nature, and it is not surprising that a preoccupation with destiny lies at the heart of the Florentine Renaissance.

Despite its perils, Florence triumphed. The prime source of its strength and wealth lay in its arti, the guilds that united its merchants and skilled craftsmen. One of the earliest to be organized was the arte di Calimala, and it held its dominating position throughout the golden age of Florence. The Calimala was a guild of merchants who brought undressed cloths from England, Flanders, and France to Florence, where they were reworked into fine materials and dyed in the splendid, vivid colors that Renaissance painters have made so memorable - the blues and crimsons and reds in which they dressed their saints and Madonnas. They exported the finished goods throughout Europe, and the stamp of the guild became a guarantee of worth and workmanship. The guild, which became a model for others that would dominate Florence in the late twelfth and thirteenth centuries, was meticulously ruled and its members subjected to strict discipline, both in their public and moral lives. Including the Calimala, there were seven guilds - the wool merchants, silk weavers, bankers, notaries, druggists (members of this guild also dealt in spices and precious stones), and furriers. These seven included all the great merchants of Florence, who formed the heart of its economic life. But Florence was a large town, with many influential shopkeepers who formed their own guilds, known as the lesser arts - the innkeepers, shoemakers, carpenters, blacksmiths, grocers, bakers, and the like - fourteen in all. Each guild had consuls, notaries, and a banner-bearer, as well as a church in which it held its special masses, for these merchants were deeply steeped in religion. (At the head of each page of one of their surviving account books is the sign of the cross, made to make forgery hell-worthy.) The Florentine guilds were small worlds unto themselves, closely regulated, self-conscious, jealous of their rights and customs, and fully aware of their power.

Relations between the greater and lesser guilds were often uneasy. The lesser guilds felt their numbers gave them a right to power; the greater knew that their money sustained the government of Florence both in peace and in war. Yet there were never more than 3,000 or 4,000 men in these twenty-one guilds, and Florence had a population of nearly 100,000. Most people worked for a day wage - spinning, dyeing, weaving, carding, or hauling the great bales of wool and cloth and silk – the people who had fought for the liberties within the city and for its rich territories and within whose hearts Savonarola's words burned like fire. They were organized into four districts, each with four quarters led by a banner under which each citizen was enrolled to fight, if necessary, for the city. From these quarters, the governors of the city, who made up the Signory, or council, that ruled Florence, were selected; they made peace or war and levied taxes. Naturally, the Signory was highly ceremonial and its chief officers, the priors, lived in luxury, but their tenure was brief, for they ruled for only two months. To control this complex governmental machine, men fought in the streets, assassinated, exiled, pillaged, and destroyed each other generation after generation, so that one Florentine gloomily remarked there were enough citizens in exile to populate another city. The main strife revolved around who was worthy to be prior - whether power should be widely distributed or kept close - and whether the major arts or the minor arts should dominate the government. There was strife not only within the ranks of the guilds but among the restless public, often swayed by hunger due to the economic storms of uncontrolled capitalism. Over the centuries, power in Florence drifted into the hands of oligarchs only to be snatched out, but never for long.

During most of the Renaissance, political power in Florence was in the hands of a group of wealthy merchants, led by the Medici family. This closely knit oligarchy controlled all the elections, and more importantly, they handled the city's taxes. They were also the inheritors of vast wealth from the four quarters of Europe.

Suspicious and guarded, these merchants clung tenaciously to their power, willing to serve the Medici only as long as the Medici served them. Their greed and envy occasionally brought them close to conspiracy, and the Pazzi family's plot to kill two Medici sons in the Duomo was considered treasonous. Politically and financially these men had little foresight: They exploited their power to siphon the city's riches into their own pockets. Yet they had one saving grace: They had been born into a tradition of civic patronage. Their fathers, and their fathers before them, had endowed monasteries, beautified churches, and established charities. Because a sense of sin still clung to usury and to the banker's trade, they felt the need to return a tithe on their profits. Naturally, they were encouraged by particular acts of God's goodness, and their piety turned quickly into patronage. But around 1400, this tradition began to change.

A war between the literary and artistic movements in Florence resulted in a remarkable leap forward in painting, sculpture, architecture, philosophy, and countless other arts and crafts. The change was as dramatic as water turning into ice.

By 1343, after failing to secure Tuscany by force, Florence had resolved to ally with neighboring city-states, to protect rather than absorb. As Coluccio Salutati, chancellor of Florence and one of its first great humanists, wrote, the Florentines who hated tyranny at home were willing to defend the liberties of others. The city's governing circles felt strongly that Florentines were the true heirs of Rome; Salutati, Leonardo Bruni, and Poggio

Bracciolini studied Cicero in addition to running Florence's diplomacy and collecting its taxes and began to believe that the good life could only be attained if people dedicated themselves to civic virtues. They talked about Rome, Cicero, and Plato with the artists they patronized. They knew they were right in their interpretation of the past and the present when, in 1402, Florence withstood the might of Gian Galeazzo Visconti, who was poised to overwhelm the city and bring all of Lombardy and Tuscany under his sway. Then Gian Galeazzo died. The threat to Florence passed, but in passing, a mood turned into an attitude about life.

The Florentines did not consider their salvation an accident. For them, it was a matter of steadfast republicans thwarting tyrants. The ancient Roman virtues had been reborn in Florence, giving the city an identity with the past. The year 1402 presented a new freedom, a breaking of the shackles of the immediate past, invigorated not only by philosophy and history but also the arts.

Interest in classics and in ancient art, delight in new techniques of painting, sculpture, and architecture existed before the cataclysmic struggle with Milan, but no one can doubt that it gave an immense impetus to the Florentine Renaissance. At the height of the struggle, the city appointed Chrysoloras, the first and the most deeply influential teacher of Greek, a public lecturer. A belief that classical learning could mold citizen's character, a conviction that a strong moral code could be derived from studying its philosophy, became deeply embedded in the Florentine tradition. When the Medici founded and encouraged a Platonic academy and patronized the great philosophers, the purpose of their patronage was widely understood: It would strengthen a singularly Florentine attitude. And the encouragement to classical studies given by the humanistic Renaissance in Florence was in harmony with scholarly activity scattered throughout the courts and cities of Italy.

Yet the greatest gains from this identification with the antique were in the arts, particularly sculpture. As in ancient Athens, statues informed citizens about their public life. The David of Donatello and the David of Michelangelo both told the Florentines that their city had always been a giant-killer, proud of its liberty: The citizens dragged Judith and Holofernes from the Medici palace and set it up in front of the Palazzo della Signoria to underline what should happen to tyrants. In no other place were sculptors so handsomely patronized or so deeply admired. The works of Florence's great masters graced Rome, Venice, Milan, and the lesser cities of Italy. In architecture, while Milan and Venice lingered in the grip of the Gothic, and Rome lay in ruins, Filippo Brunelleschi was recreating the austere harmonics of the classical world and giving the Florentines a setting for their intense civic consciousness. In painting, there was the same sense of gravitas, the weight of human character, the power of human destiny, particularly before the self-indulgence of the High Renaissance produced a more esoteric cultivation of art. Even so, Michelangelo recalls the tradition of his city created by Giotto and Masaccio.

The struggle with Milan did more than render humanism fashionable or stimulate the arts. It consolidated the power of the oligarchy, and peculiarly so, as the death of Gian Galeazzo plucked them from the jaws of destruction and set them on a course of military success. Florence, still free, still republican, enjoyed a prosperity, a fame, and an unparalleled serenity that she owed to the antique virtue of her government and its citizens. Oligarchies, however, are rarely stable for long; after the death in 1417 of Maso degli Albizzi, the most powerful member of the ruling oligarchy, a struggle for power between the old class and the guilds erupted once more. By exploiting their jealousies, Giovanni de' Medici, and subsequently in 1429, his son Cosimo, were able to establish their family so securely in power that Cosimo s grandson Lorenzo enjoyed the power if not the title of a prince. Yet even at the height of the family's greatness, respect was always given to the letter of the republican constitution. The survival of the Medici and the ease with which they defeated later conspiracies against them were due to the loyal support of their fellow merchants as well as their dependents.

During this half-century of Medicean rule, Florence dominated the intellectual and artistic life of Italy: Cosimo spent enormously on buildings, sculpture, and paintings. Feeling himself in God's debt, he reconstructed and embellished his favorite monastery in San Marco, as well as his parish church in San Lorenzo. Following in his footsteps, his son Piero ordered a sumptuous cabinet for the miraculous crucifix in San Miniato al Monte and another at Santissima Annunziata, where the marble alone cost 4,000 florins. Cosimo built his own modest palace strictly according to the style of the day; he patronized Donatello for as long as he lived, and as might be expected from such a dedicated Florentine, sculpture was his greatest passion after architecture. He preferred his sons to deal with painters and decorators.

Cosimo's grandson, Lorenzo the Magnificent, amazed by the staggering sums that his grandfather had spent, preferred the less expensive patronage of philosophers. Nevertheless, he maintained the tradition of his ancestors, and as the beauty and splendor of Florence grew, the citizens were regaled with pageants, tournaments, and carnivals. It was a reckless world in which capital was easily squandered on military maneuvers, diplomatic activity, and Lorenzo's desire to maintain his standing in Italy whatever the cost.

As Florence's fame reached new heights, so did its debt (not that the debt worried the oligarchy - they lent the money on excellent security and at a spectacular interest). The world was a rich man's oyster; Florentine trade stretched from Cairo to the Cotswolds, and even the shocks and disasters in the eastern Mediterranean - the spread of the Ottoman Turks and the fall of Constantinople - seemed for a time to be to Florence's advantage. The loss of Byzantine alum vital to the luxury cloth trade was immediately countered by the discovery of huge deposits at Tolfa in the Papal States, for which the Medici secured the concession. Secure and self-indulgent, the leaders of Florentine society tried to evade present and future disasters while the Florentine government tried to survive with the use of mercenaries, diplomacy, subsidies, and bribes. The call to civic virtue and the mobilization of the city's wealth and the city's men no longer appealed to a bourgeois aristocracy. Their exclusive world was too full of delights to be foolishly risked. In the soft elegance of Lorenzo di Pierfrancesco de' Medici's villa, young men might listen to Marsilio Ficino's explanations of the hidden meanings in Sandro Botticelli's Primavera, which adorned its walls; for them, bales of wool, rolls of cloth, stacked hides, and piled spices were a necessity, not a way of life, and although they could use the dagger and the sword, they were not compelled to sweat amid the horrors of war for the future of their city. Lorenzo used all his skill and authority to avoid such bleak necessities. This elegant world depended on Lorenzo's subtlety and statesmanship to prevent it from collapsing into domestic strife.

The Florentine renaissance has captivated generations by its artistic and scholarly achievements - from the serene perfection of the work of Leonardo da Vinci to the tragic realism of the observations of Niccolò Machiavelli - and all too often the grievous toil of the laboring men and women who made it possible is forgotten. The tragic situation of the common people stirred the creative imagination not only of Michelangelo, but also of Botticelli, who reflected the bright elegance and exclusive charm of the Florentine world more faithfully than any other painter. The rantings of Savonarola haunted them both.

The last decades of the fifteenth century brought a sharp reduction of Florentine trade. Englishmen were beginning to make their own cloth, and the Flemish were skillfully dressing and dyeing it. In 1478, the London bank of the Medici was closed; in 1483, the Tolfa alum concession had to be abandoned; for a time, the merchants of Florence even lost their traditional role as papal bankers. Trade with the eastern Mediterranean wasted away. Renewed wars, with expensive alliances and even more costly condottieri, added further strain to an economy which already had far too many obligations. The Florentines had been dealing in futures for too many generations, and as skillful as their financiers were, they could not conjure increased wealth from diminishing trade. For centuries, poverty had helped breed diseases that raged ferociously through the dirt-encrusted slums. Plagues, fevers, and consumption made death a constant visitor at the houses of the poor, who pleaded for the intercession of the Virgin and the saints. Religion assuaged the wounds of their poverty and its pain. For them, the elegant, exclusive domain of the scarlet-wearing burghers in their city was a bright, elusive world. The sufferings of Christ and the pity of God were easier to comprehend, and in their lives, the priest was as necessary as bread. This contradiction - poverty amid a world of profusion, extravagance, and delight - made the philosopher Pico della Mirandola seek the solace of Savonarola's mysticism; this drew Botticelli away from the gaieties and urbane moralities of the antique to accept Savonarola's prophecies; this fused Michelangelo's tragic sense of human destiny with Savonarola's apocalyptic vision.

The story of Savonarola is a mixture of tragedy and hysteria, in which genuine pity for the human condition became enmeshed in hate and muddled by political intrigue. His denunciation of worldliness, his burning of vanities, his condemnation of a lazy and corrupt clergy, were a part of the lament of the life of Europe. But Savonarola spoke at a time when the young Piero de' Medici was displaying a singular lack of his family's genius. Savonarola had the support of the discontented poor, eager for secular as well as religious hope. Those families the Medici had excluded and despised knew how to manipulate this demagogue, whose sermons could inflame a multitude. What started in evangelism ended in revolution.

The little people, the piagnoni (snivelers) as the oligarchs called them, became a power in the land. Popolo e Libertà frequently echoed in the Piazza - a cry Pisa adopted as it threw aside the Florentine yoke and claimed the protection of the French, when invasion of Italy triggered the revolution against Piero. Savonarola combined an unrealistic dependence on the French with a hatred of the papacy that bordered on insanity. His denunciations of papal sins interspersed with occasional sane bits of hardheaded diplomacy grew shriller as the French reduced their support. Pope Alexander VI - aware of and amused by his own shortcomings - tolerated Savonarola's censures only as far as diplomacy required. Time, of course, favored the pope. The French were content to use Florence, but they were not inclined to save it from itself, or to restore the Tuscan empire. In Florence, the oligarchs disliked both the rantings of Savonarola and the government of the people; the exiled Medici lurked in the wings – they were powerful in Rome. The inevitable end came:

Savonarola's supporters were defeated, and in time, the Medici returned.

The Savonarola episode is a curious mixture of idealism, ineptitude, and iniquity. Certainly Savonarola wanted a Florentine government that fully represented the citizenship - the poor and the dispossessed as well as the rich and the powerful. But he also hated life, grew drunk on his own megalomaniac visions, preferred prophecy to policy, and welcomed the disasters he had done so much to promote. Ignorance married to prejudice, blind hatred linked with a disgust for life, proved an unsatisfactory basis for statesmanship, even when practiced by a saint.

The republic was never again the same; the power of Florence was greatly diminished. For a decade after Savonarola was burned in 1498 for heresy, and after her mercenaries failed, Florence's blood and treasure were exhausted in the war with Pisa. In 1509, Pisa was captured, but the cost was much greater than the weakened resources of Florence's dwindling trade. Three years later, a refusal to act in accordance with the papacy was treated by Julius II as disrespect. His professional Spanish troops scattered the Florentine militia, followed by a papal-inspired revolution, and the Medici returned. Lacking the ability of their ancestors, they proved little better than pawns in the hands of the Medici Pope Leo X. It required further rebellions and plots, another brief republic haunted by the puritanism and religiosity of Savonarola, as well as the sack of Rome by Charles V, before Florence was finally subjected to the rule of the Medici as dukes of Tuscany. In the first three decades of the sixteenth century, the greatness of Florence faded. Economically, Florence lacked a future. The heart of its trade - cloth - was lost to England and Flanders, and banking followed trade. Florence was far more vulnerable than Venice, or even Milan, to the great decline in Mediterranean prosperity that followed the discoveries of the New World and the sea-route to the Indies.

Artists lived uneasy lives in post-Medicean Florence, for patronage grew scarce. Art and humanism no longer reflected civic virtues - these were adequately exercised by private prayer and public repentance. During the middle of the sixteenth century, the cult of sensitivity, elegance, and learning had narrowed the social basis of art and limited its appeal. In the wanderings of Leonardo and Michelangelo, in the frustrations that marred their lives and marked their art, there is a reflection of the impotence and decay of the society in which they were born and grew to adulthood.

Yet the tradition of individual destiny the Florentines had cultivated so carefully in their heroic days remained strong enough not only to sustain them throughout their tribulations, but also buoyed up a number of lesser geniuses - Il Bronzino, Jacopo Pontormo, Andrea del Sarto, and Fra Bartolomeo. And to history, the decay of Florence provided a greater stimulus than its climb to greatness. The Florentine catastrophes opened creative vistas for Machiavelli and Guicciardini. Even in its last, sad days, republican Florence still produced an astonishing array of genius, and no city of so small a compass has ever, before or since, made a greater contribution to art and letters within the brief span of a 150 years.

Profile:
LORENZO DE' MEDICI

Ralph Roeder

Although Lorenzo de' Medici was, first and last, a financier, he was much more than that. Politician, statesman, patron of art and letters - these were functions developed by his forefathers, which he inherited along with the fortune of his family. His biography begins before he was born, and he sits for his portrait under his family tree.

His great-grandfather, Giovanni di Bicci de' Medici, was the first millionaire of the family. The working-class Medici had risen through prosperous trade to the front ranks of the nobili popoiani - the merchant princes of the major guilds. But they had not abandoned their common roots, and it served them well in their subsequent rise to power. The banking business Giovanni built with branches in sixteen European capitals entitled him to a leading position among the eighty banking firms of Florence, and would have assured him a corresponding spot in the government had he chosen to claim it, since the bankers' guild supplied the capital and the connections for the state, but Giovanni prudently avoided politics. Modest and unassuming, he spent his money constructing churches, encouraging art, and practicing charity (the Foundling Hospital built for him by Brunelleschi, and the church of San Lorenzo rebuilt for him by the great architect as a family temple, were his monuments), and as long as he confined himself to such modest activities, he passed for a safe man and received quiet praise. When summoned to the Signory, he revealed a different sort of public spirit, however, by supporting, against powerful opposition, a tax reform, which substituted for the universal poll tax and the arbitrary assessment of a 1.5 percent levy on capital. This innovation was a boon for the poor, and since it was enacted when an unsuccessful war was about to be resumed, and the tax rate increased, it won him high favor with the little people. But it incensed the rich. "Since the burden was to be distributed by law and not by men," Machiavelli, the official biographer of the family, observed, "it weighed heavily on the powerful citizens and was received with extreme displeasure by the mighty." Their anger turned to alarm when the little people proposed to make the reform retroactive to compensate them for losses they had suffered in the past, but Giovanni convinced them otherwise, and having done his duty impartially, retired to private life. When he died in 1429, he was missed and mourned by those he had benefited.

The eldest son of this model Medici followed closely in his footsteps. Equally modest and unassuming and no less charitable, Cosimo also minded his own business carefully, but that business was constantly growing, and with it the motives to ruin it. The rich had not forgotten the tax reform imposed on them by his benevolent father, nor the good will he won with his churches and his charities. For four years, Cosimo went untouched, but in 1433, the Albizzi, a rival family which had been conspiring with the former nobles to uproot the Medici, judged the moment ripe to strike. In front of a Signory predisposed in their favor and a gonfaloniere in their debt, they accused the family of being a danger to the state because of their wealth and ambition. Among other proof, they cited a new mansion Cosimo was building. The evidence, based on prejudice and suspicion, was sufficient to have Cosimo arrested and imprisoned. The Albizzi, bent on obtaining the death penalty, summoned a popular assembly to appoint a balia - a commission created in emergencies and entrusted with absolute power for a limited length of time – but the balia, composed of 200 leading citizens, could not reach a decision. Many were for death, many for banishment. Many more, moved by compassion or fear, remained silent. For four days, Cosimo refused food until a friendly jailer shared it with him, and with his help Cosimo smuggled a substantial bribe to the gonfaloniere, and the sentence was commuted to ten year's banishment for himself and his family. A year later, a friendly Signory canceled the decree and recalled him. "Seldom," said Machiavelli, "has a citizen returning from a great victory been greeted by such a concourse of people and with such demonstrations of affection as Cosimo on his return from exile." After failing to seize the government by force before his return, the Albizzi family fled, and 200 of their partisans were banished or fled. When Cosimo was reproached for such a drastic purge of prominent citizens, he replied that new nobles could be made with two lengths of crimson cloth and that states were not ruled by prayers. "Better a city destroyed than lost," he added.

As a result of this experience and to prevent its recurrence, Cosimo secured a controlling influence in the government. The republic was adapted to suit his purpose. He served a brief term as gonfaloniere, but soon abandoned public office in favor of a less conspicuous but far more permanent and powerful position as banker to the republic and confidential adviser to the government. With his foes gone, his friends assumed office, and he kept them there by the customary methods of the politician. One was purely Florentine - the balia - employed whenever a direct appeal to the people was needed to support his authority, but discarded when he could afford to restore normal elections and humor his enemies. The other was money. Reviving the famous tax reform of his father and enforcing it in favor of his friends and against his foes, he wielded it as a weapon more deadly than daggers.

Neither of these methods would have lasted long, however - they served him for thirty years - had he not identified his interests completely with those of the state and guided and guarded them wisely. As banker to the commonwealth, he put the republic in his pocket by liberal loans and assumed many public expenses himself to lend it luster and prestige. He entertained distinguished visitors at his own expense and went out of his way to attract them to Florence. Once he traveled to Ferrara where a council of the Pope, the Primate of the Eastern Church, and one of the last Byzantine emperors was sitting, and induced them to move their deliberations to Florence, where he lodged them magnificently and converted the city for a season into a political, religious, cultural, and commercial convention town. The council accomplished nothing, but it left a lasting impression on Florence, where the painter Benozzo Gozzoli commemorated the exotic costumes of the Eastern dignitaries on the walls of the Medici chapel.

In foreign affairs, Cosimo took the same risks as a statesman. Like his father, he loved peace and avoided war, and with a single exception, he made war to secure peace. Reversing the traditional alliance with Venice against their mutual enemy, the aggressive duchy of Milan, he hired a soldier of fortune, Francesco Sforza, with money and means to overthrow the Visconti dynasty, and won an equally peace-loving friend in their place. When Venice and Naples turned against him, he paralyzed their military operations by calling in his loans.

Like his father, he was a builder of churches and a patron of art. Brunelleschi and Michelozzo di Bartolomeo Michelozzi, Donatello and Luca della Robbia, Fra Angelico, Filippo Lippi, and Benozzo Gozzoli worked for him building or adorning his monuments - the monastery of San Marco, the church of San Lorenzo, the Medici palace, among others - and he added to his laurels by the encouragement of learning, for he was uncommonly well educated. His agents abroad searched for rare prizes to fill his library and found the best at home: Tommaso Parentucelli, Bishop of Bologna, a fellow collector who borrowed from him to satisfy his passion for books, repaid him first by cataloguing his library and later, when he became Pope Nicholas V, by awarding the management of the papal finances to the Medici bank in Rome, whose books showed a fair profit in the Jubilee year of 1450.

But it was in the art of politics that Cosimo shone. Remaining in the background of government, he was recognized, nevertheless, both at home and abroad as the real head of state by virtue of financial sovereignty and adroit maneuvers without the support of force. Living simply and soberly, he reached the ripe old age of seventy-five, but as he aged he was crippled by gout, his grip on the government weakened, and his last days were darkened by fear for the future of his family. His fears were well founded: One of his sons was an invalid and the other died before he did, and his grandsons were mere boys. His party, once loyal and obedient, became unruly and insolent without opposition, and outraged Florence by its unbridled oppression, corruption, and excesses which the ailing, aged Cosimo could no longer control. It was a tribute to his moderation and political tact that he maintained public respect to the end, and when he was laid to rest with his father in 1464, his countrymen inscribed on the tomb of the man who had given them thirty years of domestic peace and external stability the title Pater Patriae, or "Father of the Country."

Cosimo's son, Piero, was hampered by gout, timidity, and treacherous advisers. Finding that his father's generosity had left his financial affairs in confusion and disorder, he consulted a trusted friend of his father's, who advised him to call in his loans, counting on a panic to wrest the state from his hands. Piero fell into the trap, many business failures followed, and he was denounced by his debtors as an ungrateful miser and accused of jeopardizing the prosperity of Florence to protect his capital. Piero survived this blow as well as two attempts to overthrow him by force of arms.

His five brief years as head of state, marred by civil dissension, saw one event which was to set the reputation of his son and successor. Cosimo had gilded the Florentine lily so well that Louis XI of France conferred on Piero the right to add the French fleur-de-lis to the five red balls of the Medici coat of arms, and Piero took advantage of the favor. He married his nineteen-year-old son Lorenzo into the house of Orsini, one of the great feudal families of Rome, but as this was a departure from custom (Cosimo had made it a rule to marry the Medici at home), the match was unpopular in Florence. Malcontents complained that the middle class was too ambitious, that the Medici were satisfied with nothing less than a foreign and baronial alliance, and that they would soon be assuming the style of princes themselves. The marriage was celebrated by a tournament, an aristocratic spectacle so foreign and unfamiliar in Florence that Machiavelli felt it necessary to explain it: ". . . a scuffle of men on horseback in which the leading young men of the city contended with the most renowned cavaliers of Italy; and among the Florentine youth the most famous was Lorenzo, who carried off the prize not by favor but by his own valor." Splendidly attired in ornate armor, bearing the French fleur-de-lis on his shield and the Medici coat of arms on his banner, the powerful young athlete easily unseated all his opponents, and the pride his countrymen took in his prowess reconciled them to his marriage. It was superbly celebrated, and Piero, who had once been called a miser, made ample amends with the wedding feast. As Machiavelli added slyly, "Piero decided to celebrate the nuptials of his son Lorenzo with Clarice of the house of Orsini magnificently, and they were held with the pomp of apparel and all other manner of magnificence befitting such a man." Long before he earned the title of Magnificent, Lorenzo learned its political value and developed an appetite for it.

Such was the heritage of Lorenzo de' Medici. "Two days after the death of my father," he wrote in later life, "although I, Lorenzo, was very young, being only in my twenty-first year, the principal men of the city and the state came to our house to condole on our loss and encourage me to take on myself the care of the city and the state, as my father and grandfather had done. This proposal being contrary to the instincts of my youthful age and considering that the burden and danger were great, I consented unwillingly, but I did so to protect our friends and our property, for it fares ill in Florence with anyone who possesses great wealth without any control in the government." Lorenzo, more fortunate than his father, however, found faithful friends who loyally rallied to him and due to their devotion, he succeeded him peacefully. With the backing of eminent citizens bent on banishing civil dissension from Florence, he began governing under favorable conditions, and the first years were fairly easy both at home and abroad.

For nine years, Lorenzo was indeed the most fortunate of his family. His father had been called the most mediocre of the Medici, but no one could say that about his son. Sheltered by his family tree and with no opposition to overcome, Lorenzo encountered only critics. Political writer and statesman Francesco Guicciardini was one of them, and he echoed many others. Lorenzo, he said, "desired glory and excellence above all other men and can be criticized for having had too much ambition even in minor things; he did not want to be equaled or imitated even in verses or games or exercises and turned angrily on anyone who did so." Unlike his father and grandfather, who were mature men when they became heads of the house, he was still young and wanted the pleasures and the carefree enjoyment of life. Besides his other accomplishments, he was a poet - another variation from his ancestors, who although they took many risks, never ventured to write verses - and he composed fluently for festive occasions. Improving on his father, he entertained Florence continually with masquerades, pageants, and processions, engaging the best artists to design the masks and decorate the floats, and taking part in them himself; for these he wrote his Trionfi, his Canzoni a Ballo, and best of all, his famous carnival songs. Later historians were scandalized by their obscenity and lamented that Lorenzo catered to the taste of the common people, forgetting that Lorenzo was young, virile, and lusty. A more serious charge was raised by his elders, who saw in these lighthearted frolics a profound political design to charm and divert the people from public affairs, as his father had done. But this was crediting Lorenzo with wisdom beyond his years and unwarranted guile, for these were untroubled times of peace and plenty, and public affairs went well. If ever history could be happy, it was then, and he made the most of life while he could sing:

> How passing fair is youth,
> Forever fleeting away;
> Who happy would be, let him be;
> Of tomorrow who can say?

An uneasy premonition of doom prompted the haunting refrain, for, in fact, the time was approaching.

In every generation, plots had been laid to ruin his family. They were part of his heritage, and his turn came in 1478 with the Pazzi conspiracy. The Pazzi were an old and numerous family with aristocratic pretensions even grander than those of the Medici, and they had old scores to settle with Lorenzo.

Wealthy and proud, the Pazzi had been denied public office and the honors to which they were entitled, and they bore the discrimination and abuse bitterly. The most sensitive of the family, Francesco, unable to suffer any longer, fled to Rome, where he fell in with a nephew of the Pope, and between them, they hatched a plot for their mutual benefit. As ambitious as he was lowborn, Pope Sixtus IV was burdened with six covetous nephews, three of whom he placed profitably in the Church, and a fourth in Imola, one of the poorest and smallest of the papal fiefs. When Francesco proposed to create a vacancy in Florence, Sixtus consented to second the Pazzi in ousting the Medici. Encouraged, Francesco returned to Florence to enlist his family. Jacopo de' Pazzi, the head of the house, hesitated until he was convinced that the scheme had the blessing and the backing of the Pope.

On the surface, the scheme was senseless: A foreign potentate aiming to add Florence to the papal domain and impose a papal cub on a fiercely freedom-loving people, and relying on an ambitious Florentine family to fill the vacancy, the plot was a patchwork of cross-purposes calculated to fail. Yet it nearly succeeded.

The Pope opened hostilities by canceling the concession of the Medici bank in Rome and transferring it to the Pazzi. Then he appointed as Archbishop of Pisa a member of another family hostile to the Medici, the Salviati. Notwithstanding these unfriendly acts, Lorenzo seems to have suspected nothing. In April 1478, the conspirators assembled in Florence and were entertained in Lorenzo's villa at Fiesole, where they planned to kill him during a banquet. However, his brother Giuliano was absent, and since the murder of both was essential to success, they postponed until the following morning, during the celebration of High Mass in the Duomo, where both were scheduled to appear for the celebration of Easter Sunday. The hired assassin, however, suffered an attack of conscience and shrank from committing sacrilege, as well as murder in the cathedral. Francesco de' Pazzi, a priest, and another accomplice assumed his duties, but an additional hitch developed. Giuliano was missing when the service began, and they were forced to fetch him to the slaughter, coaxing him out of bed, where he was nursing a bad knee. They braced him between them, feeling his body to make sure that he was unarmed, and brought him limping to the altar. Having finally united the victims, they struck. The church was crowded; the signal for attack was the moment the officiating Cardinal raised the Host and hundreds of heads bowed devoutly. Giuliano bent obediently, the priest behind his back struck the first blow, and Francesco finished him off with eighteen more - so furiously that he hacked himself in the leg and in the confusion was mistaken for one of the victims.

Lorenzo escaped with a gash in the neck and ran into the sacristy, where his friends bolted the doors and waited for help. In the meanwhile, Archbishop Salviati, entrusted with the most difficult part of the undertaking, entered the palace to seize the government. His confederates waited below in the chancery, where they locked themselves in by mistake, while he climbed to the upper floor to talk with the Signory. His agitation aroused their suspicion, and before he could call for help the gonfaloniere hanged him, stammering, from the window. The city was now in an uproar. Francesco de' Pazzi, weak from loss of blood, took to his bed and begged his uncle to rally the people to their cause. With 100 armed men, Jacopo de' Pazzi ran through the streets crying "Liberty!" without arousing a response, and encountering a mob acclaiming the Medici, turned and fled. Lorenzo, escorted by his friends, returned home unharmed.

The mob avenged him loyally. Francesco de' Pazzi was dragged from his bed and hanged beside the body of the Archbishop, dangling limply with a cluster of comrades overhead. A furious manhunt followed: Everyone even remotely connected with the conspiracy was brought to justice or mobbed; seventy perished in the first four days, and 200 more before the tumult subsided. Jacopo de' Pazzi, was caught and killed, but not allowed to rest in his grave: A horde of scavenging boys unearthed his body, dragged it through the streets, and flung it naked into the Arno. Of his ten sons and nephews, two were beheaded; the survivors were sentenced to prison or exiled, and the name Pazzi was banned.

Infuriated by the failure of the plot, the Pope demanded that Lorenzo surrender and that the Florentine government answer for the sacrilege committed against the Archbishop. Lorenzo protested that his only crime was not allowing himself to be murdered; the Signory seconded him, circulated the confession of one of the conspirators exposing the Pope's complicity in the plot, and appealed to the sovereigns of Europe for support. When the sovereigns of Europe sided with the Medici, the Pope excommunicated the Florentine state; the Florentine clergy outlawed him in turn, and the Pope declared war. Brandishing both his spiritual and temporal arms, he forbade the faithful to trade with the rebellious republic, broke their previous alliances and prohibited any state from forming new ones and summoned the Sienese republic and the King of Naples to invade Tuscany. Florentines were losing, and Lorenzo volunteered to surrender himself, but the issue had long since outgrown a personal sacrifice, and the Signory refused to abandon him. He insisted, however, and sailed for Naples to negotiate with King Ferrante. Ferrante was a notoriously treacherous monarch, but, impressed by Lorenzo's daring, he treated him as a guest, listened to his arguments, and consented to abandon the Pope. The Pope fumed, but an incursion of the Turks in Calabria compelled him, like Ferrante, to make peace.

The Pazzi conspiracy failed, but it marked a turning point in Lorenzo's political career. To prevent its recurrence, he surrounded himself with an armed guard and adopted precautions which his enemies denounced as a tyranny. He tightened his grip on the government, subordinated the Signory and the councils to a privy council responsible to himself alone, and converted the controlling influence created by Cosimo into absolute personal rule. Before the Pazzi conspiracy, he was the most fortunate of the Medici; after it, the most masterful. But the crisis had a further effect: His powers as a statesman were diligently devoted to preserving the balance of power and keeping the peace in Italy.

His critics immediately called his expedition to Naples a rash, foolhardy, and unnecessary adventure. They argued that he could have attained the same success sitting safely at home instead of risking his life at the hands of a faithless enemy and returning to Florence as a hero. Instead of antagonizing the Pope and playing the injured party, if he had handled him gently he might have averted a war that caused the greatest damage to the city, especially in trade and taxes. Also, his punishment of the Pazzi was cruel. Some considered him vindictive and heartless for imprisoning the innocent young men of the family and preventing the Pazzi women from marrying and giving birth to more of their kind. But even Guicciardini admitted that "the event was so bitter that it is no wonder that he was extraordinarily angered by it. And it was seen later that, softened by time, he gave permission for the maidens to marry and was willing to release the Pazzi from prison and let them go and live outside of Florentine territory. And also it was seen that he did not employ cruelty in other matters and was not a bloodthirsty person." But while suspicion lingered, he intervened in domestic affairs, prevented powerful families from intermarrying, arranged matches to suit himself, and permitted no important marriage in Florence without his intervention and consent.

As soon as peace was restored, he returned to his pleasures and won his final and most undeniable triumphs in the patronage of art and letters and the pursuit of women. He increased his family's fame by his generosity. Florence became the mother of arts and the cultural capital of Italy, unsurpassed by rival states. Other princes were compelled to compete, but he was the highest bidder for the services of scholars and artists and carried off all the prizes for the glory of Florence and the greater glory of the Medici. In Pisa, he founded a branch of the University of Florence for the pleasure of surpassing rival schools, paying the highest salaries and sparing no expense to secure the best-known teachers in Italy. In Florence, the Platonic Academy formed part of his household and boasted the best philosophers he could find. Sharing the passion for ancient learning, he made philosophy a household word, collecting intellectuals at his table to discuss it and teach Florence that no one could live without it. "When my mind is disturbed by the tumult of public affairs and my ears are stunned by the clamor of turbulent citizens," he confessed to a friend, "how could I bear such dissensions unless I found relief in learning?" Study was a refuge from politics and an escape from statecraft. Educated as a boy by humanists, he was one of them and collected them to preserve his most precious treasure, his peace of mind. Poggio, Poliziano, Mirandola, and Ficino were the friends who formed his intellectual family. He spent more than half the annual income of the state on books alone, and his bounty for art was unbounded. Ambitious to be the most glorious of the Medici, he befriended all the arts, and they flourished abundantly at his bidding. "For vernacular poetry, music, architecture, painting, sculpture, and all the fine and mechanical arts he showed the same favor, so that the city overflowed with all these graces," Guicciardini acknowledged. Artists flocked to Lorenzo de' Medici from far and near, not merely for financial reward, but because he appreciated their gifts, understood their problems, and defended them against fools.

When it came to his other ruling passion, Guicciardini found it difficult to forgive his infidelity: "He was licentious and very amorous and constant in his loves, which usually lasted several years. In the opinion of many, this so weakened his body that it caused him to die comparatively young. His last love, which endured many years, was for Bartolommea de' Nasi, wife of Donato Benci, who was by no means beautiful but with a style and grace of her own . . . . What folly that a man of such great reputation and prudence, forty years old, should be so infatuated with a woman who was not beautiful and already well along in years, that he was led to do what would be disgraceful in any boy!" Physically, he also found fault with him: "Lorenzo was of medium height, his countenance coarse and dark in color, yet with an air of dignity; his voice and pronunciation harsh and unpleasing, because he spoke through his nose." But the fact remains that he was attractive to women; neither his nasal voice nor his coarse features displeased them.

As he matured, he became as tolerant of his critics as they expected him to be. Though Guicciardini was one of them, he was the most indulgent and judicious of his judges, and his final verdict was fair. "Though the city was not free under him, it would have been impossible to find a better or more pleasing tyrant. From his natural goodness and inclination came infinite advantages, but through the necessity of tyranny some evils although they were restrained and limited as much as necessity permitted . . ."

Twelve uneventful years followed the Pazzi conspiracy, until Lorenzo succumbed to gout and to a graver affliction. He neglected his financial affairs, which fell into confusion and disorder, and the fall was fatal. Machiavelli blamed his misfortunes on mismanagement by his banking agents abroad, stating that Lorenzo, to avoid further reverses, abandoned his mercantile enterprises and turned instead to "possessions, as a more stable and firm form of wealth." Among his possessions was the state, and his forays into the public coffers left Florence nearly bankrupt. In 1490, a commission was created to reform the fiscal administration of Florence; the currency, previously the most stable in Europe, was depreciated to a fifth of its face value, and the government was driven to desperate measures to avoid bankruptcy. Lorenzo managed to save his private fortune by withdrawing it from commerce and investing in real estate, but at the cost of his good name. Financial acumen was the foundation of the Medici political fortunes, and without it, his enemies gained power against him.

Under these gathering clouds, his last days were also darkened by a new adversary. An agitator in Florence echoed the complaints of his enemies, and the sermons of Savonarola kindled new and unexpected contention. From the pulpit of San Marco - a Medici foundation - a foreign reformer called Lorenzo to account for his political sins. The festivities with which Lorenzo entertained Florence were denounced as political snares: "The tyrant is wont to busy his people with spectacles and festivities, that they may think of their pastimes and not of his designs, and becoming unaccustomed to the conduct of the commonwealth, leave the reins of government in his hands." The old and familiar charge could no longer be ignored, and it was followed by graver ones. Summoned to preach before the Signory, Savonarola said: "Tyrants are incorrigible because they are proud, because they love flattery, because they will not restore their ill-gotten gains. They allow bad officials to have their way; they yield to adulation; they neither heed the poor nor condemn the rich; they expect peasants and paupers to work for them gratis or they tolerate officials who do so; they farm out the taxes to aggravate the people more and more . . . The people are oppressed by taxes, and when they come to pay unbearable sums, the rich cry: Give me the rest . . . When widows come weeping, they are told: Go to sleep. When the poor complain, they are told: Pay, pay." The preacher was popular, his following grew, and in 1491, he moved into the Duomo, where, before a packed congregation, he preached inflammatory sermons which terrified his hearers, predicting a coming calamity, ordained by divine wrath, which would sweep away the princes of Italy, including the Medici. Lorenzo was tolerant but troubled: What the Pazzi failed to accomplish, the prophet promised to perform. He attempted to mollify him but was rebuffed. He sent a delegation to reason with him and threatened Savonarola with banishment. "Tell Lorenzo to do penance for his sins," the priest replied, "for God will punish him and his. I do not fear your banishments. Though I am a stranger here and he a citizen, and the foremost in the city, I shall remain and he will go. I shall remain," he repeated proudly, "and he will go." He predicted the death of Lorenzo within a year.

A year later, Lorenzo lay dying in his villa at Careggi. He was in great pain, suffering from an abdominal disorder aggravated by his physicians, who fed him powdered pearls, and he sent for Savonarola to relieve his soul. Savonarola came. According to a popular but probably fictional account of the scene, the priest's price of salvation included the restoration of all ill-gotten gains and the restitution of liberty to Florence. Lorenzo agreed to the first, but he died without absolution before he could consent to the second.

Machiavelli was kinder. He acquitted Lorenzo of his political sins and wrote a gracious obituary. "Of Fortune and of God he was supremely loved, wherefore all his enterprises ended well and those of his enemies ill . . . All the citizens mourned his death and all the princes of Italy . . . and that they had good reason to grieve the result soon showed; for Italy being deprived of his counsels, none of those who remained found any means of curbing or satisfying the ambition of Ludovico Sforza, the governor of the Duke of Milan . . . as soon as Lorenzo died, all those bad seeds began to sprout which not long after, he who could quell them being no longer alive, ruined and are still ruining Italy."

His words proved true. Lorenzo was the pivot of Italian politics, and his eldest son, Piero, was born to be unfortunate - for himself, for his family, and for Florence. Two years after Lorenzo died, a revolt broke out, the Medici were driven into exile, and their palace was sacked by a mob of vandals. Nothing was left of Lorenzo but the memory of him. The financier was a failure, the politician and the statesman were transient, and of all the titles he left for posterity, only the patron of culture was remembered.

5
MILAN
CITY OF STRIFE

Milan seemed particularly favored by nature. To its south over the Apennines lay the great seaport of Genoa, a city so majestic that the Venetians feared its power and envied its wealth. To the west and north swept the great arc of the Alps. The few mountain passes that led to France or southern Germany gave Milan control of the routes from Genoa to the markets of the North. Seen spread across an atlas, the fertile valley of the Po seems one of the more natural places in Europe for a strong, unified state. Between the fall of the Roman Empire and the unification of Italy in the nineteenth century, such unity was achieved only once - by Napoleon. The history of Lombardy is one of invasion and war. For more than 1,000 years, some of Europe's bloodiest battles were fought there.

Part of the trouble was due to the fertility of the alluvial plain: The great walls of the Alps and the Apennines made it similar to a hothouse. Crops grew easily, and heavy crops meant a large and prosperous population. Lombardy was studded with thriving cities – Alessandria, Bergamo, Bologna, Brescia, Ferrara Lodi, Mantua, Padua, Parma, Pavia, Piacenza, Turin, Verona, and Vicenza, among others. Only in times of desperation were these cities capable of acting in unity, as when Emperor Frederick Barbarossa attempted to exert his power over them; otherwise they were content to plot and fight among themselves. From time to time, a city or a family arose like a bubble in this boiling cauldron and burst. Furthermore, the Holy Roman Emperor often found it advantageous to strengthen his aristocratic allies at the expense of the communes, for the emperor preserved the legal right of overlordship, even if he often failed to exercise it. What he never failed to do, however, was to angle for greater power in these troubled but fish-laden waters. He was not alone. The princes of Savoy found the Lombard plain far sweeter than the granite wastes of the Alps, which their country bestrode. Beyond Savoy were the French, whose king was willing to try to hold Savoy in check - at a price - or urge her forward if they went unpaid. And, of course, the two great parties, the Guelphs and Ghibellines, which polarized so many ancient feuds, thought they could manipulate the great European powers to their advantage.

Milan and its satellite cities failed to do what Florence and the Tuscan towns had succeeded in doing - they never subjected the feudal nobility to the authority of the merchant class. It is not surprising that men harassed by invasion, ruined by petty strife, and hamstrung by vendettas should dream of a "natural" state in which princes - powerful, all-wise, and intensely patriotic - should succeed generation after generation, wielding an iron authority that brought peace and fame. At times, imaginations soared and saw the princes of Milan, whether Visconti or Sforza, adding the kingship of all Italy to the duchy of Lombardy. There were three Milanese dukes - Gian Galeazzo Visconti, Francesco Sforza, and Ludovico Il Moro - who, for the brief periods of their rule, removed the absurdity from this vision, although they were far too realistic ever to indulge in such fantasies themselves. Nevertheless, they created a state equal in power and wealth to Florence and Venice. Milan, the epitome of the Renaissance state, is best seen reflected in the lives of its three greatest dukes.

The Visconti's emblem was a viper, and they needed all the serpent's cunning to survive the vicissitudes of a fickle and bloody fortune and grow in riches and in authority. By the time Gian Galeazzo Visconti was born in 1351, his family had played a leading part in Lombard affairs for more than 200 years. They had resolutely defended the interests of the merchants, acquired increasing judicial authority from the Holy Roman Emperor to provide a legal basis for their power, and arranged their marriages with dynastic prudence. Nevertheless, Gian Galeazzo's father had been forced to fight for his inheritance, for the death of a Visconti ruler, followed by the division of his lands among his heirs, always provided an opening to rebels and exiles in discontented cities on the fringes of their lands. Galeazzo II shared the Visconti territories with his brother Bernabò, who ruled in Milan, while he remained at Pavia. As Bernabò struggled to regain Bologna and Galeazzo pushed westward to the Alps, they aroused a hornets' nest, and in 1373, were nearly overwhelmed. It was a typical story of treachery, turbulence, and violence that fed the darker side of Galeazzo's nature - his suspicion, greed, and hate. His son, Gian Galeazzo, born from his diplomatic marriage with Bianca of Savoy, was pointed as quickly as possible to dynastic ends. At the age of nine, he was married to Isabella of Valois, a princess of France, and by the time he was fourteen, they had a son. Gian Galeazzo proved equally precocious in battle and diplomacy, but when he inherited his father's lands in 1378, his position was far from enviable. His brutal, violent uncle Bernabò still ruled in Milan, and he had five sons, all ambitious, all land-hungry.

Gian Galeazzo was known for his resource and cunning, but the latter got the better of his discretion, and he made a sudden wild bid for greatness. He secretly negotiated his engagement (his first wife had died at twenty-three) to the heiress of Sicily - but the agreement was only valid if he consummated the marriage within twelve months. The news outraged the Italian princes, and they made certain that the bride never got within hundreds of miles of her groom. While Gian Galeazzo wrestled with his problem of logistics, his uncle Bernabò extorted concession after concession from him, to make certain that the Visconti of Pavia would not be linked with Sicily to the embarrassment of the Visconti of Milan. When the year had passed, Gian Galeazzo found himself without a wife and tied tighter than he had ever been to his uncle, for Bernabò insisted that Gian Galeazzo wed his daughter Caterina as quickly as possible.

Gian Galeazzo complied, and brooded. He cultivated his garden. He devoted his considerable intelligence and concentration to the problems of government. He reduced taxes, reformed administration, weeded out corruption, and spent his spare time adorning his palace, conversing with scholars, and consulting with astrologers. Although he enjoyed a reputation for piety, he placed his trust in the zodiac rather than prayer, and when the stars aligned in his favor, he set out on a pilgrimage to the

Madonna del Monte at Varese. Although he took along a large entourage, he was fearful of entering Milan, so his uncle and his cousins rode out to meet him. After an affectionate greeting, he took them prisoner, and Gian Galeazzo entered Milan to cries of "Long live the Count, and down with the taxes!" Gian Galeazzo's wife seems to have taken the destruction of her father and brothers with a composure suitable to a Renaissance princess. His boldness was widely admired, and even Geoffrey Chaucer in far-off London wrote a few verses on the event in his Canterbury Tales.

This success gave Gian Galeazzo confidence, and since he was highly intelligent, he learned from it. More important than the timing was that the Milanese welcomed him as a liberator - a sentiment he quickly repaid by distributing some of Bernabò's treasure to those he needed as allies. For the next seventeen years, he exploited the paternalism of his government so that he might achieve his insatiable dynastic ambitions. In order to impose his control, he posed as the liberator of cities and men. His success was aided by good fortune and blended with a good deal of contingencies. "He was wont," wrote his chronicler, Giovio, "to give himself up to meditation during solitary walks, to hold discussions with those who were most experienced in every branch of affairs, to quote instances from the annals of the past. He found relaxation for his mind in the conversation of scholars and in constant reading." Not for him, "the delights of hunting or hawking, nor games of dice nor the allurements of women, nor the tales of buffoons and jesters." He thought, he planned, he acted. In two swift campaigns, having made certain that treachery was rife in the cities he wished to conquer, he had seized all of eastern Lombardy except Ferrara and Mantua.

The Florentines, of course, were deeply disturbed to see one tyrant control all the Alpine passes on which so much of their trade depended, and they used their powers of persuasion, primarily the florin, to raise a confederacy against Gian Galeazzo. This merely succeeded in enlarging Gian Galeazzo's ambitions, for he quickly realized that his gains could never be consolidated as long as Florence remained unsubjected. He proceeded with skill and caution; each city-state had its party that hated Florence or the powers that ruled it. He fought wars when he had to, but he avoided a head-on collision with the combined powers of Florence and Venice. By 1402, he had acquired control of Bologna, Perugia, Pisa, and Siena and could easily strangle Florence politically and economically. But just as the foundation of a great northern Italian kingdom seemed within his grasp, he caught a fever and died.

By then Gian Galeazzo had done more than enlarge the boundaries of his dukedom, he had created a state as well as a despotism. He centralized government, reformed administration, and removed inequalities and special rights and privileges. Wherever possible he weakened the feudal nobility and encouraged the merchant class. He tried to fulfill the ideal his humanists at Pavia had spelled out - that of a "natural prince" whose state was based on justice and equality - and had created the duchy of Milan, a coherent state that was to last until Napoleon swept it away. In many ways, he was the prototype of the Renaissance prince - unscrupulous, yet deeply concerned for the welfare of the state; passionately ambitious, yet aware of the needs of his country; scholarly, remote, and dedicated to the pursuit of power.

Gian Galeazzo's death broke up his empire. His captains of war took their pickings as the Tuscan and Umbrian cities, mindful of the power of Florence, threw off their allegiance. The Venetians' indifference to Gian Galeazzo's success turned to alarm, and his demise brought about a fundamental change in their policy. They decided to secure control of the Alpine passes they needed for their trade, and sufficient territory to give them ground to maneuver against a resurgent Milan. Once again, the great feudal families whose power Gian Galeazzo had attempted to reduce returned with a vengeance. The Colleoni, Anguisola, Cavalcabò, and Correggio demanded their pounds of flesh, and the plain of Lombardy again reeked of blood and slaughter, pillage and rape. In the midst of this, the core of the Visconti state held firm. It is a measure of Gian Galeazzo's success that it did, for in some ways his heir was a greater disaster than the war that consumed Lombardy. Although it is untrue that he fed his hounds on human flesh, the Milanese had no difficulty believing the story. His assassination in church in 1412 caused no surprise. Perhaps as a tribute to his brother's memory, his successor, Filippo Maria Visconti, had the murderers put to death by the most refined tortures. By nature, Filippo Maria was not excessively cruel, merely neurotic. He was obese to the point of ridicule and ugly to the point of embarrassment. His portrait was never painted, his marriage never consummated, and he rarely appeared in public. Nevertheless, he ruled with skill and maintained the machinery of the state and kept his head above the turbulent waters of Italian politics. Precluded by nature from the pursuit of martial glory, he was content to employ one of the best condottiere - Francesco Sforza - at least from time to time, for Filippo could never trust anyone for long.

Sforza, son of one of the first great Italian condottiere - Muzio Sforza - came, as most condottieri did, from the Romagna, which had little to sell but the strength of its men. Sforza proved himself a great captain. His direct manner, tough physique, and aggressive nature made him an excellent general, and his attention to detail, ferocious discipline, and deep personal loyalty brought him devoted and skillful soldiers. His personal magnetism won the enduring friendship of the two most outstanding men of his day - the sophisticated and cultivated banker Cosimo de' Medici and the equally cultivated condottiere Federigo da Montefeltro. In the hard, tough school of war he won a vast reputation and a small territory, too small for his purse or his ambition. The situation in Milan was as clear to him as it was to his friends. Cosimo de' Medici did not relish the steady advance of Venetian power across the Lombard plain (the Alpine passes were vital to Florentine trade, and the Venetians were traders first and republicans second). A powerful, friendly Milan was necessary to Florence, so Cosimo provided Francesco with good advice and handsome loans. Federigo, a generous condottiere, admired Francesco's prowess as only a professional could, but he preferred that Francesco should win his kingdom in Lombardy and not on his doorstep in the Romagna, where the Sforza had their patrimony.

Filippo Maria did not need to be told their thoughts, for he was as subtle as his father, if less ambitious. It was hard enough for him to weld together the Visconti lands, bring the stubborn nobles and cities to subjection and withstand the encroachments of Venice. For these projects, he needed Francesco, and to stay alive in his castle of Milan, he had to keep Sforza both expectant and dependent. So Francesco rattled his sword, and Filippo Maria dangled his daughter - not a legitimate daughter, of course, but his mistress had been more skillful than a wife, and Bianca was the result. The wrangle resulted in a long engagement that ended in a wedding that produced a son and heir. Before his succession had been determined, however, Filippo died. At the time, Francesco was away from Visconti territory.

The Milanese, in republican sentiment, abolished the dukedom, and chaos ensued. Neither Venice nor Florence was amused by the advent of a sister republic and gave no help as its troubles multiplied. Sforza moved cautiously until the republic crumbled, and when he finally entered Milan, the citizens cheered with delight, rushed him and his horse into the Duomo, and proclaimed him duke. For many years, that was the sole right the Sforza had to their dukedom - that and the sharp edge of their swords - for the emperors refused to acknowledge them. The powers of Italy, however, lacked the prejudice of the Germans, and while Francesco consolidated his power with military precision, the Medici got a bank in Milan, and alliances were formed with Florence, France, Naples, and Savoy. The Sforza obstinately insisted on peace and stability. There would, of course, be wars, but Sforza wanted them local, petty, and contained.

The Milanese dukes became accepted in the major state-system of Italy as Francesco Sforza completed the work Gian Galeazzo Visconti had begun. No condottiere had yet won such a prize, and Francesco, the tough captain who had once stood amazed by the luxury of Pavia and the splendor of its library, now enjoyed the prosperity of his sword. War or no war, the Milanese thrived. Francesco settled his court at Milan, the heart of his dukedom, and, until his death in 1466, ruled his subjects as he had once led his troops - wisely, directly, decisively. Unhappily, his children proved more devious, more extravagant, and even more brutal than their Visconti ancestors. The story of Milan and its Renaissance reaches a climax in the rule of Ludovico Sforza.

Francesco was a great warrior - in love as well as in war - and his brood of Sforza, legitimate and illegitimate (the difference in Renaissance Italy was scarcely remarked - Francesco himself was illegitimate), numbered twenty. At number six, (legitimate), Ludovico's prospects of the throne of Milan were remote, but his one advantage was that he was the first legitimate child to be born after Francesco had been acclaimed Duke of Milan. He would have to wait to claim his right, however, for his brother Galeazzo Maria Sforza intended to enjoy the power and the riches their father had bequeathed him. Indeed, his court left no doubt that the Sforza had arrived, that the wealth of Milan was vast, that neither the doge in Venice, the pope in Rome, the Medici in Florence, nor the Aragonese kings in Naples could outvie them in magnificence. The great Castello Sforzesco, built like the Tower of London on the edge of the city, witnessed some of the most remarkable spectacles of the fifteenth century. Galeazzo loved shows. He made Saint George's Day the military spectacle of the year; tournaments, pageants, processions gave his mania full rein, and he thought nothing of ordering 1,000 or more costly velvet costumes to adorn his servants. An even greater pleasure was to take a visiting prince or ambassador to his jewel house, where rubies, emeralds, sapphires, and diamonds lay in heaps - a treasure King Christian of Denmark called "unbefitting a true and generous prince." Galeazzo's taste in music, however, was more refined. After searching Italy, he combed Flanders for the singers who were almost the dominating passion of his life. But Galeazzo's greatest pleasures were the enjoyment of his courtiers' wives and the exercise of his personal power; neither endeared him to his subjects, and the latter was his undoing. Rumors of his cruelty were inflated to the heights of a Gothic fairy tale and rendered just as macabre by the duke's pious, almost morbid, insistence on the strictest observance of religious ritual. So perhaps it was fitting that his assassins murdered him in church. They were a typical Renaissance bunch: a penniless noble, a cousin avenging the rape of his sister, an old, disreputable master of rhetoric who had preached and practiced too publicly the Greek way of life, and a youthful republican intoxicated by the idea of killing a tyrant, who murmured, as he was slowly and carefully torn to pieces, "Mors acerba fama perpetua est" - "Death is bitter, but glory is eternal, the memory of my deed will endure."

Galeazzo's wife was deeply troubled that her husband had gone to his grave unconfessed. She made a list of his sins and was appalled. He was, she wrote, "Versed in warfare, both lawful and unlawful; in pillage, robbery, and devastation of the country; in extortion of subjects; in negligence of justice; in injustice knowingly committed; in the imposition of new taxes which even included the clergy; in carnal vices; in notorious and scandalous simony and innumerable other crimes." Obviously, Galeazzo's torments in Purgatory would be long and grievous, so the duchess implored the aid of the pope. The pope, moved by her distress, and a considerable subsidy for the papal army, granted absolution.

Galeazzo left a child, Gian Galleazzo Sforza, and five brothers, so the years after his death proved dramatic for both Milan and Italy. Conspiracies in Genoa and Parma were linked with greater conspiracies engineered by the pope and the King of Naples in Florence. Brother Ludovico tried to kidnap the child duke, but he failed until the tumult in Florence gave him the backing of the Holy Father and Naples's King Ferrante. With luck and good judgment, aided by the silliness of the Duke's mother and the misguided cunning of her lover, Ludovico became regent of Milan. He imprisoned the duchess, ousted her favorite, and chopped off the head of Cecco Simonetta, the talented ducal secretary who who had devotedly served the Sforza throughout his life, for attempting to secure an undivided inheritance for the legitimate heir. Fortunately for Ludovico, his most active and ambitious brothers died during the struggle for power, and his nephew was so weak in intellect and character that it was unnecessary to kill him. As soon as this family fight was over, Milan settled down and pushed the memories of Galeazzo aside. The child duke was betrothed to Isabella of Aragon, and Ludovico took Beatrice d'Este, the daughter of the Duke of Ferrara and granddaughter of the King of Naples, for his bride. Although their marriages were long delayed, the festivities celebrating their nuptials provided the chroniclers of the court of Milan a subject worthy of their hyperbole. Men and women were dressed, or undressed, as pagan gods and goddesses. Fabulous animals were wondrously contrived, knights jousted in Moorish costumes, and wild men, dressed by Leonardo da Vinci, scared the ladies. Dwarfs, giants, and hunchbacks provided robust fun as poets produced verses by the ream to immortalize the occasion. The best musicians of Milan - certainly the best in Italy - played and sang through the day and night. Leonardo da Vinci created masques with elaborate scenery, and ingenious fireworks linked the intervals between gargantuan banquets. Ludovico's generosity drew the interest of painters, sculptors, engineers, historians, philosophers, and poets; Leonardo, frustrated and restless in Florence, was one of the first to seek his patronage.

Ludovico's extravagance was not mere self-indulgence. He intended to demonstrate not only the wealth and power of the Milanese state but also his supreme control. He was a highly intelligent man with a deep sense of cunning, who was acutely aware of the insecurity of both his realm and his dynasty. Prosperity, he thought, would cure the former, diplomacy the latter. He diligently cultivated the rich Lombard plain and encouraged new crops, particularly rice. He fostered trade and manufacture. And his interest in Leonardo da Vinci owed as much to the artist's inventive genius in mechanics and fortifications as to his genius as a sculptor and painter. He created the sinews of power and exploited them with his wit.

Milan's dangers were first Venice, then France, then the Holy Roman Emperor, and lastly the Swiss, who could be manipulated by the others. Milan had been intermittently at war with Venice since the beginning of the fifteenth century when the Venetians decided to become a mainland power. The problems represented by the Emperor and France were interrelated. For Ludovico's Visconti ancestors, who had been the Emperor's legal representatives, the Emperor had been a safety factor, but the Sforza were not, and the legal basis of their power rested on popular acclamation. To further complicate matters, the Visconti had intermarried with junior branches of the French royal family, and this had given the French dynastic claims to Milan. Furthermore, the French had always coveted Genoa, which was a linchpin of the Milanese economy, and they supported the Anjou claims to the throne of Naples. To create some stability in this dangerous world, Ludovico, Lorenzo de' Medici, and Ferrante, the King of Naples, had enacted the Triple Alliance. Together they had presented the threat of sufficient force to make external or internal powers hesitant to attack them. War had not been abolished, but the Triple Alliance had diminished it, and Ludovico was the beneficiary. Besides the Triple Alliance, Milan had other reasons for friendship with Naples. Ties between the two cities had been strengthened by the marriage of the young Duke and Ferrante's granddaughter, Isabella of Aragon. Or so it seemed. Reasons of state and reasons of strategy were at odds, however, with Ludovico's personal ambition. He wished to be Duke of Milan, legally as well as in fact. That meant killing the young Duke, whose wife already resented the incongruence of her position and the slights, real and imagined, from Ludovico's wife - the intelligent, formidable, and indiscreet

Beatrice d'Este. Naples might align behind the wronged wife, and so might France; the Duke of Orleans had better dynastic claims than Ludovico. So might the Emperor, who could bestow the title of Vicar on whomever he wished. It was a complex situation, and Ludovico worked his astrologers hard, and the conjunction and combination of the stars became his daily concern. He reached the point of desperation when his nephew came of age and fathered an heir before Beatrice d' Este produced a son for Ludovico. While the arrival of the heir to the dukedom was received with modest celebrations, much to Isabella's fury, the banquets, jousts, pageants, and Te Deums that celebrated the birth of Ludovico's son were as splendiferous as they were prolonged. No doubt remained as to how the Regent's mind was working.

Ludovico's opportunity came when Charles VIII of France, who, after settling his quarrel with the Emperor and acquiring the Anjou claims to the Neapolitan throne, thought he might exercise his nobility and seek honor and reward by invading Naples. Ludovico encouraged this folly, and in return for his benevolent neutrality, Charles supported Ludovico's request to the Emperor to be appointed Imperial Vicar of Milan - a legitimization of power never yet won by a Sforza. His luck improved dramatically when his nephew, the Duke, died. Ludovico immediately proclaimed the infant Francesco duke, but not surprisingly, the Council would not have him. They begged Ludovico to assume the title with the power. Ludovico complied, achieving a bloodless and perfectly timed coup d'état. With Charles VIII occupied by his successful campaign in Naples and the imperial edict safe in his pocket, Ludovico suddenly changed sides, and as Charles began to withdraw from Italy, Sforza eagerly hurried him on his way. Then, sensing the possible benefits, he seized the opportune moment to switch allegiance to Charles once again.

Ludovico had his years of triumph. He could boast that the Pope was his chaplain, the Emperor his condottiere, Venice his chamberlain, and the King of France his courier. For a time Milan was prosperous, the court brilliant, the prince magnificent. But then death took a hand. Beatrice, who had brought Ludovico's subtleties to decisive action, died in childbirth. Charles VIII of France also died, and his successor, Louis XII, claimed Milan and regarded Charles VIII's failure to take it as a disgrace. Apart from Naples, which feared a fresh invasion, the powers of Italy jumped as quickly as possible onto the French bandwagon and were overjoyed that the victim beneath the juggernaut's wheels should be Ludovico. The French won, Ludovico retreated to the Tirol, the French puppet outraged the Milanese, and Ludovico returned. So did the French, who won again with consummate ease. This time they packed Ludovico off to France, where he was imprisoned and finally died in a tiny, lightless underground cell in the dungeon of Loches.

It was not the end of the Sforza. They had become pawns in the battle between the great European powers who used Lombardy as their tilting ground. Sforza's son, Massimiliano, was brought back by the Swiss, and after a brief and extravagant career he was removed, after the Battle of Marignano, by Francis I and pensioned, not imprisoned, in France. These two wars, which devastated Milan, were soon followed by a third, when Charles V, who combined the formidable power of his Holy Roman Empire with that of Spain, decided to expel the French from Lombardy. This he did in 1525 outside the great Visconti capital of Pavia. It was a fitting place, for with that battle the last gleams of Milanese independence disappeared. Although Milan possessed natural frontiers and great wealth and an able ruling house, as a state, it never acquired the stability of Florence or Venice or even Naples, simply because its class struggles went unresolved. The feudal nobility were never uprooted; they constantly quarreled with each other and readily supported any adventurer, internal or external, who favored their personal ambitions. This powerful aristocracy thrived on the divisions and jealousies of the merchant class which hated it. Finally, Milan was disrupted by cities almost as great as itself, all with rich, ambitious, jealous guilds of merchants who seesawed between wanting the stability the leadership of Milan could bring and its humiliation. In such an unstable world, the abilities of the Visconti and the Sforza were largely wasted.

Profile:
LEONARDO DA VINCI

Jacob Bronowski

Leonardo was born outside the small town of Vinci, near Florence, on April 15, 1452. The birthday is hardly worth remembering, but the year is, for its remoteness remains a constant surprise. Leonardo appears to us as such a modern man, and so relevant to our lives, that we have to remind ourselves he was born more than 500 years ago. He lived long before William Shakespeare and Rembrandt and Isaac Newton. Leonardo was dead before Nicolaus Copernicus ascertained that the earth goes around the sun; he was an old man, unhappy and full of regrets, when Martin Luther began the Reformation, and he was past middle age when Christopher Columbus sailed for the New World.

Leonardo was the illegitimate son of a lawyer and a woman who may have been a servant in the house of Leonardo's grandparents. The boy's father took several wives - each a member of a good Florentine family - but for over twenty years, Leonardo was his father's only child.

Italians in the Renaissance were not outraged by the thought that a bright child had been conceived out of wedlock. Illegitimacy was common; men were proud of making their own way, and churchmen and condottieri, artists and statesmen, boasted that they were born out of wedlock. This was no stigma. As the historian Jakob Burckhardt wrote, "The fitness of the individual, his worth and capacity, were of more weight than all the laws and usages which prevailed elsewhere in the West."

Nevertheless, we get the feeling that Leonardo never walked easily in the houses of the great, and that this wariness goes back to his childhood. There is something hooded and withdrawn about his character that evokes a picture of a child celebrated and yet not at home in the house of his birth. All his life he hated to see suffering. The story is told of Leonardo buying birds in the market place, holding them in his hand for a moment, and then setting them free. It is evident that in that rough, insensitive time, he was one of the few men who could not bear to see animals caged or in pain.

When Leonardo was about fourteen, in 1466

or so, his father apprenticed him to Andrea del Verrocchio, one of the foremost artists in Florence. Florence was aglow with the wealth and splendor of the Medici. Here the display of riches was almost a ritual, a public announcement of status and authority.

The workshops of Verrocchio and other artists supplied this society with its beautiful treasures and trinkets. Verrocchio was a painter and sculptor as well as a goldsmith and a decorator. His studio was his workshop, and his business there was to create a picture or a chair, a statue or a goblet, a golden chafing dish or a ceremonial suit of armor. Verrocchio could do all these things himself, however, he was a rather wooden painter and turned more and more to sculpture.

One reason Verrocchio turned from painting was that his apprentice Leonardo was so good at it. The artist who ran his studio as a workshop had to conserve and to divide its labor intelligently and expediently; and when he had an apprentice who could paint, he let him do just that and did something else himself. Tradition has it that Leonardo was still a boy when he painted an angel in one of Verrocchio's religious commissions and made it more lifelike than his master could.

The story of the boy painter who outdoes his master is characteristic of the Renaissance, for this was an age in love with surprises, eager to discover genius, native and untaught. But the story is true of Leonardo. There is at least one picture by Verrocchio, The Baptism of Christ, in which one of the angels is unlike the rest, and has clearly been painted by a more sensitive and subtle hand. Moreover, the landscape of the Baptism, the detail of trees and grasses, has an intimacy and vivid lucidness which belong to no painter before Leonardo. At least one other landscape in a painting by Verrocchio shows Leonardo's hand. Verrocchio must have known that young Leonardo was not merely a better painter: He was a new painter.

Leonardo finished his training with Verrocchio about 1472, when he was twenty or so, and continued to work in Florence for another nine or ten years on a variety of projects. He is described as tall and handsome, graceful in his actions and apparently had a fine singing voice. He was interested in mathematics and mechanics, particularly in the mechanics by which living things move: He constantly drew birds in flight and studied human anatomy.

For a painter, these were odd interests, yet for Leonardo, it was necessary to examine the structure of natural things. Later in life, he wrote simply about this: "And you who say that it is better to look at an anatomical demonstration than to see these drawings, you would be right, if it were possible to observe all the details shown in these drawings in a single figure, in which, with all your ability, you will not see nor acquire a knowledge of more than some few veins, while, in order to obtain an exact and complete knowledge of these, I have dissected more than ten human bodies, destroying all the various members, and removing even the very smallest particles of the flesh which surrounded these veins without causing any effusion of blood other than the imperceptible bleeding of the capillary veins. And, as one single body did not suffice for so long a time, it was necessary to proceed by stages with so many bodies as would render my knowledge complete; and this I repeated twice over in order to discover the differences."

This is an account of an anatomical study, but Leonardo did not want to cure men: He wanted to know how their bodies were made and worked. He distrusted doctors and medicine and chemical science, which saw nature as an interplay of occult qualities. Leonardo looked at nature directly, not through the mind but through the eye. And his eye, sharp and abrupt as a camera, could stop a bird in flight and fix the muscled movement of its wing. He did not speculate about the soul of the bird; he wanted to understand the mechanics of its flight: "A bird is an instrument working according to mathematical law, which instrument it is within the capacity of man to reproduce with all its movements, but not with a corresponding degree of strength, though it is deficient only in the power of maintaining equilibrium. We may therefore say that such an instrument constructed by man is lacking in nothing except the life of the bird, and this life must be supplied from that of man."

Leonardo's preoccupations with the structure of things seem to have grown from the time he began to work for himself, and distracted him from the opportunities that Florence in the 1470s offered to artists who could display the warm beauty of the surface of things.

At this time, Verrocchio was working on a statue of the great condottiere of Venice, Colleoni, and he left Florence to finish the work in Venice. Perhaps Leonardo felt that Florence was no longer the center of art it had once been, or perhaps he could not resist the urge to create a statue better than Verrocchio's; although he was not a sculptor, he wrote to Ludovico Sforza in Milan, offering, among many other things, to make a statue of his father, the condottiere Francesco. In that same letter, he described in detail his talents as a military engineer and inventor (two abilities likely to appeal to a Sforza), and soon after, at the age of thirty, he left Florence, carrying with him a silver lute he had made in the shape of a horse's head, to spend nearly twenty years at the turbulent court of Milan.

For the most part, Leonardo was a self-taught, self-willed man who did things almost truculently at times. Some of his paintings have perished due to bad luck; others because he insisted on mixing pigments with curious ingredients or drying them in new and different ways. He was an innovator, an experimenter, who was never satisfied with the accepted or acceptable, and he left Florence because Florence was a city of tradition, living on its golden dreams of the past. When Leonardo chose Milan, he was not merely choosing a different city: In a sense, he was choosing a separate culture.

Leonardo was one of the first men in whom the Renaissance expressed itself not as a recovery but as a discovery. He was an unscholarly, unlettered painter: He did not know Latin (he learned it later in Milan), and he never aspired to Greek. This is a subject he returned to heatedly and often in his notebooks: "I am fully aware that the fact of my not being a man of letters may cause certain arrogant persons to think that they may with reason censure me, alleging that I am a man ignorant of book-learning. Foolish folk! Do they not know that I might retort by saying, as did Marius to the Roman patricians, 'They who themselves go about adorned in the labor of others will not permit me my own.' They will say that because of my lack of book-learning, I cannot properly express what I desire to treat of. Do they not know that my subjects require for their exposition experience rather than the words of others? And since experience has been the mistress of whoever has written well, I take her as my mistress, and to her in all points make my appeal."

Leonardo expressed his contempt for the new aristocracy of Florence, for the rich men who leaned on the talents of others and whose taste was unoriginal: "Whoever in discussion adduces authority uses not his intellect but rather memory." He also set up a new standard for the creation of works of art: an original mind that goes directly to nature, without intermediaries: "The painter will produce pictures of little merit if he takes the works of others as his standard: but if he will apply himself to learn from the objects of nature he will produce good results. This we see was the case with the painters who came after the time of the Romans, for they continually imitated each other, and from age to age their art steadily declined. . . . it is safer to go direct to the works of nature than to those which have been imitated from her originals with great deterioration and thereby to acquire a bad method, for he who has access to the fountain does not go to the water-pot."

Here we have the crux of the principle that separated Leonardo from his predecessors. The medieval Church had taught that the universe could only be understood spiritually, as a God-given and abstract order; that the beauty of humankind and nature only tempts us away from that stark understanding. The Renaissance contradicted those dogmas, insisting instead that fleshly and natural beauty is not sinful, but on the contrary, an expression of the divine order. Yet this humanistic belief took different forms at different times. The pioneers of the Renaissance took their ideal of man and nature from the texts of the classics and the ancient works of art. But the new men of the Renaissance like Leonardo were not content with anything second hand. They wanted to see, to understand, to enter into nature for themselves. Above all, Leonardo wanted to discover his own humanity.

When Leonardo left Florence, he was turning his back on the classical Renaissance and looking for other men who shared his thirst for a more popular Renaissance. Milan was larger than Florence, less dependent on its wealthy men, less self-satisfied, and more cosmopolitan than the rest of Europe. Printing had been invented before Leonardo was born, but had spread little into Italy; now, in the 1480s, it became important in Milan, along with mathematics and mechanics. Leonardo was drawn toward mathematics, and in Milan he drew the pictures for a book, The Divine Proportion, which the mathematician Luca Pacioli wrote and later printed. The divine proportion is the geometrical ratio now called the golden ratio, a term coined by Leonardo da Vinci.

Intellectually, Leonardo was drawn to Milan because he was seeking a more down-to-earth expression of Renaissance humanism than Florence offered. Emotionally, there was also something about the brutal power of the court of

Milan that attracted him more than the classical air of Florence. Ludovico Sforza was hardly a gracious man, yet something in his sinister directness, his naked quest for power, his simple and single will, fascinated Leonardo. Like other sensitive people, he found satisfaction in watching others impose themselves ruthlessly on a world in which he himself was so ill at ease.

It was Leonardo's search for the simplest, most rudimentary forces in people and in nature that took him to Milan and made him accept Ludovico Sforza's whims in a way he would not have accepted Lorenzo de' Medici's. Despite his other faults, Ludovico was an admirable patron. The fact that his patronage lacked the literary overtones of the Medici made it more attractive to Leonardo, and the variety of the work Leonardo was called upon to perform appealed to his ingenuity, his curiosity, and his interest in experimentation. In Milan, Leonardo used his powers of invention to entertain the court, painted portraits of Ludovico's mistresses, and designed the costumes and scenery for the court masques. To celebrate a visit from the King of France, he made a mechanism shaped like a lion, which spilled a shower of lilies from its breast. He drew maps and engineered irrigation, founded cannon and installed central heating, planned engines of war and palaces, and designed a dozen schemes that Ludovico disregarded. And he made countless sketches of the most stupendous surprise of all, a statue of Francesco Sforza, Ludovico's father and creator of the Milan his son now ruled, astride a rearing horse. (It is interesting that he considered the animal the center of the monument, and that he referred to the statue simply as "the horse.") But like everything else that Leonardo did for his patron, this came to nothing.

But Leonardo's years in Milan were not wasted. In an odd way, he could allow his curiosity to run rampant here. The pageants and the plans he executed hardly filled his time, and Ludovico was too busy to pester the court sculptor about his unfinished commissions. In Milan, Leonardo did not have to earn his keep by painting, which is a pity for us: If Leonardo had had to deliver his work for cash during the years in Milan, when his gifts flowed most easily, we would have more great paintings and fewer sketches. But we can be grateful that, in his middle life, Leonardo did not have to undertake commissions that were becoming distasteful to him. In Milan, he grew impatient with his talents: He did not enjoy painting; he disliked the likenesses that he could catch so swiftly, the tricks of light and shade, the surface appearances. He was more and more interested in the structure of things, and his notebooks are full of sketches in which he dissected nature in order to understand it.

An indication of how his mind worked during these years can be seen in *Lady with an Ermine*, the beautiful portrait of Cecilia Gallerani, Ludovico Sforza's mistress, painted soon after Leonardo arrived in Milan. The ermine she holds in her arms was an emblem of Ludovico and is also a pun on the young woman's name. In a sense, the whole picture is a pun, for Leonardo has matched the ermine with her. In the skull under the long brow, in the lucid eyes, in the stately, beautiful, stupid head of the girl, he rediscovered the animal nature without malice. The carriage of both the young woman and the ermine, the gesture of the hand and the paw, explore the character with their anatomy. The painting is as much a research into man and animal as Charles Darwin's Origin of Species.

Leonardo's notebooks – consisting of some 5,000 pages - are as unexpected and as personal as everything else about him. Each page is a wonderful jumble of drawings and notes, in which a piece of geometry, a horse's head, an astronomical conjecture, and a flower stand side by side. A photograph shows all this with Leonardo's transparent clarity, but it fails to show the delicate scale on which Leonardo worked. Many of the pages in the notebooks, crowded with detail, are no bigger than a man's hand. This is yet another expression of Leonardo's introverted character, as is the mirror writing Leonardo used, writing with his left hand. The shading in his drawings is left-handed also, but it is not certain that he painted with his left hand. He may have damaged his right hand in Florence and afterward used it only for the most delicate parts of his pictures. The pocket notebooks, the left-handed shading, the mirror writing, express something else in Leonardo's character: a determination to do everything in his own way, down to the smallest detail. His anatomical drawings, for example, showing the hollows and blood vessels in the head, are so exact that they resemble photographs made by X-ray or radioactive tracers. It is not just the enormous scope of his research that is impressive, it is the absorption, the meticulousness, and the intensity of his vision. Leonardo was not merely an original thinker, he had a passion for looking with new eyes at everything that came into his life, no matter how trivial.

Leonardo's notebooks from this time are full of his observations of nature, particularly his anatomical drawings, and are also filled with his sketches of flying machines. He had long been absorbed by the flight of birds, and was now inspired to invent a parachute and a type of helicopter. That the latter did not work can be blamed on the fact that the age in which he lived did not have the capacity to create the mechanical energy necessary for flight. He observed, 100 years before Galileo, that the pendulum could be used to make a clock keep time. He recognized that red light penetrates through mist and that blue light does not and devised practical rules for giving depth to the painting of landscapes. Mechanisms detailed in his notebooks included designs for various types of bridges, a mechanical excavator, machines for grinding needles and mirrors, a rolling mill, an automatic file cutter, an instrument for measuring wind speeds, and a self-centering chuck. Here is a characteristic invention:

A Way of Saving Oneself in a Tempest or Shipwreck at Sea

It is necessary to have a coat made of leather with a double hem over the breast of the width of a finger, and double also from the girdle to the knee, and let the leather of which it is made be quite air-tight. And when you are obliged to jump into the sea, blow out the lappets of the coat through the hems of the breast, and then jump into the sea. And let yourself be carried by the waves, if there is no shore near at hand and you do not know the sea. And always keep in your mouth the end of the tube through which the air passes into the garment; and if once or twice it should become necessary for you to take a breath when the foam prevents you, draw it through the mouth of the tube from the air within the coat.

As Leonardo grew more absorbed in the mechanisms of nature, the work he had come to Milan to do was put off further and further. At last, in 1493, he could put it off no longer. Ludovico Sforza was arranging to marry his niece to the Emperor Maximilian. Leonardo made a full-sized model in clay of the statue of Francesco Sforza on horseback. The bronze to cast the statue was gathered, but that had to be sent off the following year to make cannon for Ludovico's allies.

After Ludovico's failed attempt at increasing his power through a French alliance, Leonardo, a defeated man nearing fifty, fled Milan. The French archers had used the clay horse and its rider as a target, and there was little left of Leonardo's in Milan except a painting of the Last Supper that had begun to molder on its damp convent wall even before the artist died. The prior had complained that Leonardo had been remiss in finishing even that, and in revenge Leonardo had said that he would paint the prior into the figure of Judas for eternity. Yet, when it came time, Leonardo had done something more profound: He had moved Judas out of the place that the Middle Ages had assigned to him and had put him on the same side of the table with Jesus.

Leonardo lived for twenty years after the fall of Milan, wandering aimlessly from one city to another, and from one commission to another, without ever settling down. In 1502, he briefly served as Cesare Borgia's military engineer on the same treacherous campaign with Niccolò Machiavelli - the one that provided the Florentine diplomat with a portrait of undeviating ambition for *The Prince*.

Soon after, Florence commissioned two patriotic pictures of battle scenes, one from Leonardo and one from Michelangelo. Leonardo's drafts of the picture survive, but the painting itself deteriorated almost immediately. During this time, Leonardo painted a portrait of the wife of a local merchant named Giocondo. This is the Mona Lisa, admired in its day for the warmth of its flesh tones, which time and varnish have now turned the faint green of ice in a landscape of rocks.

Leonardo went back to Milan from time to time to make sketches for another horse and rider. The rider this time was to be Gian Giacomo Trivulzio, an Italian condottiere who had fought on the side of the French in the battle for Milan and had overthrown Ludovico. Again, nothing came of this monument. Then, in 1513, the son of Lorenzo de' Medici became Pope Leo X, and Leonardo went to Rome, where Raphael and Michelangelo had been working for some years and received several papal commissions. The story goes that Leonardo, upon his arrival, began to make the varnish for one picture before he started to paint it, and Leo X observed, sadly and wisely, "This man will never do anything, for he begins to think of the end before the beginning."

The King of France at last offered Leonardo a retreat without obligation near Amboise, and there he spent the last four years of his life, from 1516 until

1519. His self-portrait, drawn a few years earlier, shows him looking much older than his sixty years, full-bearded and patriarchal, his eyes veiled against emotion and his mouth set bitterly. The distress of an old age full of regrets for the wonderful things that he had planned and never finished filled his notebooks. Once he had been so sure of his gifts that there had seemed to be an infinity in which to fulfill them. In those confident young days he had written: "I wish to work miracles; I may have less than other men who are more tranquil, or than those who aim at growing rich in a day."

Now he was conscious of the merciless erosion of time, which leaves nothing of the vigor and beauty of a man if he has not perpetuated them in his own creations. Leonardo is looking into his own face when he thinks of Helen of Troy and, borrowing from Ovid, writes: "O Time, thou that consumest all things! O envious age, thou destroyest all things and devourest all things with the hard teeth of the years, little by little, in slow death! Helen, when she looked in her mirror and saw the withered wrinkles which old age had made in her face, wept, and wondered to herself why ever she had twice been carried away. O Time, thou that consumest all things! O envious age, whereby all things are consumed!"

The works of art that Leonardo left behind are sadly few - not a whole statue, about a dozen finished paintings, some fine anatomical and mechanical drawings, and thousands of sketches. For artists with one small gift, this might be enough. But when we consider the prodigious talent of Leonardo, the instant eye, the exact hand, and the penetrating mind, we understand why he scribbled desperately on page after page of his later notebooks: "Tell me if anything at all was done . . . Tell me if anything at all was done . . ."

Leonardo may have been right to think that he had wasted his life, but he was wrong to think that he had wasted his gifts. His true gifts were not those of a painter, for his painting, original as it was, was not out of the reach of his contemporaries. Leonardo's most profound gifts were of another kind, and make him seem to be our contemporary, 500 years after he lived.

The first gift that made Leonardo a pioneer was his obsession with the structure and mechanism of nature in an age where science was still dominated by a magical view of man. The power-seeking alchemists of Leonardo's time believed that they could command nature only by casting a spell which would make nature function contrary to her own laws. Leonardo realized, as his contemporaries did not, that we command nature only when we understand her, when we enter into her processes and allow them to work naturally. He was full of contempt for those who wanted to force nature to do the impossible: "O speculators about perpetual motion, how many vain chimeras have you created in the like quest? Go and take your place with the seekers after gold."

Leonardo's second pioneering gift was to see that the structure of nature also reveals her processes, which are perpetually in movement and in development. The way a skeleton is hinged, the way a muscle is anchored, the way a leaf is veined – all tell something about the functioning of the organism, and in the end, about the whole cycle of its growth. Leonardo looked for the strict mechanism by which living things move and act and saw that mechanism as something dynamic. This dynamic quality is present even in his simplest sketch of a machine, and in his old age, it expressed itself in a growing preoccupation with plants and flowing water. Leonardo did not think that a scientific analysis of the processes of nature deprived them of life; on the contrary, he expected the analysis to express their changing and living movement.

Third, and most important, Leonardo understood that science is not a grand parade of a few cosmic theories, of the kind that Aristotle and Saint Thomas Aquinas had propounded. Until Leonardo's time, a theory was expected to give a general explanation of some large phenomenon, such as the motion of the moon, and no one thought to ask whether the theory could also match the precise times at which the moon rises and sets. The detail was not considered important, and any discrepancy between theory and fact was shrugged off as inconsequential. Leonardo elevated the detail so that it became the crucial test of a scientific theory. He was seldom misled by what the classical medicine of Galen said about the functioning of the heart or the way that the eye sees; he drew what his dissection showed him and then asked how it could be squared with the currently accepted vague medical beliefs.

Because of Leonardo's eye for detail, because he was a painter for whom nature lived not in generalities but in the specific shape of a flower or a waterfall, he was at the opposite pole from the theorizing scientists of his own age. Leonardo did not lose interest in science: He transformed it. Only a painter could have forced science to change its outlook by dedicating his art to discovering the natural order of living beings by studying the minute detail of their structure. Leonardo was that painter, the true pioneer of science as we practice it.

His interest in what was new made him unwilling to look back; his gaze was outward and forward. His passion for the exact turned him toward mathematics, his passion for the actual urged him to experiment, and these two dominant themes - logic and experimentation - have remained, since Leonardo's time, the basis of scientific method.

With these gifts, it was natural that Leonardo quarreled with the classical and literary Renaissance in which he was brought up and turned to a more popular and naturalistic Renaissance. It was natural that he gave up pictures for machines and that his machines had a subtle quality of human intelligence, of one operation controlling another, which today we call automation. It was natural that these interests took him from the rich merchant culture of Florence to the brutal thrust for power of the Sforza and the Borgia. And it was natural and inevitable that a life spent at the courts of such men had the modern ring of our own age, the pointless planning of pageants and machines of war, the aimless postponement of constructive schemes, and the final despair of a great mind that from childhood was baffled by an alien world. At the end of his life, Leonardo wrote constantly of his visions of the cruelty of people, and what he foresaw links his age to ours:

Of the Cruelty of Man

Creatures shall be seen upon the earth who will always be fighting one with another with very great losses and frequent deaths on either side. These shall set no bounds to their malice; by their fierce limbs a great number of the trees in the immense forests of the world shall be laid level with the ground; and when they have crammed themselves with food it shall gratify their desire to deal out death, affliction, labors, terrors, and banishment to every living thing. And by reason of their boundless pride they shall wish to rise towards heaven, but the excessive weight of their limbs shall hold them down. There shall be nothing remaining on the earth or under the earth or in the waters that shall not be pursued and molested and destroyed, and that which is in one country taken away to another; and their own bodies shall be made the tomb and the means of transit of all the living bodies which they have slain. O Earth! what delays thee to open and hurl them headlong into the deep fissures of thy huge abysses and caverns, and no longer to display in the sight of heaven so savage and ruthless a monster?

6
ROME SPLENDOR AND THE PAPACY

Rome was a city caught, like the aged, in memories, delusions, and dreams. Even when fighting – not very successfully - the little town of Tivoli, medals were struck bearing the proud title, Roma caput mundi: Rome, the world's ruler. By 1400, however, even the impressive days of the Middle Ages seemed gone forever. For most of the fourteenth century, the popes had lived at Avignon in France, in the great and luxurious Palais des Papes that looms above the Rhone, where the broken Roman bridge became a symbol of the Church's break with its own past. To Avignon went the clerics, lawyers, and merchants who harvested and spent the wealth that a pious Europe poured into the papal lap. It was to Avignon that Francesco di Marco Datini, the famous merchant of Prato, went to make his fortune as an ambitious boy of fifteen. And he did, in his determined, hardheaded, Tuscan way, selling silks, jewels, works of art, damasks, swords, silverware, cloth, even salt - anything that would make money, although the profits on his insurance and his banking interests nagged at his conscience. Through men like Datini, Avignon prospered and Rome lost, and of course, the artists also went where the money was, and Sienese men painted the frescoes that adorned the Palace's walls.

In Rome, a few cardinals still flaunted their courtesans, and a few individuals continued to dedicate themselves to the worship of God and the relief of the poor. But the absence of the papacy was killing Rome. The ruinous buildings, combined with constant plague, stifled hope, depressed the spirit, and bred despair. In this dark world, the furious Roman tribes - the Orsini, the Colonna, and the Frangipani – made their sport, tossing each other into the Tiber, and when a pope ventured into Rome, they chased him into the fortress of Sant'Angelo or frightened him into the remote corners of the patrimony.

They terrorized the citizens, raped the nuns, robbed the monks, and pillaged the churches. To compound the confusion, from 1378 to 1429, there was an antipope as well as a pope, and in 1409, three authentic successors of St. Peter provided a glorious opportunity for rebellion, riot, and plunder. King Ladislaus of Naples prowled about the broken-down streets of Rome, extorting what he could and decapitating whom he dared. Popes and kings hired the toughest, most brutal condottieri – including Braccio da Montone, who enjoyed the sufferings of others and for his pleasure would throw men from the highest towers in Rome or drop a prisoner into a boiling cauldron. After years of anarchy, Romans were willing to believe anything and nothing. When antipope John XXIII, afterwards struck from the list of the popes and accused of a catalogue of crimes, the least important of which were incest, sodomy, and murder, swore that he would defend them to the death, they replied that they would rather eat their children than surrender to his enemies. That same night, John fled in the darkness, taking all the portable wealth he could lay his hands on.

Amid such brutality and violence, no one in 1425 could have foreseen that Rome was about to be reborn - not spiritually, for the Renaissance popes were not men of the spirit, but physically, artistically, and politically. St. Peter's, the Vatican, the churches, the tombs, the squares, the palaces and gardens of Rome, which enchant the eye and delight the heart, encouraged the pursuit of beauty that the stern moralities of the Counter Reformation could not stop. For 200 years, the splendor of Rome became the pride of the papacy. The downward plunge into anarchy and destitution and poverty was checked by Martin V (1417-1431), a Colonna and a Roman who mended the dreadful split in the Church. He proved to be such a good administrator and a fearsome personality that he secured peace for the city. He held the robberies, violence, and murder in check and stimulated the city's trade. With the papal court back in Rome, the pilgrims and supplicants and merchants returned to the city, as did the financial lifeblood of Rome - the papal tax that was harvested from Europe's peasantry. And so the Roman soil was fertilized again, for without wealth, no Renaissance was possible.

The next pope, Eugenius IV, had to flee down the Tiber in a rowboat, disguised as a monk, and barely escaped capture. For years, he kept his court at Florence, where he patronized the humanists and bided his time, while he left Rome to be pacified by a ferocious bishop, Giovanni Vitelleschi, who razed cities, hanged and decapitated barons, slaughtered right, left, and center, and probably met his own end by poison (possibly with Eugenius's assistance). By these murderous methods, the popes were reestablished. The calculated savageries of Cesare Borgia that astounded a later generation were unusual only in the beauty and dexterity of their timing.

To be secure in Rome, the papacy needed to control the states of the Church, which stretched diagonally across the long leg of Italy. During its residence at Avignon and the Great Schism (1378 to 1417), men and cities had usurped papal rights and privileges, and what they won by force they would not yield by persuasion. Excommunication, sanctions, and cursing left them unmoved. These had been flung about so wantonly by rival popes that they lost much of their force. Indeed, it seemed to the popes that the Church could only get back its own by acting like any other power in Italy. Only by alliance, diplomacy, and war could the Church wrest its possessions from alien hands. The Church could afford to hire the ablest condottieri, including Francesco Sforza and Federigo da Montefeltro. Having been the pawn of warring powers, Church leaders, seeking to secure independence, looked for tough, worldly men with powerful personalities and the ability to make quick decisions to lead them. And as the power of the Papacy steadily grew through battle and diplomacy, so did the need for a similar pope. This is what so many now find difficult to understand about such popes as Alexander VI and Julius II. Alexander VI, whose lusts repelled even the tolerant in the age in which he lived, was a hardheaded diplomat and excellent administrator who pursued what he thought to be a necessity for the Church - temporal power, expressed in the overlordship of central Italy. Julius II, even as pope, loved war, loved to get on his horse and feel the weight of his armor and hear the blood-call of battle.

By and large, the Renaissance popes were worldly men, pragmatic, tough, and concerned with power. Like many ambitious men, they did not wish to be outshone by their rivals. They built enormous churches and palaces and magnificent fountains; employed the finest painters, sculptors, and craftsmen; collected the loveliest antiquities, resplendent jewels, remarkable books, and exquisite manuscripts. These things, like their armies, were necessities of state, and the cost was irrelevant. The resurgent power of the papacy went hand in hand with the artistic Renaissance in Rome, and because the popes controlled more wealth, the result was more splendid than anywhere else.

Rome was full of priests, monks, nuns, churches, monasteries, convents, holy relics, miraculous shrines, healing images. Every year thousands of pilgrims from all corners of the Western world made their way to it in penitence and in hope. Most were simple people to whom the sight of a piece of the True Cross or a saint's leg justified the dangers and tribulations of their journey. They didn't care about the rumors of the Pope's children, his poisonings, murders, or even the alarming sexual liberties of the Borgia. Twenty thousand of them worshipped Alexander VI in the great Jubilee year of 1500 - unmindful of his lusts. For them, the mounting grandeur of Rome was a wondrous thing, visible proof of the glory of their Church. Criticism of the Church's corruption and immorality fell on deaf ears. A Savonarola or a Bernardino of Siena might momentarily incite this multitude with a sense of the world's unrighteousness, but the majority of the Western world was locked in accepting piety, and the glaring sins of the popes and cardinals were a matter for gossip, not radical rage. Throughout the Renaissance, with its political and personal immorality and its intellectual skepticism, Rome remained the center of the Western world's religion. From this atmosphere of worship, no pope could escape, and it became subtly interwoven in the Renaissance in Rome.

There is no need to follow the twists and turns by which the Papacy gradually re-established its dominion over the Patrimony or to describe how from time to time this was threatened by popes trying to create hereditary dominions for their children, a tendency which scores of Orsini and Colonna died bloody deaths to prevent. While the treaties, battles, and plots have faded to oblivion, the treasures of the Vatican - its library, antiquities, sculptures, and paintings – remain. And the Vatican is but a fragment of Renaissance Rome; the statues of Laocoön and the Apollo Belvedere belong to it as much as St. Peter's or Via Giulia; a reverence for her own past grew with her new delight in beauty.

The revival of Rome began, like the Renaissance itself, with literature. At the time of the Schism, the Italian Papacy had many Tuscans in its service, among them Poggio, one of the luckiest of the humanists. After Petrarch's discovery of the lost letters of Cicero, the search for ancient manuscripts intensified, and Poggio's instinct lead him to his target. Perhaps he was more thorough, more remorseless than the rest; whatever the cause, his haul was prodigious. In the Swiss monastery of St. Gall, he unearthed the entire works of Quintilian, poems of Lucretius, discourses by Cicero, treatises on architecture by Vitruvius, and on agriculture by Columella. The rich patrons of Italy rushed to buy them or to have them copied and illustrated, for the competition to possess first-rate classical manuscripts splendidly illuminated was as keen as that for French impressionists among present-day millionaires. Tommaso Parentucelli, who became Nicholas V, was as addicted to books as the Borgia family was to women. "What was unknown to Parentucelli," said Pius II, "lay outside the sphere of human learning." He encouraged his secretaries to ransack old monastic libraries, and he employed an army of copyists. Terrified by the fall of Constantinople, he sent his emissaries to Greece and collected Greek manuscripts, paying extravagant prices for the work of translation as well as for the books themselves: He offered 10,000 gold pieces for a translation of Homer. He employed the best classical scholar, Lorenzo Valla, who had proved some of the most hallowed documents in the papal Curia to be forgeries. As well as being a genius, Valla was a satirist with the bite of acid, and his favorite targets were priests, monks, and cardinals. During the pontificate of Eugenius IV, Rome had been too hot for him, but Nicholas V welcomed him and employed him. And, of course, the Pope created a fitting setting for his great library: the books were housed in the Vatican and exquisitely bound in red velvet with silver clasps. Philosophers, poets, historians, grammarians, and teachers of Latin and Greek were all welcome in the new palace of the Vatican that Nicholas was creating, whether their work fortified or undermined the authority of the Papacy. Only a few setbacks marred Nicholas's triumphant development. As with so many aspects of the Renaissance, Sixtus IV was also involved in the extension and adornment of the Vatican library. Even Alexander VI added to it, although his interest in learning expressed itself in the patronage of the University of Rome. Nicholas and Sixtus laid the foundations and secured some of the rarest treasures of the greatest library in the Western world.

Although the reverence of most popes for ancient literature was profound, their attitude toward the visible remains of ancient Rome was more haphazard. As early as 1400, a few cardinals had collected coins, bronzes, and statuary, and as the fashion for antiquity spread, so did the desire to acquire the classical art of Rome and Greece. But the ruins of Rome were a different matter. Palatine Hill, upon which had stood the immense palaces of the emperors, was now an incoherent mass of rubble - broken arches, paths, and masonry covered in sage and thyme and rosemary, crowned with olive trees, and grazed by sheep. It was a desolate, rural place - a paradise only for the humanist brooding on the mortality of greatness. The Arch of Constantine was buried in ruins and covered by houses; the Colosseum was a mound of tumbled marble; everywhere throughout the ruined city there were broken columns, remains of theaters, circuses, and stadiums. These vestiges of a glorious past were harder to cherish, and although an occasional pope paid lip service to the need to preserve them, the majority happily plundered them for building materials or razed them to the ground for new projects. Nicholas V removed 2,300 wagon loads of marble from the Colosseum in a single year, as well as quarrying from the Circus Maximus, the Forum, the Arch of Titus, and the Temple of Venus. Even Sixtus IV built a bridge across the Tiber from the masonry of the Colosseum. A few dedicated men dug and measured and drew the ancient buildings, but most men were drawn to them, like the robbers of the pyramids, by the hope of a lucky find, for the search for antiquities had revealed masterpiece after masterpiece of ancient art. Even though the powerful plundered the ruins or ignored them, humble scholars were still fascinated. The best of these was Ciriaco de' Pizzicolli, sometimes called the

Father of Archaeology, who wandered throughout the classical world, measuring, sketching, and further describing the visible remains. Antiquarian studies, however, were largely confined to medals, coins, inscriptions, marbles, and bronzes, things which could be collected and displayed. There were, of course, not enough, and forgeries soon abounded, to the confusion and despair of posterity.

Although the popes had little wish to preserve the ruins of Rome, they earnestly desired to restore its architectural supremacy. The popes recovered a ruined city shrunk to a fraction of Imperial Rome, with fields and orchards and wild, overgrown places. Fortunately, Nicholas V possessed a touch of megalomania. He not only dreamed, but also planned, a vast new Rome, dominated by a new St. Peter's, a new papal palace, and protected by an invincible Castel Sant'Angelo. The medieval popes had lived in the indefensible and oft-burned Palace of St. John Lateran, but on their return from Avignon it was in such disrepair that they took up residence in the Vatican Palace, which had been the guest palace for emperors and kings. Nicholas V sent for the great Florentine architects Bernardo Rossellino and Leon Alberti, men as addicted to the classical as the Pope and totally hostile to the Gothic. Cost did not daunt the Pope, who tore down the ancient Roman temples near St. Peter's and slowly began to lay the foundations of his new basilica. At his death, all of what is now Vatican City was scarred with trenches for the huge walls of his dreams. They were never fulfilled, but Sixtus IV, Alexander VI, Julius II, and Leo X completed the destruction of medieval Rome and created the new city of the Renaissance that would prove worthy of him.

Sixtus IV, born in poverty, ruthlessly pursued greatness. Sensual, self-indulgent, decisive, a gifted administrator and generous patron, he showered gold on his nephews (one of whom was to become pope as Julius II) and stopped short of nothing to achieve his political ends. He helped promote the Pazzi conspiracy, and furious when it failed, censured all of Florence. His personal immorality gave rise to wild rumors, but his lack of restraint provoked an extravagance that was ultimately beneficial to posterity. Not since the days of the emperors had Rome witnessed such indulgences. Here is a description of the food at the banquet given by Sixtus when a bastard daughter of the King of Naples arrived in Rome to meet her future husband: "Before them were carried wild boars, roasted whole in their entire hides, bucks, goats, hares, rabbits, fish silvered over, peacocks with their feathers, pheasants, storks, cranes and stags; a bear in its skin, holding in its mouth a stick; countless were the tarts, jellies, candied fruits and sweetmeats. An artificial mountain was carried into the room, out of which stepped a liveryman with gestures of surprise at finding himself in the midst of such a gorgeous banquet; he repeated some verses and then vanished. Mythological figures served as covers to the viands placed on the table. The history of Atlas, of Perseus and Andromeda, the labors of Hercules were depicted life size on silver dishes. Castles made of sweetmeats and filled with eatables were sacked and then thrown from the loggia of the hall to the applauding crowd. Sailing vessels discharged their cargoes of sugared almonds . . ." Many of Sixtus's indulgences were less fleeting. His taste in building was as simple and as austere as his delight in food was riotous and fantastic. He widened streets, constructed bridges, built hospitals, erected churches, and gave land to anyone who would build houses and palaces. He encouraged his cardinals to foster the splendor of Rome: The market was expelled from the Piazza Navona and the building of its churches and palaces begun. There was scarcely a ward of the city that Sixtus did not improve or adorn, but his greatest glory is the chapel in the Vatican that bears his name. Simple in design, it served merely as a frame to be adorned, and for this purpose, Sixtus brought the best artists in Italy to Rome to paint glorious frescos - Signorelli, Botticelli, Perugino, Pinturicchio, Ghirlandaio, Rosselli. Later, Julius II, who wished to complete his uncle's work, employed Michelangelo to paint the ceiling for which the Sistine Chapel is so famous. The galaxy of painters in Rome in the 1470s founded the guild of St. Luke, which afterward developed into the famous academy. Although painters and sculptors and architects had been patronized by the popes long before Nicholas V and Sixtus IV, with papal patronage, they moved into a new dimension that touched all aspects of art and learning. With unlimited wealth and authority, many of the popes shared the magnificent visions of Nicholas V. The Basilica of St. Peter's - the work of a plethora of geniuses: Alberti, Bramante, Raphael, Michelangelo, Bernini - is the most impressive Christian monument in the world, yet it is essentially a product of the Renaissance. The treasures of the Vatican Palace - paintings, sculpture, antiquities, ancient manuscripts, and rare books - are incomparable, yet in 1420, the Papacy possessed no more perhaps than 300 books and scarcely any antiquities or pictures or statues of merit. Rome owes a great deal of its present beauty to the sensual, warlike, popes who ruled from 1471 to 1521.

These popes make a strange gallery, yet they are as much creatures of the Renaissance as Michelangelo's Adam or Donatello's David. Without question, the strangest of all is Alexander VI, a man of animalistic passions driven remorselessly by his instincts, whose name has become synonymous with lust and cruelty. His attachment to his mistress, Vannozza dei Cattanei, who bore him the terrible Borgia brood, was profound and life-lasting, no matter what other temporary indulgences he permitted himself. He loved his children with a fierce physical passion. When one son was stabbed and thrown into the Tiber, probably by another son, Cesare Borgia, his grief was so deep that he tearfully swore not only to reform his own life, but also the Church's. But his animal spirits, soon reasserted themselves, and his devotion to Cesare became the bane of Italy when he resolved to create for him a great Italian kingdom. After spectacular victories in which, with French aid, Cesare overcame the seemingly impregnable fortresses of the Romagna and the Urbino, he seemed to Machiavelli to be destined to rule Italy. Machiavelli admired the way Cesare welcomed his enemies as friends and then neatly strangled them. By such stratagems were the Orsini obliterated. The speed, decision, and timing of Cesare had an almost physical perfection. Yet fate had a bitter end in store. Before Cesare could consolidate his power, his father died, and at the time, he was ill with a loathsome and debilitating sickness. Stripped of his power, he became a pawn of popes, was banished to prison in Spain, and finally was killed in a brawl in Navarre. Alexander's daughter, Lucrezia, suffered a similar irony of fate. The Pope loved her with an almost incestuous passion and heaped wealth on her; nothing was too sumptuous or too lascivious to be denied her. No husband was worthy of her charms: One was declared impotent by Papal Bull; another was assassinated.

But Lucrezia lived long after her father's death, her life threaded with tragedy and stultified by a piety that mocked her past. The depth and ferocity of the Pope's passion for his children have made him an ogre of history, making men forget his dignity, physical charm, and immense presence as well as the vitality that made him as tireless at work as at pleasure. His irresponsible virility scarcely was in keeping with the papal crown, but his pontificate was far from disastrous for the Papacy. He brought its possessions firmly under control.

That control was brilliantly exploited by Julius II. At sixty, he possessed the strength and decision of a man half his years. He loved action, hated the French, loathed the celebrated Roman families, and detested the tyrants of Perugia and Bologna, who usurped the power of his Church. Defeat only increased his energy, and in all his dealings, this tough, thickset priest was bold, decisive, and single-minded. His goal was the Papacy's absolute independence from emperors, kings, or Romans, for without that, its claims to universality in a world of national states would be meaningless. Julius never vacillated, either in politics or in art, nor did he play it safe. When he heard of the abilities of the young Raphael, he sent for him from Florence and ordered him to obliterate paintings by Piero della Francesca, Signorelli, Perugino, Il Sodoma, and the rest and to cover the walls with subjects of his own choice. The result – known as the Stanze of Raphael - is one of the glories of Renaissance Rome. In architecture, Julius showed the same sweeping vision and decisive action. He patronized Donato Bramante, a man whose dreams were as grandiose as Julius's, accepted his colossal plans, and taxed the faithful. Julius always stared life directly in the eye and contemplated death with the same robust realism. Michelangelo's designs for his tomb entranced him; it was the largest and most ornate mausoleum conceived in Europe since Theodoric's. But he could not bridle his impatience with the sculptor's slow progress, creative doubts and endless reconsiderations, which drove the Pope to such fury that Michelangelo left Rome in anger and the project came to a standstill. Reconciliation failed to hasten the work - long after his death, a part of Julius's tomb went up in the little church of San Pietro in Vincoli; his bones lie in an undistinguished grave in the Vatican.

Upon Julius's death, the triumph of the Renaissance Papacy was realized in the young Giovanni de' Medici, son of Lorenzo, who became pope in 1513 at the age of thirty-seven. Bull-necked, popeyed, red-faced, he lacked the presence and ferocity of Alexander VI or Julius II. The cardinals in conclave had had enough of aggressive, virile temperaments. Leo X was subtle, intuitive, and sophisticated. He charmed with his generosity, affability, and sweetness of manner. Discretion veiled his private life, and his character and education gave him a range of intellectual interests and sympathies unmatched by a pope since Nicholas V. Bred in riches and nurtured in luxury, he had no compunction in using the wealth of the Church in spectacular pageantry. Not since the days of the emperors had the Romans witnessed a procession comparable to his, as it made its way from the Vatican to St. John Lateran. Cardinals and bankers vied with each other in their displays of artistic treasures or the construction of ceremonial arches. Banker and patron Agostino Chigi erected an eight-column arch and festooned it with his best pictures and sculpture. The best antiquities Rome had to offer lined the processional path, along with newly painted apostles and prophets of Christendom. The procession itself, with 250 abbots, bishops, patriarchs, and cardinals matched by the representatives of Italy's great families - equaled its setting. The Gonzaga, Este, Sforza, Bentivoglio, Colonna, Orsini, Baglioni, nobles of Florence, patricians from Venice, the Duke of Urbino in black velvet, Lucrezia Borgia's husband released from excommunication for the occasion, and the rebel Cardinal, Alfonso Petrucci, whom Leo would later have executed, were set like jewels among chamberlains, standard-bearers, guards, and attendants. No stones were hurled, no angry shouts drowned the singing, no daggers flashed in the cruel sun. All paid homage to the fat, perspiring, red-faced, white-clad Pope, sitting sidesaddle on his white horse. Eighty years earlier, no pope could have risked his life and throne in such a spectacle.

Although Rome steadily increased in splendor, and the Pope's authority waxed majestic, violence, turmoil, and treachery still filled the papal annals with battle and murder. The French, Milanese, and Spaniards had not given up their dynastic ambitions, and the Venetians had not given up their belief that they could only achieve security by raping the Church of its northeastern possessions. What's more, the Church's wealth proved insufficient for its needs. Taxes grew severe, and the sale of indulgences became more blatant. Across the Alps, criticism of clerical worldliness, monkish foolishness, papal avarice, and Roman decadence was sharp and prolonged and developed a political and social purpose. Martin Luther, who might easily have met his end at the stake like Savonarola, became the founder of a reformed Christianity that came to see the Pope as Antichrist and Rome as the whore of Babylon. The tribulations of Luther's Reformation dimmed the luster of the Papacy. But it was a more immediate tragedy that jolted the Romans and the Church out of the gilded sweetness of Medicean rule into a sterner, harsher world. In 1527, the soldiers of the great Hapsburg ruler Charles V, whose dominions embraced the Spanish as well as the German Empire, sacked Rome efficiently, brutally, completely. After the death of Clement VII, another

Medici who succeeded Leo X, the growing rift with Protestantism and the shock left by the devastation of Rome bred a sterner spirit in the Church and Papacy. The more flamboyant aspects of the Renaissance were suppressed: Speculation went out of fashion, dogma was more sharply defined, the Holy Office maintained its purity; the new order of Jesuits dominated the school and the confessional, and men of ruthless will and unbending morality sat on the throne of Saint Peter, marshaling and leading the resurgent forces of Catholicism. These men deplored paganism; repressed the debauchery of the Romans, both religious and secular; insisted on sacred subjects in art and clapped fig leaves on ancient statues. But no matter what they did, they could not stop the Renaissance. For centuries, Rome continued to grow in beauty and became, as no other city, the embodiment of the arts, if not the spirit, of the Renaissance.

Profile:
POPE PIUS II
Iris Origo

The road that winds up from the eleventh-century pieve (a rural church with a baptistery) of Corsignano - roughhewn in the golden stone of the region and containing the font in which Aeneas Silvius Piccolomini was christened - to the perfect little Renaissance city of Pienza - named after Pope Pius II - is a short one. But the ascent it symbolizes was unusually swift and high even in a period in which able men quickly made their mark - the ascent that led a clever country boy from a humble secretary's desk to Peter's throne. A shrewd statesman, an elegant humanist, an inquiring traveler - keenly addicted to the learning of the past, but equally alive to new ideas or discoveries of his own time - witty and urbane, skeptical and adaptable, he might be considered an entirely typical figure of the Renaissance, had he not, at the very summit of his career, devoted his last years to a vast and impracticable idea which was more closely in harmony with the spirit of an earlier age: the last Crusade. To carry out this plan, he cast aside every obstacle and hastened, knowing well that his scheme had failed, his own death.

Aeneas Silvius Piccolomini, the son of an impoverished country nobleman who had been a soldier of fortune, was born in 1405 in the little Tuscan village of Corsignano, on the bare, dust-colored hills of the Val d'Orcia. A clever boy, he was sent by his father at the age of eighteen to Siena, the city he called "sacred to Venus." There, while certainly not neglecting the charms of the beautiful Sienese women, he ardently pursued his legal studies with the celebrated jurist Fausto Sozzini, and later continued his classical studies in Florence with Filelfo. Too poor to buy all the books he needed, he would sit up at night copying long passages from the volumes lent to him by his friends - once even setting his nightcap on fire, as he nodded over his work. Cicero, Livy, and Virgil were his first models, and when first he began to write verse, Petrarch. His first glimpse of the efficacy of eloquence, when he saw the whole congregation of Siena swept off its feet by the sermons of the famous popular preacher Saint Bernardino, excited him so much that he pursued him to Rome, to ask whether he, too, should not follow the same path.

But Saint Bernardino firmly dissuaded him, telling the future Pope to return to the worldly pursuits for which he was apparently more fitted.

It was then not as a priest but merely as a young scholar with some legal training that Aeneas's career began. Cardinal Domenico Capranica, passing through Siena on his way to Basle to claim redress from the Ecumenical Council in his quarrel with Pope Eugenius IV, took him along as his secretary - and in Basle, the young man found ample scope for his talents. The Council - which had recently reaffirmed its supremacy even over the Pope, and which had the support of both the King of France and the Emperor Sigismund - was confronting two enormous tasks: the destruction of heresy and the reformation of the Church. There Aeneas made the acquaintance of most of the great European prelates and observed their intrigues and counter-intrigues; he fostered the cynical detachment already inherent in his Tuscan blood; and he acquired the adaptability, the breadth of vision, and the persuasive eloquence that would lead him to success. In his Commentaries he related, with disarming vanity, that he once held his audience so riveted by his words that for two hours no one even spat!

For twenty years, he led a wandering life through Switzerland, Germany, and Austria. He was sent on missions all over Europe: to James I of Scotland -

probably for the purpose of inciting fresh border raids against England - to the Hussite heretics of Bohemia, and to the hermit-duke Amadeus of Savoy, whom he described as leading, in his luxurious hermitage on the Lake of Geneva, "a life of pleasure rather than of penitence." He became known in Germany as "the apostle of humanism." He accepted a post in the chancery of Frederick III, negotiated the marriage of the young Emperor to Eleonora of Portugal, and later went to escort the young bride and her bridegroom to Rome. Ambition, he quite frankly admitted, was the chief spur to every human activity. But he also found time to make love to many pretty women (declaring chastity to be a philosopher's virtue, not a poet's, and sending home one of his illegitimate sons to be brought up by his father at Corsignano, "so that another little Aeneas may climb on your and my mother's knees") and to write some scurrilous tales and a little satirical treatise on the miseries of life at court, as well as the poems which caused him to be crowned as poet by the Emperor. To all this he added a formidable list of serious works, which included treatises on education, rhetoric, the Holy Roman Empire, and even on horses; histories of Bohemia, the Goths, the Council of Basle, the Diet of Ratisbon, and the Emperor Frederick III; and some Lives of Illustrious Men - and finally, after becoming Pope, the famous Commentaries.

It was not until the age of forty that he returned to

Rome, obtained the forgiveness of Pope Eugenius IV, and conducted the negotiations which led to the reconciliation of the Papacy with the Empire - and it was only two years later, in 1447, that he took orders. After this, the speed of his advancement was remarkable. Within a year he became Bishop of Trieste and resumed his travels between Italy, Austria, and Bohemia; in 1449, he was made Bishop of Siena; in 1456, Calixtus III nominated him Cardinal of St. Sabina; two years later, in 1458, he was elected Pope.

Success comes most swiftly and completely not to the greatest or perhaps even to the ablest men, but to those whose gifts are in harmony with the taste of their times. The Renaissance man admired versatility, scholarship, eloquence, diplomacy, and an inquiring and balanced mind; above all, he valued style, both in life and letters. All these qualities the new Pope possessed to a very high degree. "Aeneam rejicite, Pium suscipite" (Reject Aeneas and accept Pius), he wrote, harking back to the Virgilian phrase which had also determined the choice of his new name - and it is certainly true that he abstained for good, after his ordination, from the loose living and scurrilous writings of his early years, and lived a life of great industry, sobriety, and benevolence. "I do not deny my past," he wrote to his friend John Freund, "but we are old, nearer to death . . . I have been a great wanderer from what is right, but I know it, and I hope the knowledge has not come too late."

He was not exempt from one fault of many other pontiffs: nepotism. Three members of his household (including his nephew Francesco) were given the cardinal's hat at the same consistory, another nephew, Antonio Piccolomini, was made commander of Castel Sant'Angelo, and his sisters were richly endowed with both money and palaces.

The fullest picture of his daily activities can be found in the book which was the mirror of his times and of himself: his Commentaries. This is not only one of the most readable autobiographies ever written, but also a historical record of many of the important events of his time, seen with a sharp eye and a ripe judgment, and enlivened by sketches of men and places, and by perceptive reflections on human nature. "Nil habut ficti, nil simulati" - nothing was there in him of deceit or pretense, wrote one of his earliest biographers - and indeed this book carried these qualities so far that when it was first published in 1584 (during the Counter Reformation), it was thought necessary not only to prune it severely, but to ascribe its authorship to its copyist, Gobellinus of Bonn, so that "matters which the heretics gladly seize upon" should not come from a pope's pen. Now that the full text is again available, however, we are afforded an unvarnished picture of the Pope's contemporaries. It is not always flattering. He described the Florentines as "traders, a sordid populace who can be persuaded to nothing noble." "When once

Pius asked the Bishop of Orta what he thought of Florence and he replied that it was a pity that so beautiful a woman had not a husband, the Pope replied, 'She lacks a husband, but not a lover.' As though to say she had no king, but a tyrant, meaning Cosimo." Of the Bolognese he wrote: "They are cruel rather than brave at home, while abroad they are known to be cowards," and many pages were filled with attacks on the Venetians, who drew back from their promises of alliance against the Turks, while he said, "They favored the war against the Turks with their lips but condemned it in their hearts." "Glorious deeds," the Pope said, "are not embraced by democracies, least of all by merchants, who, being by their nature intent on profit, loathe those splendid things that cannot be achieved without expense."

The tyrants of the Italian states were described with an equally sharp pen. Cosimo de' Medici, indeed, was admitted to be "more lettered than merchants are wont to be," but Borso d'Este was depicted as "listening to himself when speaking, as though he pleased himself better than he did others," and as a man "whose mouth was full of flattery mixed with lies." And Sigismondo Malatesta, for all his brilliance of mind, artistic sensibility, and military skill, was described as "a man essentially pagan" and "so avaricious that he never shrank not only from looting but from theft, so ruled by his passions that he raped his daughters and his sons-in-law.

He surpassed all barbarians in cruelty." The Pope publicly declared that, just as some holy men are canonized, so Sigismondo should be "enrolled as a citizen of Hell." On the steps of St. Peter's his effigy was burned, bearing the inscription: "Sigismondo Malatesta, son of Pandolfo, king of traitors, hated by God and man, condemned to the flames by the vote of the Holy Senate."

It is when he is writing of the members of his own Curia, however, that Pius II's indictments are most startling. Shortly before his death he addressed a secret consistory of his cardinals: "Like businessmen who have failed to pay their creditors, we have no credit left. The priesthood is an object of scorn. They say we live for pleasure, hoard up money, serve ambition, sit on mules or pedigree horses, spread out the fringes of our cloaks and go about the city with fat cheeks under our red hats and ample hoods, that we breed dogs for hunting, spend freely upon players and parasites, but nothing in defense of the Faith. Nor is it all a lie!"

Yet when Pius met true saintliness or valor, he was swift to recognize it. It was he who canonized Saint Catherine of Siena and who, in describing the entry into Vienna of the humble Franciscan friar Giovanni da Capestrano - "with so tiny a body, so advanced in years, so dried up, exhausted, all skin and nerves and yet always serene" - at once recognized in him the attributes of a saint. He also gave a singularly detached and impartial account of the story of Joan of Arc, "that astonishing and marvelous maid," ending with the comment, "Whether her career was the work of God or a human invention we would not like to say."

But where his regard was not awakened, no figure was so eminent as to escape his darts. He described James I of Scotland as "smallish, hot-tempered, and greedy for vengeance," and said of his former master, the antipope Felix V, that when he appeared without his beard, he looked like "an unsightly monkey." Before the assembled Curia he referred to the Cardinal of San Marco, Pietro Barbo as "the buffoon of your Order," and to the brilliant, unscrupulous French Cardinal Guillaume d'Estouteville of Rouen as "a slippery fellow who would sell his own soul," And here is his account of another prelate, Jean Jouffroy, Cardinal of Arras - a man "made mad by too much learning . . . He wanted to appear devout and would say Mass, sometimes in the Basilica of St. Peter's, and sometimes elsewhere. By face and gesture he would show how much he was carried away, sighing deeply, weeping and, as it were, conversing with God. But before he had taken off his sacred vestments and left the altar he had cuffed one or another of his servants who had made some slight mistake in his ministration . . ."

His description, too, of the assembly by which he was elected Pope is as cynical as it is convincing. "The men having most power in the College ... summoned the others and demanded the Apostolate for themselves or for their friends. They implored, promised, threatened; some, even, without a blush and forgetting all modesty, spoke in praise of themselves..." Aeneas's chief rival was the Cardinal of Rouen, and many intrigues took place in the latrines of the Vatican ("as being a private hiding place"). The French Cardinal openly distributed promises of honors and posts to those whose support he thought he could obtain, but the next morning Aeneas called upon his friends - appealing to the loyalty of one prelate and the vanity or self-interest of another. In the end, nine votes for him and six for the Cardinal of Rouen were dropped into the golden chalice. But still the required majority had not been obtained. For a while, no man dared to commit himself. "All sat in their places, silent, pale, as though they had been struck senseless. No one spoke for some time, no one opened his mouth, no one moved any part of his body, except the eyes, which turned this way or that. The silence was astonishing, astonishing, too, the appearance of those men, as though you had found yourself among their statues ... Then the Vice-Chancellor Rodrigo [the future Pope Alexander VI] rose and said, 'I accede to the Cardinal of Siena!' And his words were like a sword through Rouen's heart..." Another followed him, but still one vote was lacking, that of the old, fat Cardinal Prospero Colonna. As he rose he was seized by each arm by the cardinals of Nicaea and Rouen, who tried to hustle him out of the room. But before they could do so, he shouted, "I, too, accede to Siena, and I make him Pope!"

Pius II's Commentaries, however, are not now read chiefly for their account of the intrigues of the Curia or of the politics of the Italian states. What gives them their peculiar flavor is their revelation of the point of view of a Renaissance man. "My spirit is an inquiring one," Aeneas wrote of himself in his youth, and in this he never changed. As an antiquarian, his curiosity embraced Christian and pagan monuments alike. In England, he admired the stained glass windows of York Cathedral and the shrine of Saint Thomas Becket in Canterbury, "at which it is a crime to offer any metal less than silver," but he was no less interested in the translation of Thucydides in St. Paul's Cathedral, and in being told that Newcastle was founded by Julius Caesar. In Hadrian's Villa, he tried to reconstruct the origins of the ruins. On his visit to Federigo da Montefeltro, the Pope and condottiere discussed not the politics of the day, but the arms used in the Trojan War. On his way to the Congress of Mantua, he turned aside to search for the labyrinth of Clusium described by Pliny, and visited the house called Virgil's Villa. Even in his last years, crippled with gout, he was carried in his litter to Tusculum, Tibur, and Falerii; he examined "with great pleasure" the Roman ship recently dug up in the Lake of Nemi, and rowed down the Tiber to Ostia, speculating about the Latin name of the fine sturgeons he was given, and the site of one of the Roman palaces. At Albano, he visited the old monastery of San Paolo, which its new owner, the Cardinal of Aquileia, had transformed into a fine villa surrounded by gardens, and the deserted church belonging to the Cardinal de Foix, which was "without roof, altar, or doors" and served only as a stable for cattle and goats. "These," he dryly commented, "are the Canons appointed by the Cardinal of Albano to perform God's service day and night." With regard to the preservation of ancient monuments, however, his own conduct was somewhat inconsistent. When, on the Appian Way, he found a man digging up some stones of the Roman pavement, he sharply rebuked him, bidding Prince Colonna never again to allow the public road to be touched, and he even issued a Bull forbidding the use of ancient columns and statues for making mortar. But he himself used, to build the Loggia della Benedizione and the marble steps leading up to St. Peter's, many fragments from the Colosseum, the Forum, or the Baths of Caracalla, and he constructed most of the great new fortress at Tivoli with material from the amphitheater of that city.

He was in some ways singularly free from the superstitious beliefs of his time, rebuking Borso d'Este for "heeding the pagan folly" of his astrologers, and refusing, even after being racked with fever for seventy-five days, to summon a magician who was "said to have cured of fever 2,000 men in the camp of Niccolò Piccinino." But he told a Saxon student who asked him whether he knew of a Mount of Venus in Italy, in which the magic arts were taught, that "in Umbria . . . near the town of Nursia [Norcia], there is a cave beneath a sharp rock, in which water flows. There, as I remember to have heard, are witches, demons, and dark shades, and the man who is brave enough can see and speak to the ghosts and learn the magic arts."

In his travels, he always investigated eagerly, if skeptically, any local legend or tradition. In Scotland, he was fascinated by the legend of the Barnacle Geese, which told "of a tree growing on a river bank, whose fruit rotted if it fell to the ground, but if it fell into water, it came to life and turned into birds; but when he [Piccolomini] went thither and made inquiries, eager for a miracle, he found that it was a lie . . . " When he visited the slopes of Monte Amiata, he looked for the herb called Carolina because, according to tradition, "it was once revealed by God to Charlemagne as a cure for the plague" and he succeeded in finding it - "a herb with prickly leaves which cling to the ground and are set around a flower similar to that of a thistle." He added, however, "Pius considered it a fable invented by Charlemagne's admirers."

He had an observant eye, too, for the different sorts of men and manners that he met upon his travels. In Scotland - where he spent one night in a rough farmhouse, with the goats picking the straw out of his pallet - he observed with interest that the white bread and wine that he had with him were such rarities that "pregnant women and their husbands drew near to the table, fingering the bread, sniffing the wine, and asking for a taste." He noticed, too, that "nothing gives the Scots more pleasure than to hear the English abused." In Basle he was impressed by the well-built stone houses and well-kept gardens, with fountains "as numerous as those of Viterbo," and in Vienna - according to his Life of Frederick III - by the comfortable dining halls with stoves and glass windows, where songbirds were kept, as well as by the fine churches and spacious cellars. He even described a convent for the redemption of penitent prostitutes, "who sing hymns in the Teutonic language day and night. . . . But if one of them is caught sinning again, she is cast into the Danube." But he also complained of the rough German table manners, of a court in which any falconer or stable boy was more welcome than a scholar, and above all, of the gross drunkenness. He described how Heinrich, Count of Gorizia, would wake up his two little boys in the middle of the night to pour wine down their throats. When the sleepy children spat it out, he turned upon his wife, a virtuous Hungarian lady, shouting, "Strumpet, these brats are none of mine!"

Perhaps the most delightful passages in the Commentaries, as in Pius's letters, are those which reflect his passion for natural beauty. He might, indeed, be considered, with Petrarch, the first of the Romantic travelers. At Viterbo, he went out almost every day at dawn "to enjoy the sweet air before it grows hot and to gaze at the blossoming sky-blue flax." At Bolsena, he insisted on being rowed out to the islands in the lake, and whenever possible, he preferred to hold his consistories out of doors, especially in the great beech woods of Monte Amiata, "beneath this tree or that, and also by the sweetly running stream . . . Sometimes it happened that as the Pope was signing documents the dogs flung themselves upon some huge stag hiding nearby, which would drive them back with its horns or its hoofs and make off with all speed for the mountains." Often, too, he picnicked with his Curia in a meadow or poplar grove - though whether his cardinals, mostly elderly and urban gentlemen, enjoyed this habit is not related. One evening, as the Pope was returning home through some meadows, a cowherd, "seeing the golden litter carried by its porters and surrounded by horsemen . . . milked a cow that was near him and, full of joy, offered to the Pope the bowl which he used for eating and drinking, filled to the brim with milk . . . Pope Pius . . . was not too proud to put his lips to the black and greasy bowl."

One of Pius's most endearing traits was his simple enjoyment of homely pleasures: the cheese of Monte Oliveto, "which Tuscans consider the best in the world," the fresh trout which he saw caught on the Monte Amiata, and the engaging antics of his sister's baby. He even devoted a whole page to the misadventures of his poor little puppy, Musetta, who first fell into a cistern full of water and, when rescued at the last gasp, "was taken to the Pope, to whom she continued to whimper for a long time as if she wanted to tell him about her danger and stir his pity," but then was bitten by a large monkey, and finally, having climbed up on a high window sill, was seized by a violent gust of wind and dashed upon the rocks. The Pope sadly commented that, like some men, she was plainly foredestined to a violent end.

He described with relish the horse and foot races in Pienza, where a small and beardless grown-up slave inserted himself among the boys and defeated a little boy from Pienza, "with fair hair and a beautiful body, though all bedaubed with mud, who . . . bewailed his fortune and cursed himself for not having run faster. His mother was there, a handsome woman, comforting her child with gentle words and wiping off his sweat with a towel." "The Pope and cardinals" - so ends this chapter – "watched from a high window with no small merriment, though in the intervals they were busy with affairs of state."

The occasion of these events was the inauguration of the cathedral and palace which the famous Florentine architect Bernardo Rossellino had built at Corsignano - now renamed Pienza - as a summer residence for the papal court. The little city is still as perfectly harmonious a work of art as the early Renaissance has produced - the cathedral being flanked on one side of a little, paved square by the papal palace, and on the others by the episcopal palace and town hall. Some smaller palaces were built nearby for the cardinals and their courts. The cost, however, was so much higher than the original estimate that everyone expected the architect to be cast into prison. But the Pope, after inspecting the buildings, sent for him and said: "You did well, Bernardo, to lie to us about what this undertaking would cost us. Had you spoken the truth, you had never persuaded us to spend so much money, and this fair palace and this church, the loveliest in all Italy, would never have existed. . . . We thank you, and we consider you deserving of special honor." And he issued a Bull forbidding the defacing of any of the church's walls or pillars, the building of any other chapels or altars, or any other change that might mar the church's perfect symmetry. "If any do otherwise, may he be anathema and absolvable only by the authority of the Bishop of Rome, except in the hour of death."

This happy return to his native city was perhaps the last carefree incident of the Pope's life. His remaining years were obsessed by a single idea: The coercion of the reluctant princes of Christendom to fight against the Turks.

It is not difficult - even without attributing to Pius II the religious fervor of an Urban II or a Saint Catherine - to understand his motives. He was well aware of how closely Hungary and Austria, and beyond them Italy herself, were threatened by the rising ambition of that astute and designing sultan, Mohammed II. His historical imagination was intensely conscious of the ancient traditions of the Holy Roman Empire, and of the Papacy as the savior of Christendom. And as he himself would have been the first to admit, his sense of drama was fired by the image of himself as the central figure in the most significant of all wars, once again leading princes and peoples against the Crescent in the name of the Cross.

Long before his accession, Aeneas had tried to awaken the European princes to the Turkish menace. At the coronation of Frederick III, he had pointed out that Hungary had become the last bulwark of Christianity, and when Constantinople fell he was among the first to realize that thenceforth the doors of Europe would always remain open to the Turk. "I see faith and learning," he wrote, "destroyed together." Aeneas implored both the Emperor and the Pope, Nicholas V, to convoke a European congress at which the princes would agree to a truce with each other, "and turn their arms instead against the enemies of the Cross." A Diet was actually held at Ratisbon, at which the few delegates who came voted for the Crusade, but only a few months later, when another congress was held in Frankfurt, most of them had already changed their minds. "They would not listen to the names of Emperor or Pope, but said they were deceivers and greedy men, who wanted to make not war but money." Aeneas was still struggling to persuade them to confirm their promises, when the sudden death of the Pope "rent the web that had been so long in weaving."

Immediately after his accession, Pius returned to the charge. He summoned another congress at Mantua and, though crippled by gout and suffering from stone and bronchitis, decided to attend it himself. "It is all-important," he had written, "that a war should begin well, for the end of a war is often implicit in its beginnings." Certainly the beginning of this one foreshadowed its failure. The Pope set forth for Mantua with most of his cardinals, but when he arrived there, he found himself almost alone. His court implored him to go home again. Had they been brought here, they asked, to discuss a Crusade with the Mantuan frogs? Messengers from Thomas Palaeologus of the Morea (the southern part of the Peloponnesus) brought desperate appeals for help, but there were few to listen to them. The Duke of Burgundy now said that he was too old to come.

The King of France, exasperated by the Pope's recent support of the accession to the Kingdom of Naples of Ferrante of Aragon, sent word that he could join no Crusade so long as he was still at war with England. England - torn by the Wars of the Roses - sent a similar message. Frederick III was engaged in invading the Kingdom of Hungary, while the envoys of that country - which alone, in the recent past, had defended Europe against the Turks - bitterly complained of this new menace. No single voice was raised to echo the old Crusading cry: "Deus lo vult - it is God's will!" Of the Italian rulers, Borso d'Este declared that his astrologers forbade him to attend; Malatesta suggested the employment of Italian mercenaries, but only to get their pay for himself. The Florentines and Venetians both feared the loss of their eastern trade, but Venice promised to furnish sixty galleys, if every expense was paid from the general treasury and she was given the supreme command of the naval forces and awarded the spoils of the war. "To a Venetian," the Pope commented, "everything is just that is good for the State; everything pious that increases the Empire."

Yet when at last he was in the presence of those envoys who did come, the Pope showed much of his old fire. He had learned to conceal his physical pain so well that it was only revealed by his yellow color and drawn features and by an occasional compression of his lips. The French, in return for their participation, demanded the re-establishment of the Angevin rule in Naples, and believed that the Pope's illness would at once cause him to yield. But he declared: "Though I should die in the middle of the assembly, yet shall I reply to that proud-stomached delegation!" Speaking with as much eloquence and energy as in his youth, his cough ceased, and the color returned to his old cheeks. Even his most bitter opponents admitted that he had "spoken like a Pope." Moreover, in an attempt to shame the princes into following his example, he declared that he himself would lead the Crusade. "We can be borne in Our litter to the camp." On January 14, 1460, the Holy War was formally declared, and, discouraged but not defeated, the Pope started on his long journey home.

Before actually embarking on the Crusade, however, Pius II made one last curious effort to come to terms with the infidel - one which, if successful, might well have changed the course of European history. In a long and eloquent letter, he attempted to convert the Sultan Mohammed II to Christianity. If he accepted baptism, the Pope wrote, a second Roman Empire might arise in the East, with Mohammed at its head. Pius reminded the Sultan that Clovis had brought Christianity to the Franks, and Constantine, to the Romans; he depicted a Europe once more united and, for the first time in centuries, at peace. The epistle - which now reads more like a fine literary exercise than a political document - was widely circulated in Europe, but whether it ever even reached the Sultan is not known. Certainly no reply was ever received in Rome.

It was now plain that the Turks could be conquered only by arms. In a last attempt to arouse the Roman people, the Pope decided to display to them - in what Gregorovius calls "one of the most curious scenes of the Roman Renaissance" - a singularly precious relic: the skull of the Apostle Andrew, which the exiled Despot of the Morea, Thomas Palaeologus, had brought to him – "the symbol of the Empire of Constantine and Justinian, and of the Church of Origen and Photius." Three cardinals, who had gone to fetch the head at Narni, were met at the Ponte Molle by the Pope and the other cardinals, and after a solemn Te Deum they accompanied it in procession to St. Peter's. "It was a splendid spectacle," Pius wrote, "to see those old men walk on foot through the mud holding palms in their hands and wearing miters on their white heads . . . Some who till then had lived delicately and could hardly move 100 paces except on horseback, on that day . . . walked two miles through mud and water with ease." All along the route, windows were hung with tapestries and lit up with torches and oil lamps; altars were set up at street corners, branches of fragrant shrubs were set alight. "Any man who possessed paintings or a fine and lifelike statue displayed them in the portico before his door." Little stages were set up, on which children, dressed as angels, sang or played musical instruments.

Finally, on reaching St. Peter's, the Pope stood at the top of the marble stair before the church and displayed the head to the assembled crowd, renewing his own vow to the Apostle "to recover thy sheep and thy dwelling-place on earth," and calling upon God to deliver Christendom from the Turks. "Then there arose a great sound, like the murmur of many waters."

In the following spring, since the Turkish army was engaged in Bosnia, the Venetians, who had concluded an alliance with Hungary, decided that the moment was propitious to send off their own fleet to the Peloponnesus. "We are already at war," they declared. Pius had no illusions about the Venetian motives, but, as he pointed out to the Florentine envoys, even though the Venetians were "seeking the Peloponnesus and not Jesus. . . . if Venice is victorious, the Church will be victorious. . . . This war is our common war." Moreover, at just this moment, a most fortunate event had come to strengthen the Pope's hand. In the wooded hills of Tolfa, which were within the Patrimony, some mines of alum, the precious dye until then imported from Turkey, were discovered. This Pius declared to be a miracle, and at once set aside all its profits for the Crusade. On October 22, 1463, he issued the Bull Ezechielis, repeating his determination to lead the troops of Christendom himself. "In our spirit, old as it is, and in our sick body there is a determination to make war upon the Turks."

Already, however, he realized that many of his allies had failed him - in particular, Francesco Sforza of Milan, Louis XI of France, and his vassal the Duke of Burgundy. The Venetian troops in the Peloponnesus had been swiftly defeated by the Turks, and their commander killed. The only troops to reach Ancona were a handful of unscrupulous adventurers, greedy for gain and loot. The Archbishop of Crete was appointed to weed them out, rejecting all those who had neither arms nor money.

Nevertheless, on June 14, 1464, in a solemn ceremony at St. Peter's, the Pope took the Cross, and four days later, so ill that he had to be carried onto his barge, he set forth. Turning back at the Ponte Molle for a last glimpse of Rome, he bade his city farewell, declaring, "You will never see me alive again." In all the history of the Crusades, there are few episodes more pathetic than this journey of the dying Pope up the Tiber and across the Apennines - well aware that his enterprise was doomed. Often, as they drew near the coast, his attendants would draw the curtains of his litter, so that he might not see the bands of deserters who, scenting the prospect of defeat, were fleeing home before they had even begun to fight.

When the Pope reached Ancona, no Venetian ship was to be seen, and day after day, from the windows of the bishop's palace at the summit of the town, Pius scanned the Adriatic in vain for the galleys of Saint Mark. The city was now short of food and water, and a pestilence had broken out, and the Pope himself was wasting away with dysentery.

When at last, on August 12, the Doge Cristoforo Moro sailed in with twelve ships, Pius was too ill to receive him. "Until now," he said, "it was a fleet that was lacking. Now the fleet has come, but I shall not be there." Two days later, feeling his end to be near, he summoned to his bedside the prelates who had come to Ancona with him, gave them his blessing, and told them that he was leaving them to finish what he had begun. Then, left alone with his nephew, his secretary, and his old friend Cardinal Ammanati, he once again exhorted the latter not to draw back. "Urge my brothers to go on with the Crusade . . . Woe befall you if you draw back from God's work." Asking for his friend's prayers, he lay back and died before the dawn.

On the next day, his body was carried to the cathedral, where the Doge pronounced a long and insincere oration over it and then at once set sail for Venice, while the cardinals hurried back to Rome to elect a new pope. The last Crusade was over, with the death of the only man who had believed in it.

7
VENICE
THE GOLDEN YEARS

On Ascension Day in 997, Pietro Orseolo, the Doge of Venice, anchored his galleon in the Grand Canal that joins the Venetian lagoon with the Adriatic Sea and poured an offering in the sea. He received the blessing of the Roman Catholic patriarch and then sallied forth to annihilate the Dalmatians of Croatia. For 800 years, as Venice grew wealthier and more powerful, that ceremony increased in complexity and grandeur until it became one of the great ritual pageants of the Western world. The huge state barge of the doges, the Bucentaur, blazing with cloths of crimson and gold, drew away from the Piazza San Marco to the chants of massed choirs. The Council of Ten, the Signory, the patricians and ambassadors, followed in their gilded gondolas. At the Porto di Lido, the doge, standing on the deck of the Bucentaur, cast a golden ring into the waters, declaring "O sea, we wed thee in sign of our true and everlasting dominion." The mixture of paganism, Christianity, and Oriental splendor was as symbolic of Venice as the marriage to the sea.

The sea linked Venice with Byzantium, the market for its goods, the protector of its liberties, the model of its state, the teacher of its crafts, the fountain of its arts. Under Byzantium's wing, Venice had grown to greatness, great enough to ruin the empire in the Fourth Crusade, yet not great enough to save the imperial city in its days of crisis when, in 1453, the Turkish hordes overwhelmed it. The loss was grievous for Venice, but not disastrous, for by then, the sources of Venetian power were scattered throughout the Western seas.

Only twice in its history did enemy vessels sail into the Venetian lagoon, and both times the enemy was annihilated; on land, its defenses proved equally inviolate. The Venetians built their ships in the great Arsenal - two miles of forbidding fortifications enclosed the most formidable armor in the Renaissance world. There, thousands of workmen produced a new galley every 100 days. The ships were moved from the Arsenal to the lagoon as if on a conveyor belt - masts, sails, oars, stores, and weapons were quickly loaded as the vessel slowly passed each storehouse. Most fittings on each galley were standardized so that replacements could be stored in all Venetian warehouses. Any crew could be transferred to any ship without further training, or a fresh crew could be made up from survivors in battle. And every galley, regardless of its use, belonged to the state: no patrician, no matter how wealthy, could possess a Venetian galley. Such precise regimentation, such absolute control, gave Venice its preeminence over its rivals and enabled it to ship a crusading army to the Holy Land without overstretching its resources.

The other maritime powers of Italy hated Venice's supremacy. Genoa ruined herself in a long and desperate series of wars, which ranged from the Bosporus Strait to the lagoon itself, in an attempt to crush Venice and steal the wealth of its great fleet. By 1400, Venice had proved invincible and had become the center of a sea-borne empire. Crete, Ragusa, Zadar, and many Aegean Islands belonged to her; trading communities had been established in Acre, Alexandria, Constantinople, Sidon, and Tyre. Venetian merchants were as familiar with the Black Sea as the Adriatic, and its ambassadors could be found in Cairo and Isfahan; its travelers reached Ceylon and Sumatra long before Vasco da Gama rounded the Cape. And even though the Venetians never ventured as far as the Genoese at the height of their greatness, their contacts with the East were more stable, more secure, and made up in volume what they lacked in diversity.

By 1450, Venice's interests required not only a great fleet but also a complex intelligence system. Venice needed to know the intentions of the Shah of Persia, the Count of Flanders, the Sultan of Cairo, the King of France, and the Duke of Ferrara. Every merchant, every priest was expected to spy for his country's good. The Signory knew the deepest secrets of the most carefully guarded conclaves of the pope, for the patriarchs of Venice put loyalty to the state above the Catholic Church. The well-informed, judicious reports of the Venetian residents in Bruges, London, and Paris now form some of the most reliable sources not only for the history of Venice, but also for the history of England, France, and the Netherlands. In the Archivio Centrale, or Central Archives of Italy, is the greatest collection of archives ever accumulated by a single city. There are a quarter of a million books, documents, and parchments, which, if placed end to end, would circle the earth eleven times. For the fourteenth and fifteenth centuries, there are a multitude of papers, a plethora of facts, a pyramid of accounts, still awaiting the labors of the historian. The reason for it all lies in the attitude and methods of the infamous Council of Ten, who, throughout the Renaissance, were the absolute rulers of the most highly organized state west of Byzantium.

The Council of Ten believed in knowledge and facts: Nothing was too trivial, too remote. They were as interested in the words and actions of a shopkeeper in the Campo di Santa Maria Formosa as they were the gossip of the harem at Samarkand. So voracious was their desire to pry that, throughout Venice, they installed the famous Lions' Mouths by which Venetians could inform the council anonymously of their suspicions of their neighbors. The Council acted swiftly and silently on this information, for there were no public trials and no appeals. Once found guilty, the prisoner was sometimes quickly and efficiently strangled in the dungeons and thrown into a part of the lagoon reserved for the purpose, hanged by one leg from the pillars of the Doge's Palace, quartered and distributed throughout the city, buried upside down in the Piazza San Marco with legs protruding, or beheaded as a public spectacle between the statues of Saint Theodore with his crocodile and the winged lion of Saint Mark. That was how the mighty condottiere Carmagnola met his end when the Council discovered that he was prepared to sell Venice to its enemies. But most traitors went silently in the night, their broken bodies sending a shiver of horror through the waking city as dawn gilded the palaces and churches.

This formidable government ruled all departments of the state - finance, diplomacy, the navy, the army, the welfare of the city - with equal efficiency, and it tolerated no rivals. The safety of the state, for which the Council of Ten was responsible, overrode all other considerations. The powers of the doge had been so ruthlessly suppressed (he could not even display his own armorial bearings) that he had become nothing but a figurehead. The Catholic Church, too, bowed to the state. No bishops, no parish priests, could officiate in Venice unless they were Venetian born. When placed under the Interdict by Pope Sixtus IV, the doge fell discreetly ill, and the council told the clergy that they would consider any priest who refused to celebrate the offices of the church a traitor. The clergy ignored the Interdict. During the most savage years of the Counter-Reformation, the council protected the historian Paolo Sarpi, whom good Catholics regarded as little better than a Lutheran. In Venice, there were no divided powers. Its immense wealth and colossal maritime power were ruled with the iron will of a dictatorship. Unbridled capitalism might flourish on the Rialto, but the Doges' Palace was a close cousin to the Kremlin.

The Council of Ten did not abide by permanent leaders. Its powers were partly shared by the Collegio, or cabinet, and beyond these was the Senate, or Signory, from which the councils were appointed. By a 1297 decree, however, no one could sit on these bodies unless his ancestor had been a member of the Great Council between 1172 and 1297. In 1319, to make certain that the purity of this oligarchy be maintained, the officers of the republic drew up the famous Golden Book, the Libro d'Oro, as a perpetual registry of

Venice's aristocracy. This revolution deprived the majority of Venetians of all the political rights they possessed. Any murmurs or rebellions were quickly and ruthlessly suppressed, and by the time of the Renaissance, the patrician families of Venice were as secure in their political and social power as the English aristocracy of the eighteenth century. A patrician's life was not, however, one of gilded leisure. The aristocrats were expected to man the fleets and participate in trade, as well as serve as leaders in far-off territories for their government. Like the guardians of Plato's republic or the proconsuls of British India, these men were expected to dedicate their lives to the state. Power and prestige might be theirs, but they earned it with undeviating loyalty, exemplary courage, and unflagging generosity. If they aspired to the doge's throne, they were aware of the risks, the dungeons, and the assassin's silent visit. If they sought glory in battle, their spirit was steeled by the grim epics of Venice's history - Admiral Andrea Dandolo, who bashed out his brains against the timbers of his galley the night the Genoese defeated him, or the neatly folded skin of Admiral Marco Antonio Bragadin, flayed alive by an Ottoman general. In the dulcet beauty of Venice, with its time-eroded buildings bathed in the light of the lagoon, it is all too easy to forget the stern, unyielding, harsh, and dedicated spirit that inspired its rulers in their days of greatness.

Venice, however, was two-faced. Though its commerce was regimented, its aristocracy disciplined and controlled, and its people subjected, it was cosmopolitan as no other European city was. The crowded wharves of the Rialto and the Riva Degli Schiavoni saw gentile and Jew, Muslim and Greek, haggling over precious cargoes from the Orient. The Germans possessed a vast warehouse on the Grand Canal; the Turks another, which had been the palace of the Pesaro family. The Armenians followed their religion for centuries without fear of the Inquisition. All the nations of Europe mingled with the races of the Near East in Venice, brought together by the greatest market of the Western world. Anything could be bought and sold in Venice, but the principal commerce was in spices, slaves, gold, silver, glass, silks, damasks, and jewels - cargoes small in bulk but huge in worth. Throughout barbarian times, as Venice grew to greatness, Europe lacked the sophisticated skills and crafts commonplace in the Eastern Empire or Syria and Egypt; in return for products from these places, Venice could provide the cheap raw materials that a primitive Europe produced: hides and tin from England, cloth from Flanders, raw silver from Bohemia, copper and steel from Germany. And there were the pilgrims. Decade after decade, century after century, in peace or in war, rich and devout Christians won their way to heaven via the Holy Places to the profit of the

Venetians. For centuries, as the Crusaders warred in the eastern lands, they paid for their armies, their horses, their necessities - and Venetians did not believe in bargains. In spite of their wars against the Genoese, Greeks, and Turks, Venice grew wealthy on people's craving for luxury, ostentation, and self-indulgence, on the pride of life and the lust of the eye. It encouraged luxury crafts rather than industries. The glass manufacture of Murano, based on secrets learned in the East, was closely guarded by the Council of Ten: Any workman who left Venice with the knowledge of its manufacture was guilty of treason; the council ordered him hunted down and killed. Along with the monopoly in glass, the making of mosaic derived from Byzantium was practiced only in Venice. Venetian jewelers had no rivals in the late Middle Ages, and emperors and kings sent there for their crosses and scepters. Few Italian cities could rival Venice in the splendor of its silks, and none in the beauty of its lace.

In Venice, everything was for sale – including love. Venice boasted more courtesans than Rome, and their fees were thoroughly catalogued, as were their skills. They, too, had their rivals - the competition from homosexuals was so severe that the harlots complained loudly to the Council of Ten. As the wealth and prosperity of Europe lifted, the riches of Venice soared.

On the threshold of the Renaissance, Venice had unrivaled trade and a stable and immensely powerful government firmly in the hands of its patricians. Merchant Jacopo Loredan entered in his ledger: "The Doge [Francesco] Foscari: my debtor for the death of my father and uncle." After Foscari had been harried to death and his son killed, Loredan wrote on the opposite page, "Paid." In 1450, that was the spirit of Venice. By 1550, a softer, more self-indulgent atmosphere had turned Venice into a city of carnival: still strong, still rich, still capable of sacrifice, but essentially an empire in defense, longing for a secure isolation in which to enjoy its riches. This change was brought about partly through a change in strategy and partly through the spirit of the Renaissance itself.

Safe in the security of the lagoon, the strategic problems of Venice had been mostly distant and maritime. Its diplomacy had been directed solely to the pursuit of trade; the acquisition of territory had been secondary. Throughout the High Middle Ages, the Venetians had excluded themselves from Italy, but when it suited their purpose, they forgot the East and made a token gesture to the emperor of the West. This policy had been so successful that many influential doges and patricians regarded it as the foundation of Venice's glory. They felt that any deviation would ruin the state, and the deviation they most feared was that the government would succumb to those who demanded that Venice extend its frontiers on the mainland and take its place as a great power in Lombardy. The problem was one that all expanding commercial empires faced: Did the needs of commerce require political control of its channels? So long as the Lombardy plain was divided up among a multitude of petty powers, Venice had little to fear, but in the fourteenth century, as the dominant powers in northern Italy became fewer and fewer, the danger was brought home when Francesco I da Carrara, the despot of Padua, joined the Genoese in the war that Venice barely won in the lagoon in the great Battle of Chioggia. The safety of the lagoon, let alone Venetian trade, depended upon the control of the rivers - the Brenta and the Piave - that had cost the republic huge sums to canalize and divert from the lagoon. Beyond the rivers were the easy Alpine passes, particularly the Brenner, through which Venetian trade flowed to Northern Europe. And there were subtler motives at work - everywhere in Italy, small city-states were vanquished through the onslaught of Florence, Milan, Naples, and Rome, and if the Venetians wished to be heard in the councils of Italy, they needed to acquire far more Italian territory than a few muddy islands and river mouths in a shallow lagoon. Finally, after the defeat of Genoa and before the collapse of Constantinople, Venice had plenty of money and young aristocrats ready for a venture.

Although the debate, particularly at the time of Doge Foscari, seemed bitter and prolonged,

Venice was inevitably drawn into the vortex of Italian politics and war. Once embroiled, strategic needs forced it to push its frontiers westward and southward against Milan and Rome. Its fluctuations were many, but its successes built and continued to grow. There were years of danger, particularly when Venice struggled singlehandedly to keep the Turks confined to the eastern Mediterranean; there were darker days when all the princes of Italy combined with its enemies in the League of Cambrai to ruin it. But Venice triumphed. Its boundaries stretched from Lake Como in the west to Trieste in the east, from the high-Alpine valleys in the north to Ferrara in the south. These rich territories were ruled with wisdom and restraint. No local customs were violated, no local law nullified, no families uprooted. The possession of Bergamo, Brescia, Padua, Treviso, Verona, Vicenza, and the rest added enormously to Venetian wealth in spite of the costly wars their capture entailed.

The patricians found they could tap the riches of the terraferma, as they called the Lombard plain, far more easily than they could the Oriental trade, rich as it was. The Turks were in Constantinople, and the frequent, costly struggles there made eastern trade more difficult than it had been in the time of the Greek emperors. That trade had always entailed risks, from pirates, shipwreck, or the hazards of the sea, but farms on the rich alluvial plains brought a high, steady financial return. There were choice opportunities in the captured towns - real estate, banking, insurance, partnerships in trade and industry – but it was the land that attracted the Venetians. For centuries, rich families had built their villas and landscaped their gardens on the islands of Giudecca and Murano to escape the heat and stink of Venice. But tenements and warehouses crept along Giudecca, and much of Murano was consumed by the ever-expanding glass works. The sweeping curves and gentle slopes of the valley of the Brenta and the hills of Cadore, on the Austrian border, drew the Venetian aristocracy to the rustic but sophisticated life of the countryside. There Andrea Palladio built the exquisite villas that would inspire the architects not only of eighteenth-century England, but also the planters of Virginia. Here they created an indulgent life that stood in harsh contrast to the battle-scarred days of Venice's heroic growth. Here the strength of merchants was sapped by the delight in being landed gentlemen.

The same spirit was at work in Venice itself. The city had become stuffed and bloated with possessions. Although it clung tenaciously to what it had, it grew indifferent to adventure. No Venetian galleys probed the secrets of the New World; no hardheaded merchants sought gold in tropical Africa. Perhaps it is not surprising that the early heroic phase of Renaissance exploration passed Venice by. Only when the market in Renaissance goods was established did Venice enter it, but it did so with a panache and brilliance all its own. Furthermore, its proud independence and its indifference to the ideological strife of the sixteenth century enabled the spirit of the Renaissance to flourish long after it had been strangled elsewhere in Italy. Venetians, by their nature, were quick to adopt technical improvements and to exploit the commercial possibilities of artistic development. The Flemish discovery in oil painting was quickly adopted by Venetian artists; the market for bronzes was flooded by Venetian craftsmen; family portraiture was commonplace in Venice while it was unusual elsewhere. Whenever a Venetian entrepreneur saw a chance, he seized it. Printing, scoffed at in Rome and patronized in Milan, became a luxury industry with a growing mass market in the capable hands of Aldus Manutius and his family, who produced the first comprehensive, standardized set of books known as the Aldine Classics. They lacked the beauty and rich ornamentation of the earlier books that attempted to mimic illuminated manuscripts, but they exhibited a spare and efficient functionalism. Elegant, moderate in price, and easy to read, they were all that a book should be. Yet this was one of more than 200 presses in Venice in 1500. Here the new printing trade, nurtured and protected by the state, flourished as nowhere else.

Venice skillfully exploited the bourgeois pleasures that satisfied the increasingly affluent public. Indeed, as its political and military power ebbed, it became a symbol of self-indulgence and sensuous living - a city of extravagance, urbanity, and sophistication in which the future was forgotten in the day's delights. In the end, stripped of all but the pageantry of power, the Venetians, as hardheaded as ever, plucked their profits from the provincial nobility of Western and Northern Europe. But between 1450 and 1570, there was still vigor enough in Venetian commerce and achievement in Venetian arms to create legitimate pride. The lords of Venice lived in an aura of greatness without any sense of falsity. Yet the weakening, the softening, spread throughout the decades like self-indulgent fat on an old warrior. This transition, though exceptionally fertile for Venetian art, sapped its power.

The Signory had always believed in the value of art as propaganda and was willing to pay high prices for huge frescoes in the Doge's Palace that celebrated the heroic deeds of the republic or the noble acts of its great men. When it came to a pageant, their hard fists opened willingly, and they delighted in parading the might and splendor of the republic. Saints' days, anniversaries of notable victories, the solemnization of treaties, the visits of monarchs and princes, the presentation and dismissal of ambassadors - all were opportunities for glorious display. As they wound their way through the Piazza, or in and out of the Doge's Palace, the powerless populace became acutely aware of the greatness of their masters. It was a lesson, the Signory thought, that could not be learned too often - and they commanded Venice's outstanding artists to immortalize their pageants and embellish the walls of the Doge's Palace with the glories of the republic. Powerful guilds and wealthy patricians followed suit - and the life stories of Venice's favored saints covered the schools, hospitals, churches, and monasteries of the city. Skilled craftsmen and painters had always been in demand in Venice, and Venetian artists – Giovanni Bellini, Giorgio da Castelfranco, Tiziano Vecelli, Vittore Carpaccio, and Paolo Veronese - were surrounded by traditions that went back to the early Middle Ages. In Venice, because demand had been so heavy and the commissions so large, painting had to be a family affair, a workshop, almost a factory. Every great Venetian painter was more than just an individual artist; he was the director and inspiring genius of a studio in which brothers, wives, sons, daughters, journeymen, and apprentices all worked together. Naturally, the number of people involved increased output and enabled a painter to cover acres of wall and bolts of canvas in his long and active life. Venetian art exists in abundance; indeed, in Venice, every church and monastery swarms with masterpieces. This astonishing abundance reflects the vigor, wealth, and sensuous delight of Venetian life. Of all Renaissance painting, the Venetian is the most colorful, alive in flesh and clothes and landscape played upon by light and shade. The Venetian master could move with consummate ease from painting an enormous wall glorifying the state to a display of the intimacies of physical love, yet in whatever he painted, there was warmth and the reality that the Venetian knew. The Paradise of Tintoretto, the largest painting of its age, was peopled with Venetians. In Gentile Bellini's Miracle of the Cross, canals, gondolas, rooftops, and chimneys of Venice abound. In Carpaccio's Saint Ursula, a Venetian girl sleeps in her bedroom; under the thin guise of a Christian story, the rich, sensuous life pulsates, reflecting the splendor of the city.

Although the life of Venice was glorified, individuals were not. An occasional doge (when dead), a patriarch or two, a brilliant condottiere might be immortalized in a portrait or a statue, but the majority of portraits by Bellini or Titian remain nameless, for they were of ordinary patricians whose only claim to fame was the luck to be born in Venice at a time of artistic greatness. These evocative paintings, infinite in their variety, display the sharp sense of the transience of the living and loving of the Venetians. Nostalgia emanates from things Venetian; the streets of Venice echo with a sense of loss. The poetry of existence, the sadness that veils a sensual life, flows throughout not only the best Venetian painting but also the writing of its one literary genius - Arctino di Mileto. In him were mirrored the conflicting images of man - the cosmic and the noble, the moral and the obscene - that hypnotized the creative writers of Europe for generations.

Venice at the crossroads of its destiny created an exceptionally complex society. It was still the city of hardheaded merchants, of enterprise and ingenuity, of the all-pervading, all-powerful state, of swift and terrible justice. Its claim to dominion over the sea wasn't an idle boast: The doge's had not been reduced to a quaint, old-fashioned pageant. Yet the Renaissance settled on Venice like a golden haze, sweetening life, softening the edges. The city of commerce was becoming the city of carnival. This feeling of a lost future was already pervading the attitude of Venetian men and women, drawing them to the luxuries they could easily afford, to the new delights in painting, music, architecture, and letters the Renaissance produced in such abundance. Rome itself could scarcely vie with Venice in the splendor of either its public or private new buildings. The splendid facades of Jacopo Sansovino had given the city its permanent face, and scattered about the canals and islands of the lagoon were the churches and monasteries of Palladio. Its artistic luxuries were incomparable, and its gold and silver, armor, jewelry, bronzes, glass, lace, printing, and bookbinding were practiced not only skillfully, but also so profusely that Venice, both in its lagoon and on the mainland, became the most affluent state of Italy. The splendor of its new palaces of white marble and serpentine overwhelmed generations of foreigners, while the plethora of its merchandise bewildered them. Philippe de Comines, nobleman and ambassador of France, rich, sophisticated, much traveled, was as entranced by the Grand Canal as the merry, uncouth joker Thomas Coryate of Somerset, who walked all the way there and gaped, open-mouthed with amazement. Other cities might possess nobler paintings, statues, buildings, but nowhere did the Renaissance permeate more thoroughly the daily life of a city and its people than in Venice.

Profile:
THE DOGE OF VENICE
Hugh Trevor-Roper

In 1423, the Doge of Venice, Tommaso Mocenigo, lay dying. The city's prosperity was at its height; this was indeed the golden age of the republic. But for a generation, grave problems had clouded the city's future: Should it concentrate on its empire abroad or on its base at home? Both were threatened.

The empire abroad was centered in the Aegean Sea, although it extended to Constantinople and the Middle and Far East. Here the threat came from the Ottoman Turks, now settled in Europe, who were pushing into the Balkans. All of Venice's efforts were needed to keep them out of the Aegean, and for years that had been the primary goal of Venetian diplomacy.

The threat to home came from closer quarters: New powers were rising in and around Italy. Prior to this time, Venice had been able to build up its empire abroad because its neighbors at home had given little trouble. While bishoprics, communes, and petty princes could not be ignored, their offerings could not compete with the huge profits of the Eastern Mediterranean. The republic had balanced its power with a minimum of direct intervention. But now these petty neighbors were being assimilated by greater powers who were threatening the very life of Venice. The rulers of Hungary and Naples were closing in on its Adriatic lifeline, and a menacing new state was pressing down the valley of the Po. The free republics of Italy were being converted into despotic princely states, and the most powerful of these states was the new duchy of Milan, under the Visconti family. Having crushed the liberties of Milan, the Visconti were expanding their territory around it. They had already absorbed the mercantile republic of Genoa to the south, which, being confined between the Ligurian Alps and the sea, lacked a turf on which to fight. In the east, the Visconti were pushing toward another mercantile republic squeezed between the lagoons and the sea - Venice.

How could the republic ensure its survival? According to some Venetians, the answer was to enlarge its own territory, the Venetian terraferma - a process that had already begun with the annexation of Padua, Vicenza, and Verona. But others distrusted this policy. Land wars, they said, were costly and distracted the city from its real task in the East; they created a new class of landed nobility and made the city dependent on condottieri, and it was out of the landed nobility and condottieri that the powerful new group of princes, which threatened the liberties of all Italian cities, was rising.

As the Doge Mocenigo lay dying, he summoned the ducal councilors to his bedside and delivered a famous speech. The war for the terraferma, he said, had shattered the finances of the republic and could not be continued. The wealth of Venice lay in manufacturing, trading, and shipping: only by keeping to these pursuits and to peace, would the city master the wealth of Christendom. They must be careful to appoint a sound successor to himself. Then he went down the list of the possible candidates: Pietro Bembo, Leonardo Loredan, Giovanni Mocenigo, and Gasparo Contarini - the political members of the great mercantile families who formed the closed aristocracy of Venice. But he warned them explicitly against one man: Francesco Foscari, he said, was proud, ambitious, and unscrupulous. If he were doge, it would mean war, war, and more war.

By that time, the republic had achieved its aristocratic form - a form that would last for centuries. Gone were the days when the people had power of election; since 1297, the Greater Council, the legislature and electorate of the republic, had been confined to the nobility, who, in turn, kept careful control over their membership. Gone, too, were the days when the doge exercised personal power. By now, successive "ducal promises" - the conditions which the nobility, after observing the faults of each doge, imposed upon his successor - had reduced the doge to a mere figurehead. If offered the dogeship, a Venetian nobleman was unable by law to refuse it. Once elected, his power was narrowly circumscribed. He was unable to travel outside Venice. Neither he nor his sons could marry foreigners without permission. Neither his sons nor his personal officers could hold public positions under him (except as ambassadors or naval commanders, where they could not make trouble at home), and his official councilors, without whom he could do nothing, not even open a formal letter, could not be chosen by him. His income was fixed and his expenses limited, and his authority over the citizens was reduced. He was not even allowed to give himself social airs or answer to honorific titles. To foreigners, as the representative of the wealthiest republic in Italy, he might be Serenissimo Principi (most Supreme Prince); at home, he was only Messer lo Doge. Finally, he could not even quit his job at will: Without the consent of his six councilors, ratified by the approval of the Greater Council, he could not even abdicate. Why then would an ambitious man want to be doge, and what could an ambitious man do if he were doge?

Nevertheless, Mocenigo's warning cannot have been entirely groundless. The Venetian constitution may have been altogether aristocratic, and its aristocratic character may have been preserved by a perpetual subdivision of authority and indirect elections and an intricate web of checks and balances. But even a perfect constitution is driven by human passions, and the more complex a constitution is, the more it falls into the hands of skillful politicians. And skilled politicians, even with the old rules, may play a new game. In the fifteenth century, a new game was being played in all the republics of Italy. Their old constitutions were crumbling, and new politicians - sometimes patricians rising out of their midst, sometimes condottieri in their service - were building up despotic rule. This had already happened in Milan with the Visconti; it would happen again with the Sforza. Soon it would happen in Florence, too. Cosimo de' Medici might begin as pater patriae, "the first citizen" of the republic, but he would end by founding a dynasty that would last for centuries. Remembering this fact, no one can assume that even the Venetian constitution was a guarantee against being overthrown by an ambitious doge who might build up a new form of patronage and power. At least that may have been the fear that inspired the Doge Mocenigo to warn his fellow noblemen against electing Francesco Foscari as his successor.

Who was the man who aroused these fears? Venetian aristocrats are always somewhat impersonal figures; the very system, with its intense jealousy of individual power, tended to depersonalize them. It was the essential character of the Venetian republic that all personality was ruthlessly subordinated to the state. Instead of the cutthroat private enterprise of Genoa, or the brilliant individualism of Florence, in Venice, we see only an impersonal state capitalism, an implacable reason of state, a culture entirely hostile to "the cult of personality." So the official records of Venice do not animate even a controversial man like Foscari. And yet he certainly was a controversial character, as was demonstrated, first of all, by the battle over his election.

Foscari was determined to be doge. As an outsider, Mocenigo and his friends feared Foscari. He was also, at fifty, the youngest of the candidates; he was considered poor by the wealthy "nabob" families, although he had enriched himself by marriage; he had held most of the powerful elective offices of the state, and above all - and this was what Venice particularly distrusted - he was the ambitious head of a party. This party was particularly suspicious to the mercantile aristocracy that customarily ruled

Venice, for it was a party of the lesser nobles, the radicals, the "Westerners" who favored war by land. It is said that as procurator of Saint Mark's, Foscari had used the large cash balances in his hands to create his following; he had relieved the wants of poor noblemen, given portions to their daughters, and made himself dangerous by their support. No doubt he had won other support by his merits, too. And finally, as was soon to be shown, he was a consummate election manager.

When the forty-one electors met, Foscari was not the favorite. He was too impulsive, too controversial, too committed to a policy. The favorite was Pietro Loredan, the admiral of the republic, who was also determined to be doge. But Loredan made the mistake of speaking confidently on his own behalf, which lost him votes. Foscari was more prudent. Although his rivals did not know it, he had already nine ballots safely in his pocket. These voters acted as a bloc, but they did not reveal themselves until they had quietly defeated all the other candidates and pretended that they, too, were opposed to Foscari. Then, at the tenth ballot, their votes carried the outsider into the ducal chair.

Thus began the longest ducal reign in the history of the Venetian republic. The flamboyant Foscari hastened to celebrate his victory. For a whole year, he dazzled the city with feasts and pageants. The new Sala del Maggior Consiglio - the Hall of the Great Council - was opened with splendid ceremony. He fetched his wife, the dogaressa, to the palace in the ducal galley, the Bucentaur, attended by the noblewomen of Venice. Then the doge settled down to the business of government.

Foscari's reign can be described in three words - pageantry, war, and dissension. There were feasts and spectacles of unexampled magnificence, but there was also - as Mocenigo had prophesied - constant war for the terraferma. Thirdly, there was the undying jealousy and hatred of those Foscari had defeated - particularly of the Loredan family. The spectacle gave his reign its outward splendor; the war its real content; and the hatred of the Loredan brought it to a tragic end.

The outward splendor was shown in many ways. New palaces rose by the Grand Canal and the lagoon. The Rialto Bridge was rebuilt. The artist Paolo Uccello worked on mosaics in Saint Mark's, Antonio Vivarini painted in San Pantaleon. Famous visitors were received with even more pomp and show. In 1428, the ducal galley, the Bucentaur, escorted by a fleet of boats, transported a prince of Portugal to a banquet attended by 250 ladies dressed in gold and silk and jewels. In 1438, Byzantium's emperor, in his time of turmoil with the Turks, came to Italy with his brother the despot of the Morea and the patriarch of Constantinople, ready to accept the supremacy of the Roman Church in return for Western aid. When the Bucentaur sailed with the imperial party from the Lido, the whole lagoon was full of boats, flying banners and playing music, with oarsmen clad in cloth of gold. In 1452, even this event was eclipsed when the Holy Roman Emperor followed the Byzantine emperor to Venice and was drawn by the Bucentaur and the gaily colored boats to the Grand Canal. By the next year, the last Byzantine emperor had perished in the sack of his capital, and the Doge Foscari would receive the fugitive scholars and salvaged treasures of that empire.

In Byzantine eyes, the fall of Byzantium was due to Venetian indifference. Throughout the reign of Foscari, it was said, the military resources of Venice had been turned too much to the West. But this was hardly a fair judgment. The threat from the West was real, as the fate of Genoa showed. Also, in the first year of Foscari's reign, there had been a great success in the East. That year, the Greek governor of Salonika, the emporium of Thessalian grain (Venice lived on imported grain) and the northern watchtower of the Aegean, sold his city to Venice rather than lose it to the Turks. The East, it seemed, was safe. Meanwhile, the republic had obtained an invaluable ally for war in the West. At this time, Francesco Bussone, known as Carmagnola, the greatest condottiere in Italy, the man who had recreated the power of the Visconti in Milan, had now deserted his master and offered his services to Venice. The Venetians could hardly resist his offer. Against this background of double security provided by Salonika in the East and Carmagnola in the West, the republic, in 1425, allied with Florence and declared war on the Visconti.

Within three years of his accession, Foscari was carrying out the policy that had always been associated with him. There can be no doubt that war was his policy: A copy of the speech with which he persuaded the republic to make war still exists. Of course, given the Venetian constitution, it's certain that this policy was not his alone, for he had only influence, not authority. Nevertheless, his influence, combined with circumstances, weighted and held the scales. Even twelve years later, in 1437, his personal prestige was extraordinarily powerful. In that year, the doge sat, day after day, at the bedside of his son Domenico, who was dying of the plague. Foscari's supporters feared that he, too, would catch the infection, and then what would they do? The lives of many, they said, depended on his: If he were to fail, the state would be in peril. Clearly, the doge was no mere chairman. The policy of the state depended particularly on him in 1437, when the advantages that had made the Western war attractive a dozen years earlier had disappeared.

In fact, neither Salonika nor Carmagnola lived up to their promise. In 1430, the Turks captured and sacked Salonika; the slaughter was terrible, the loss final. From now on, the Aegean Sea and the wealth of Venice lay open to the Turks, scattered among subject islands whose Greek inhabitants preferred (or thought they preferred) Turkish conquest to Venetian exploitation. In the same year, an attempt was made to assassinate the doge. As for Carmagnola, like so many condottieri, he proved unsatisfactory. At the head of one of the greatest armies in Italy, he somehow failed to be as victorious in Venice as he had been in Milan, and he remained suspiciously familiar with his former employer and present enemy, the ruler of Milan. The Venetians offered to make him lord of Milan if he would only conquer it, but instead he spent time and money in parades or took cures at the baths of Abano. Finally, the Venetians lost patience. With their usual wariness, they did nothing rashly or openly, but invited Carmagnola to Venice to meet the doge and discuss future strategy. He never saw the doge. Instead, he was whisked from the palace to prison, tortured, tried, and condemned. When his sentence was discussed, the doge voted for mercy, but was overruled, and Carmagnola was sentenced to death and beheaded. After that, the republic employed other, less dangerous condottieri.

By 1432, Foscari was faced with difficulties on all fronts. He sensed the obstacles and the next year asked to leave office. It is said that he made the request again in 1442 and again in 1446, and this suggests that he was an impatient man, easily discouraged by defeat. But the Venetian aristocracy would not allow him to give up his office. On each occasion, they reminded him that, by the constitution, he could not resign except with the assent of the six councilors and the Greater Council. It was an answer he would later use against his enemies.

Meanwhile, the long war for the terraferma went on, lasting, with brief interludes, for thirty years. It was also very expensive; the first ten years alone cost 7 million ducats. It had its dramatic incidents - among them bringing of Venetian ships over the mountains from the river Adige to Lake Garda. It had its disappointments, too - the most bitter being the gradual slide of the Florentines, out of commercial rivalry, toward the side of Milan. But in the end, the war was successful, and the westward frontier of the terraferma was expanded to incorporate the provinces of Brescia and Bergamo, and the doge received them as imperial fiefs along with Ravenna as a papal fief. Before his death, he inspired and signed a new treaty - a confederation with Florence and Milan, Rome and Naples, which would preserve the liberty of Italy. It would have been a great triumph had it lasted: At least it outlasted Foscari.

But what of the third feature of Foscari's reign, the enmity of his rivals? This, too, was long and bitter, as Venetian enmities always were. For if Venice, with its exaltation of state service, was free from the strife of parties that ruined every other Italian republic, it was invigorated, more so than the others, by fierce personal and family feuds. In particular, the Doge Foscari never escaped the bitter hatred of the Loredan family. They remembered their defeat of 1423, and in later years, with their allies the Dona and the Barbarigo, mercilessly persecuted him at his weakest point - his family.

At the time of his election, one objection to Foscari had been his large family, whose members, it was suggested, would feed on the resources of the state. This danger did not materialize, for four of his five sons died young of the plague. The last survivor, who alone had heirs and to whom the Doge was devoted, was Jacopo, a young man of cultivated tastes but indiscreet ways. In 1441, his marriage to Lucrezia Contarini had been one of the most magnificent spectacles the doge had given to the city. There had been boat races, feasts, and illuminations, a great tournament before 30,000 people in the Piazza San Marco, and 250 horsemen riding in cavalcade over the Grand Canal on a specially built bridge of barges. But in 1445, Jacopo Foscari was secretly denounced for receiving gifts from Filippo Maria Visconti, the ruler of Milan. At that time, Francesco Loredan, the nephew of the defeated candidate, was one of three chiefs of the Council of Ten, which also acted as the secret political police of the republic.

His ally, Ermolao Dona, was another, and council members decided to act. They ordered the arrest of Jacopo and excluded the doge and his kinsmen from their deliberations on the matter. Jacopo was exiled to Nafplio in Greece, and all his goods were confiscated. The dogaressa begged in vain to see her son: The orders were given, and the name of the doge himself was placed, with ruthless, impersonal irony, at their head. Before they could be executed, the place of exile was changed to Treviso, which was nearer and more comfortable, but the humiliation to the doge was no less. It was after this bitter defeat that Foscari made his third attempt to resign, but he was forced to remain in office.

Before long, however, the doge was able to score a point. In 1447, he made a moving appeal to the Ten, and they consented, not on grounds of humanity but (a typically Venetian reason) "because it is necessary at this time to have a prince whose mind is free and serene, able to serve the republic," to remit the exile of Jacopo, now sick in body and mind. But the reunion did not last long. In 1450, the Loredan family found another pretext and resumed their attack.

That year, one of Jacopo Foscari's judges, Ermolao Dona, was murdered, and Jacopo was at once suspected. Again the doge's son was arrested and tortured. Although nothing was proved, and he was probably innocent (it is said that another man afterward confessed to the crime), the Ten, having gone so far, were afraid to go back. They sentenced him, without proof, to exile, and he was carried off to Crete. Even in Crete, his movements were watched, and in 1456, it was reported to the Ten that he was planning, or at least discussing, revenge with foreign help. The Ten (of whom Jacopo Loredan was now one of the chiefs) immediately decided that the matter was "of the greatest importance." Once again, the doge's son was fetched back for trial.

Now began the final tragedy of the doge's reign, the tragedy which Byron converted into his drama The Two Foscari. Before this third trial, it was admitted that Jacopo's projects were entirely academic, and in Crete, he could do nothing to harm the republic. But it made no difference. He was tortured and found guilty, and the remorseless Jacopo Loredan urged that he be publicly beheaded as a traitor between the columns of the Piazza. Even the Ten drew the line at this, and the prisoner was sentenced to renewed exile in Crete, this time in prison. Before returning to Crete, he was allowed to see his father, now eighty-four years old. He begged the doge to intercede for him. "Jacopo," replied the old man, "go and obey your country's commands, and seek no more." But when his son had gone, he threw himself upon a chair, weeping and crying. Within a few months, he was shattered to learn that his last son was dead in Crete.

The doge's enemies decided to complete their victory. The doge, they said, was too old and distracted by grief - the grief they had caused him - and he could no longer attend to business. The Council of Ten met and decided to demand his abdication. Their message was brought to the doge by Jacopo Loredan.

A RESOLUTION CALLING FOR THE DOGE'S ABDICATION, VOTED BY THE COUNCIL OF TEN, THE PRIVY COUNCIL, AND THE GIUNTA, A BODY OF TWENTY-FIVE NOBLEMEN.

There is no one who does not thoroughly comprehend how useful and altogether how essential to our State and to our affairs is the presence of a Prince, without which, as becomes manifest from the results, the greatest inconvenience and detriment are apt to arise to our State which, since it has by the infinite clemency of our Creator been bequeathed to us by our forefathers hereditary and fair to look upon, we are bound to preserve with all our power and to hold dearer to us than our very life. And although this our city is furnished with holy laws and ordinances, it is of little avail if they be not executed, if the observance of the same be relaxed. The presence of the Prince besides in the councils, at audiences, in the transaction of affairs of state - how desirable it is, how glorious it is, it would be superfluous to point out. All are aware that our most illustrious Prince has vacated his dignity for a great length of time; and from his advanced age it is not at all to be expected that he will be able to return to the exercise of the functions appertaining thereto. How pernicious his absence and incompetence are is more easily understood than explained. Wherefore: it is proposed that by the authority of this most excellent Council and the Giunta the resolution be agreed to that the Privy councilors and the chiefs of the council shall repair to the presence of the most illustrious Prince and declare to him our opinion that the government of our city and State (which as his Highness knows very well is excessively arduous) cannot be carried on without the constant presence and cooperation of a Prince; also considering how long his Excellency has for personal reasons renounced all share in this government, and that there is no hope that he will be able at any time hereafter to discharge his duties according to the exigencies of this state; and [considering] that his absence is threatening to involve consequences such as we are assured from his affectionate patriotism, he can never desire to witness; - on these grounds which his Excellency in his supreme wisdom will readily appreciate, we with the aforesaid council of Ten and the Giunta have decided upon exhorting and requesting his Serenity, for the evident and necessary welfare of our State - his native land - freely and spontaneously to abdicate, which on many accounts he ought to do as a good Prince and a true father of his country, and especially as we provide that he shall have for his support and proper maintenance from our Office of Salt 1,500 gold ducats a year for life as well as the residue of his salary due to the present day. Also that if it happen that the same most illustrious Prince, on this declaration being made known to him, shall demand time to consider, he may be told that we are content to wait for such answer till tomorrow at the hour of tierce.

Now the old man turned on them the argument they had used against him in the past: By the law, he said, he could not abdicate unless the councilors proposed and the Greater Council agreed. Baffled, the Ten consulted again, reinterpreted the law to suit their convenience and told the doge of their reinterpretation. Still the doge held firm. Then they sent him an order to resign and vacate the ducal palace within eight days. If he did so, he would receive an adequate salary and a doge's burial. If not, he would be driven out, and all his goods confiscated.

It was an illegal demand, but the Doge was powerless to resist. The ducal ring was taken from his finger and the ducal cap from his head. He promised to leave the palace. Then, seeing pity in the eye of one of his visitors, he called to him and taking his hand said, "Whose son are you?" "I am the son of Messer Marin Memmo," was the reply.

The doge said, "He is my old friend. Ask him to come and visit me so that we may go in a boat for solace; we will visit the monasteries." The next day, he left the palace. Wearing his old scarlet robe of state, he stepped forth, bent but unaided except by his staff. As he went to the stone steps leading to the water, his brother Marco urged him to go to his gondola by the covered stair. "No," replied the doge, "I will go down by the same stair by which I came up to my dukedom." A week later, he died - of rage, it was said, on hearing the bells announcing the election of his successor.

The people of Venice were indignant at the indecent deposition of the doge who had reigned so long, whose figure and personality were so striking, whom the emperors of East and West had visited, and who had given them such wonderful shows. There was much murmuring against the Council of Ten, and even the doge's enemies were ashamed that they had not waited another week for a natural death. They gave Foscari a grand funeral in spite of the protests of the former dogaressa. He was buried in the church of the Frari, and a majestic Gothic-Renaissance monument commemorated his conquest of the terraferma. Meanwhile, the Ten withdrew from the limelight until the furor over their treatment of the Doge had abated. But there was no denying that they had won a substantial victory. From now on, the constitution was not only clearly oligarchical, it was also clear that the center of oligarchical power lay with the Council of Ten.

The long reign of Francesco Foscari ended as it had begun, in bitter personal controversy, and even today, historians dispute its significance. It has been said that it was Foscari who diverted the attention of Venice from East to West, sacrificing Salonika and Constantinople to Bergamo and Brescia. This diversion led to disastrous consequences fifty years later, when the powers of Europe united against "the insatiable cupidity of the Venetians and their lust for power." Yet, could any other doge have acted differently? The dilemma had been there before Foscari's time: If the land powers of Europe would not unite against the Turks, a sea power could not defeat them alone. Could Venice ignore the Western threat or the ominous example of Genoa? Other historians have focused on the fear of despotism, painting the Loredan as republicans bent on ridding Venice of corruption and protecting the constitution. But is there any evidence that Foscari entertained thoughts of altering the constitution? Perhaps he did in his early years (though we can only judge from the suspicion he inspired), but it is unlikely that an old man of eighty could have threatened the established power of the oligarchy. In the end, it was not he but his enemies who broke the constitution. He submitted to its most humiliating rules, malevolently applied; his foes broke through its last restraints in order to humble him.

Nevertheless, Foscari's reign was crucial in Venetian history. Whatever his own aims, they were ultimately subordinated and absorbed by the impersonal Venetian system. During his term in office, the Milanese republic was converted into the duchy of the Sforza, the great Florentine republic into the domain of the Medici, but the republicans of Venice, whatever their motives or personal suspicions, positively strengthened their republic. They accepted the policy and then crushed the personality of the one man who might have recreated the old ducal power. And their victory over him was final. Before 1457, seven doges had been assassinated, nine had been blinded and exiled, twelve had abdicated, one had been sentenced to death and beheaded, two had been deposed. But after 1457, there is peace inside the republic. The Venetian constitution survived intact throughout the era of the native princes, and the city kept its independence when the other Italian states fell under foreign rule. It resisted the papacy during the Counter-Reformation and was praised in the seventeenth century as a model of government for any mercantile state that aspired to be free, effective, and independent.

Profile:
FEDERIGO DA MONTEFELTRO

DENIS MACK SMITH

For fifty years, the little hill town of Urbino in the northern Marches was one of the great cultural centers of Europe. Urbino, the birthplace of Raphael and Bramante, drew sculptors from Milan and Florence, architects from Siena and Dalmatia, painters from Spain and tapestry workers from Flanders. Paolo Uccello worked inside its walls; so did Piero della Francesca and Melozzo da Forli. Baldassare Castiglione emigrated from Mantua there and was sent as the special envoy of Urbino to England, taking a painting commissioned from Raphael as a present for the English King. And as a result of Castiglione's much translated Book of the Courtier, people all over the Western world learned from Urbino a code of manners, a way of courtesy and refinement, which became the norm of polite behavior.

The duchy of Urbino and its standards of taste in art and manners were created by Federigo da Montefeltro, whose unforgettable broken-nosed profile portrait by Piero della Francesca has helped to make him one of the best-known Renaissance personalities. Earlier Montefeltro princes had won no special reputation either in politics or culture. For three centuries, they governed no more than a few dozen square miles in the Apennines, sometimes as feudatories of the Holy Roman Emperor, but usually owing nominal allegiance to the Pope. The soil and climate were indifferent, but because the precipitous hill villages were easily defensible, and their hardy mountaineers fought well, the rulers of Urbino remained independent, even though they never penetrated far down the alluvial valleys into the fertile coastal plain of Ancona. Federigo, who ruled from 1444 to 1482, was the greatest of the Montefeltro dynasty. He consolidated several scattered mountain fiefs and extended them into a state three times larger than his original inheritance. His duchy, which reached from San Marino in the north to beyond Gubbio in the south, was about sixty miles at its longest and broadest and included some 400 villages and 150,000 inhabitants. It maintained its independence by playing one potential enemy against another - Rome against Venice or Florence against Rome; luckily, two of the strongest Italian states, Naples and Milan, were sufficiently remote from Urbino and sufficiently threatened by Rome or Venice to be friendly.

Like many prominent contemporaries, Federigo was illegitimate and then went to Mantua, where he was taught by Vittorino da Feltre, one of the greatest educators of Renaissance Italy. Vittorino ran a boarding school where princes mixed with poor scholars were given a classical education based on Latin and mathematics, with a focus on forming character as well as mind and body. Federigo was taught frugal living, self-discipline, and a keen sense of social obligation. He became a connoisseur of literature and the arts and practiced riding, dancing, and swordsmanship - all the accomplishments Castiglione later prescribed for the perfect courtier. Religion and scholarship were equally cultivated, but philosophy was considered a guide to the art of living, and gracefulness and self-possession were instilled as training for public life. As Federigo later said, Vittorino had instructed him "in all human excellence."

Few details are known about Federigo's early life. In 1432, at the age of ten, he was knighted by the Emperor, and five years later, after returning from Mantua to Urbino, he was married, after an engagement which dated from his early childhood. A few months later, he set out for

Lombardy with 800 men to learn the art of war under a professional condottiere who was fighting against Gattamelata. Fighting was the customary occupation for most contemporary princes and especially in Urbino, where the Montefeltro family compensated for the poverty of their land and their remoteness from any significant trade routes by selling their services and their army to one side or other in most Italian wars. This was Federigo's chosen career. While his half-brother Oddantonio succeeded their father as ruler of Urbino in 1443, Federigo seemed doomed to the subordinate life of the poor, illegitimate relation. But in 1444, the young Oddantonio was assassinated and his body torn to bits by the town mob. At first, Federigo was refused entry to Urbino, but eventually he was chosen to succeed "by the voice of the people" after promising not to revenge the murder.

The chronicler who called this an election by popular acclaim was probably not exaggerating, for contemporaries unanimously praised the young Federigo, and later generations looked back on his reign as a golden age. Though any patron as generous as he could have bought adulation from that important group of writers, which handed down the verdict of history, there were no dissenting voices even among commentators who did not benefit from his generosity. Unlike many Renaissance rulers, he was magnanimous to his foes and was rewarded handsomely when they preferred to surrender rather than run the risk of ruin. He was also exceptional for never deserting his allies for gain, and he was never known to break his word, not even when urged by a papal legate. This honesty and trustworthiness were unusual in such a treacherous and brutal age. Federigo's great enemy, Sigismondo Malatesta, was more typical. Sigismondo was no less refined and tasteful a patron and was an equally fierce fighter, but his cruelties were legendary, and his dishonorable treatment of allies and his brutality toward subjects were common knowledge, as was his failure to withstand a prince like Federigo, whose people trusted him.

Because Federigo biographers (Raphael's father was the first) were concerned mainly with military exploits, there is little information about other aspects of his reign. We know, however, that he had to provide a charter of liberties at his accession. Taxes were to be reduced, some kind of public educational and medical service was promised, and the populace was granted some say in electing magistrates. It's likely we would have heard further about this charter if he had governed harshly. According to one chronicler, "revisers" were sent around the country to investigate grievances and relieve poverty, and grain from Apulia was stored away to keep prices steady when the harvest failed. Certainly Federigo was more accessible than most Renaissance rulers. Vespasiano da Bisticci described how at mealtimes the doors would be opened so that anyone might address him between courses. Furthermore, "When he rode out he met none who did not salute him and ask how he did. He went about with few attendants; none of them armed... He would often go afoot through his lands, entering now one shop and now another, and asking the workmen what their calling was, and whether they were in need of aught. So kind was he, that they all loved him as children love their parents. The country he ruled was a wondrous sight." This affability and accessibility were remarkable at a time when assassination was common. Federigo's benevolent despotism was famous throughout Italy. Where his brother was said to have burnt a page alive for some minor lapse, Federigo was merciful to all offenses save blasphemy. The few records indicate a just and human man, who prudently considered the welfare of his subjects. A ruler who was often away on campaign could not afford serious discontent at home.

An important reason for this domestic tranquility was the profits of successful war, which kept taxes low. Federigo's salary, together with the wages of his army as well as the booty they captured made the poor country rich, civilized, and content. His employers included two kings of Naples, two dukes of Milan, and three popes, and even when not fighting, he insisted on a substantial retainer fee from them. His loyalty commanded a good price, for Federigo never kept up relations with both sides simultaneously and never surrendered an allegiance until the end of his stipulated contract. His income also reflected his prestige. Less brilliant than many previous condottieri, he was nevertheless more successful in avoiding defeat, and both Castiglione and Vespasiano proudly, if mistakenly, boasted that he never lost a battle.

Federigo maintained exceptionally good discipline among his troops. In a battle, his usual technique was to be prudent in the early stages and impetuous and daring when he observed some weakness in his foe's deployment. He had lost an eye in a tournament as a young man, but otherwise he was fit and tough. People admired the mastery and modernity of his complicated siege works, his skill in carrying heavy guns through difficult mountain country, and his tested ability to endure fatigue, hunger, and wounds. Others admired his charity and the pains he took "to mitigate the horrors and miseries of war." Machiavelli derided the safety-first tactics of professional condottieri, and incorrectly asserted that not a single man was killed when Federigo fought Colleoni at Molinella in 1467. The two captains met after this battle to exchange civilities, but Machiavelli wrongly assumed that wars would be more decisive and more justifiable in the sixteenth century, when they became less humane and more destructive. Federigo had to satisfy his employers, or he would have been without a job. Wars of independence and imperialism were as real in the fifteenth century as later, even if they were smaller and less lethal.

Federigo's first regular patron was the powerful Sforza family, for whom in 1445 he helped to win Pesaro at the same time that Fossombrone was acquired for Urbino. His actions, at odds with papal ambitions, caused him to be excommunicated and also increased the hostility of the neighboring Malatesta. Sigismondo Malatesta's state and Federigo's were too close to avoid friction, and their insecurity and lack of natural frontiers led to quarrelsomeness and aggression. Between his struggles with Sigismondo, Federigo in 1448 raised an army for the Florentines, and several years later, he contracted to serve the Aragonese dynasty in Naples, an arrangement that would last almost all his life. The throne of Naples was being contested by the French Angevins, who found considerable support among the Neapolitan baronage, but in 1460, Federigo helped the Aragonese resist the invaders, and the following year, he captured the important town of Aquila.

While Federigo was preoccupied in southern Italy, a Malatesta army invaded Urbino and papal territory. The ferocious Sigismondo was "canonized to hell" by the Pope and burnt in effigy before St. Peter's, while Cardinal Nicholas of Cusa announced his excommunication for heresy, incest, the murder of his wife, and other crimes. As captain general of the Church's forces, Federigo seized this opportunity to destroy his rival's power for good and took Sigismondo's heir prisoner when the town of Fano fell after a difficult and damaging siege. But even though hostages were a legitimate and profitable asset, Federigo released him without ransom. In addition to Fano, he captured Senigallia and left only the town of Rimini for the Malatesta. Sigismondo, on his knees, publicly recanted his atheistical beliefs, and most of the Malatesta Empire was claimed by the Pope and the papal nephews. Federigo, however, was allowed some fifty townships, which made him more powerful than any other ruler throughout the Marches and the Romagna. Although still a pigmy among the giant states of Milan, Venice, and Naples, he sometimes held the balance of power in Italy.

At the time, the Papacy was trying to enforce its dominion and taxation rights over the ruling families of central Italy. Pius II had exploited the rivalry between Montefeltro and Malatesta, employing one to subdue the other, and in 1465, his successor, Paul II, in order to further extend papal power, appointed Federigo captain of the Church's forces. The condottiere from Urbino was now a famous man in Italy. In 1467, he was made commander of a league of states alarmed at the aggressive imperialism of Venice. The Venetians, retreating from the Turks on the other side of the Adriatic, were attempting to compensate for these losses by pushing their empire westward and southward in Italy, to the consternation of their neighbors and the Pope. Federigo's own state was among those threatened by both Rome and Venice, and this threat increased in direct proportion to his political success.

In 1468, Sigismondo Malatesta died, and the Pope tried to annex Rimini. Federigo, who had previously been more frightened of Venice, recognized the danger of further papal expansion. Even though he was a devout and loyal son of the Church, he could see that Venice and Rome were swallowing up the Romagna. Even more alarming, the popes were trying to conquer principalities for their sons and nephews before another family succeeded them in office. To protect himself, instead of renewing his lapsed condotta with the Pope, Federigo supported Roberto Malatesta's claims to Rimini. The ruler of Urbino, also captain of a league which included Naples and Milan, as well as other Romagnol signori, routed the papal army at Mulazzano.

Federigo's first wife, Gentile Brancaleoni, had died in 1457 leaving no children. He then married Battista, daughter of Alessandro Sforza of Pesaro. Married at thirteen, she died at twenty-five, leaving one son, many daughters, and the reputation of being an intellectual who had governed the state in her husband's absence. Federigo's half sisters had married into the neighboring dynasties of Sforza, Gonzaga, and Malatesta; two of his daughters were bestowed upon papal families, the Colonna and della Rovere, and a third upon Roberto Malatesta, the illegitimate son of his old enemy.

In 1472, the year Battista died, Lorenzo de' Medici asked Federigo to raise an army against Volterra in Tuscany. (Lorenzo was defending the mining interests of Florentine citizens against nationalization in Volterra.) The military task was easy, but after the town had surrendered, against Federigo's command, his soldiers sacked the town. Discipline in mercenary armies was always a problem, especially since loot was an inducement for enlisting recruits, but this was Federigo's part. After seizing a rare multi-lingual Bible for himself, he was triumphantly escorted to a civic banquet in Florence and given a helmet adorned by Pollaiuolo. Soon afterward, he received the Order of the Garter from England, and this emblem became a common motif in his palace. His reputation attracted special embassies not only from England and Hungary, but from Persia and Trebizond. A further triumph came in 1474, when Sixtus IV, acknowledging Urbino's independence and strength and recognizing his own need for military support for his nephews, changed Federigo's title from Count to Duke, sealing their alliance.

Federigo served Sixtus well. He tamed the

insubordinate ruler of Città di Castello in Umbria, and in 1479 he campaigned against Florence after the Pope tried and failed to assassinate Lorenzo de' Medici. Papal ambitions, however, soon became dangerous again when Sixtus began planning to conquer Ferrara for yet another nephew. Federigo wrote to the Pope, urging him to turn against the Muslims who had just won a foothold in southern Italy instead, but Sixtus was more anxious to establish his family than to oppose the Turks. As a result, war broke out over Ferrara, and Federigo aligned with Naples, Florence, Milan, Mantua, and Bologna against papal aggression, while his son-in-law, Roberto Malatesta, led the opposing papal forces. In the swamps of Ferrara, the rival commanders were stricken with malaria, and Federigo and Roberto died on the same day, September 10, 1482.

For a time, Federigo's son and successor, Guidobaldo, was able to maintain the model state of Urbino, continuing his father's lavish patronage of the arts until his failure as a general decreased the profits of war upon which the economy depended. When, in 1502, Pope Alexander VI persuaded Guidobaldo to loan the papal army his artillery, the Pope's son, Cesare Borgia, swept down on Urbino, forced Guidobaldo to flee, and appropriated his priceless art collection to pay his troops.

Perhaps Federigo would have fared no better. He

had been the last of the great condottieri, and lived at a time when defense was much easier than attack. After his death, heavy artillery became more common and more efficient, and the fortified hill towns and castles were suddenly vulnerable, spelling ruin for the small Renaissance princedoms. A decade after his death, the perennial conflicts between Italian cities and families led to an invasion of the peninsula by France and Spain, and these new nation-states would dominate the next period of European history. For three centuries, Italy was a convenient battleground for foreign armies; without Federigo to protect it, Urbino was open for predators. By 1530, Rome and Florence had been sacked in a series of invasions and counter-invasions, and the small city-states that had engendered the Renaissance were desolate. The surplus wealth used by enlightened princes to endow culture and the arts dissipated, and in this strange world, Urbino was too small and too awkwardly situated between rival empires to survive.

Federigo da Montefeltro is not remembered for his battles. He made no notable contribution to the art of war, and his dynasty and dukedom disappeared. What has survived intact is the memory of Federigo and his court of humanists and artists. He and his son were spoken of alongside the magnificent Lorenzo and shared his love of lavish display, a drive for self-expression, and a need for prestige. They were both devoted to art and learning and were far above all other contemporary rulers in character and intellectual refinement. Through them, Urbino became a center of culture which attracted men of talent and renown from all of Europe and where wealthy parents throughout Italy and other countries sent their children to be educated. Castiglione, recollecting that in his day, Federigo was "the light of Italy," described life at Urbino in his book The Courtier, in which he recorded a portrait of the model gentleman. As Vittoria Colonna wrote to him, "I do not wonder that you have depicted the perfect courtier, for you had only to hold a mirror before you, and set down what you saw there."

Books were Federigo's greatest joy, and Vespasiano described his efforts to build the library in Urbino:

We come now to consider in what high esteem the Duke held all Greek and Latin writers, sacred as well as secular. He alone had a mind to do what no one had done for 1,000 years or more; that is, to create the finest library since ancient times. He spared neither cost nor labor, and when he knew of a fine book, whether in Italy or not, he would send for it. It is now fourteen or more years since he began the library, and he always employed, in Urbino, in Florence, and in other places, thirty or forty scribes in his service... There are numerous Greek books by various authors, which when he was not able to get them otherwise, he sent for them, desiring that nothing should be wanting in any tongue which it was possible to acquire. There were to be seen Hebrew books, all that could be found in that language, beginning with the Bible, and all those who have commented upon it, Rabbi Moses and other commentators. Not only are those Hebrew books the Holy Scriptures, but also on medicine, on philosophy, and in all branches, all that could be acquired in that tongue.

His lordship having completed this worthy task at the great expense of more than 30,000 ducats, among the other excellent and praiseworthy arrangements which he made was this, that he undertook to give to each writer a title, and this he desired should be covered with crimson embellished with silver. He began, as has been noted above, with the Bible, as the foremost of all, and had it covered, as was said, with gold brocade. Then beginning with all the Doctors of the Church, he had each one covered with crimson and embellished with silver; and so with the Greek Doctors as with the Latins. As well philosophy, history, and books on medicine, and all the modern Doctors; in such a manner that there are innumerable volumes of this kind, a thing gorgeous to behold.

In this library all the books are beautiful in the highest degree, all written with the pen, not one printed, that it might not be disgraced thereby; all elegantly illuminated, and there is not one that is not written on kidskin. There is a singular thing about this library, which is not true of any other; and this is, that of all the writers, sacred as well as profane, original works as well as translations, not a single page is wanting from their works in so far as they are in themselves complete; which can not be said of any other library, all of which have portions of the works of a writer, but not all; and it is a great distinction to possess such perfection.

Vespasiano had helped to collect this library. "Some time before," he wrote, "I went to Ferrara, being at Urbino at his lordship's court, and having catalogues of all the libraries of Italy, commencing with that of the Pope, of St. Mark's at Florence, of Pavia - and I had even sent to England to obtain a catalogue of the library of the university of Oxford - I compared these with that of the Duke, and I saw that all were faulty in one particular; that they had numerous copies of the same work, but they had not all the works of one writer complete as this had; nor were there writers of every branch as in this." Virtually all the known classics were in the library, as well as Avicenna, Averroes, and medieval texts. Federigo was also a patron of contemporary literature, and Ficino, Landino, Poggio, and Piero della Francesca dedicated writings to this man the humanist Pietro Antonio Piatti eulogized as oraculum totius Italiae, the Oracle of Italy.

The Duke was a competent Latinist and also

an early enthusiast for Greek. He was able to discuss the Trojan War with Pius II and dared to contradict him about the geography of Asia Minor. He liked to have histories read aloud at mealtimes, and was especially fond of Tacitus and Caesar's Commentaries. "To return to letters," Vespasiano wrote, "the Duke of Urbino was well versed therein, not only in history and in the Holy Scriptures, but also in philosophy, which he studied many years under a distinguished teacher, Maestro Lazzaro, afterwards for his merits made Bishop of Urbino. He was instructed by Maestro Lazzaro in the Ethics of Aristotle, with and without comments, and he would also dispute over the difficult passages. He began to study logic with the keenest understanding, and he argued with the most nimble wit that was ever seen. After he had heard the Ethics many times, comprehending them so thoroughly that his teachers found him hard to cope with in disputation, he studied the Politics assiduously . . . Indeed, it may be said of him that he was the first of the Signori who took up philosophy and had knowledge of the same. He was ever careful to keep intellect and virtue to the front, and to learn some new thing every day."

With all this, the Duke was devoutly religious. He heard Mass daily and delighted in discussing religion with the abbot or mother superior of the monastic houses he had endowed. He not only knew the Scriptures well, but was familiar with the great Doctors of the early Church and possessed an extensive theological library. He developed "a strong predilection" for the works of Saint Thomas Aquinas. He was no puritan, yet despite his four illegitimate children he was a moral man and, as befitted a pupil of Vittorino, saw no dichotomy between humanist and Christian ideals.

Federigo's taste was embodied most obviously in his palace at Urbino, for to him architecture was queen of the arts and the summit of intellectual and esthetic activity. In 1468, after searching and failing to find an architect in Tuscany, he chose Luciano Laurana as chief architect. After Laurana, Francesco di Giorgio, the foremost engineer in Italy, dedicated a celebrated treatise on architecture to the Duke and thanked his employer for many technical hints about fortification. Five architects and engineers are mentioned in a surviving list of palace officers.

The same list reveals the royal scale of life in the great palace. There were 500 people in the court: in addition to knights and men-at-arms, these included 200 servants, four teachers, an astrologer, five "readers aloud at meals," four transcribers, two organists, and the keeper of the bloodhounds.

But Federgo's buildings were the most admired. He had furnished his palace, Castiglione wrote, "so well with every suitable thing that it seemed not a palace but a city in the form of a palace; and furnished it not only with what is customary such as silver vases, wall hangings of the richest cloth of gold, silk, and other like things, but for ornament he added countless ancient statues of marble and bronze, rare paintings, and musical instruments of every sort; nor did he wish to have anything there that was not most rare and excellent." Vespasiano da Bisticci was even more enthusiastic. "As to architecture it may be said that no one of his age, high or low, knew it so thoroughly. We may see, in the buildings he constructed, the grand style and the due measurement and proportion, especially in his palace, which has no superior amongst the buildings of the time, none so well considered, or so full of fine things. Though he had his architects about him, he always first realized the design and then explained the proportions and all else; indeed, to hear him discourse . . . it would seem that his chief talent lay in this art; so well he knew how to expound and carry out its principles."

Vasari also admired the spacious apartments of Urbino's palace, and its stairways, which were "more convenient and agreeable than any that had existed previously." Windows and doorways in admirable proportion, a graceful court with slender columns, a hanging garden, the great library, and room after room with splendid decorations in stucco and marble relief - all testified to the sensibility as well as the munificence of the Duke. Ambrogio da Milano and Domenico Rosselli of Pistoia were employed to design ornamental motifs on jambs, pediments, and chimney pieces, upon which the garter of England and the eagle of Montefeltro were frequently placed. Alongside his religious chapel was another chapel dedicated to the Muses, and in his study were twenty-eight portraits of famous men in world history: Homer alongside Aquinas, Ptolemy with Saint Ambrose, and Seneca with Solomon. An inscription around the interior court told how the great Federigo had raised this palace for his glory and his posterity.

In every respect, Federigo represented the best of his age, and his example endured long after his death. His practice of the teachings of Vittorino inspired a small but noble society which, even when conquered politically, made a conquest of all Europe. At Urbino could be found an intellectual elite which believed that an integrated and disciplined education would result in proper behavior and a sense of duty toward God and his fellow man. Federigo's classical upbringing and curiosity reinforced the teachings of orthodox religion. He embraced science as well as geometry and arithmetic. As for the arts, Federigo was enthusiastic about more than architecture. His musical tastes reflect contemporary Flanders, and as Vespasiano noted, "He delighted greatly in music, understanding vocal and instrumental alike, and maintained a fine choir with skilled musicians and many singing boys. He had every sort of instrument in his palace and delighted in their sound, also the most skillful players. He preferred delicate to loud instruments, caring little for trombones and the like."

Anything loud and harsh was anathema at the court of Urbino. Dress had to be sober, demeanor quiet, conversation lively but gentle. Women were given an active and respected place in this world, setting new standards for polite society. Vittorino's educational goal had been to create a well-rounded person who was courteous, upright, sensitive, but at the same time active. Federigo was such a man. He possessed a robust physique which resisted wounds and hardship, yet war left his finer feelings unimpaired. Everyone knew him to be a man of honor as well as courage. His official portraits show him as an intellectual, either reading, contemplating, listening to a lecture, or praying. Unlike many Renaissance princes, he lived without excess, "eating plain food and no sweetmeats," and the 500 people who composed his court followed an orderly, almost monastic regimen: "Here was no romping or wrangling, but everyone spoke with becoming modesty."

What we know about this court of Urbino gives us insight into the best of civilization Renaissance Italy had to offer. Although Piero della Francesca's work has partially perished, the ducal library was swallowed up by the Vatican, and Federigo's portraits were scattered to Florence, Milan, and Windsor. But time cannot erase his memory and example. Had he been more representative of his class, the course of the Renaissance might have followed a still more brilliant path.

Profile:
BEATRICE AND ISABELLA D'ESTE

Maria Bellonci

The stories of the two sisters, Beatrice and Isabella d'Este, are not easily interwoven in a single brief account, nor would either of them have relished such a thing, for they were lively with very different life spans. Of Beatrice, who died when she was twenty-two, we know only the proud and ambitious passions of adolescence. On the other hand, we know, step by step, Isabella's magisterial development from youth to maturity. They were born in Ferrara one year apart, Isabella in 1474 and Beatrice in 1475, preceding their four brothers - Alfonso, Ferrante, Ippolito, and Sigismondo.

The Este, one of the most ancient dynasties in Italy, had dominated Ferrara - a strategic area between Lombardy, Venice, and Emilia - and the broad luxuriant valley of the Po since the thirteenth century. They belonged to the Guelph party and for centuries had fought the Ghibellines in defense of the Church - and even fought the Church when the popes had meddled unduly in their affairs. These struggles had forged men who, regardless of their individual temperaments, were bold statesmen. The Ferrarese, proud to the point of arrogance and brave to the point of audacity (a Ferrarese proverb states that no man is too poor to own a dagger), never rebelled against their masters.

In 1402, Niccolò III consolidated the domain on a grand scale. He was a resolute soldier, an astute manipulator of circumstance, and a man of constructive intelligence, who founded a university and was so solicitous of the people's welfare that he stipulated in his will that the monies allocated for his own funeral should be donated instead to public charity. Variously magnanimous and cruel (he ordered his son Ugo and his second wife, Parisina, beheaded when he discovered that they were lovers), Niccolò had exceptional sons who reigned in succession after him, the first two illegitimate, the third legitimate. Leonello, a levelheaded, shrewd politician, sowed the seeds of humanism in Ferrara; Borso, also a peaceful statesman, was equally devoted to the arts. The first legitimate son to rule was Ercole, a man whose temperament was so icy that it won him the nicknames "North Wind" and "The Diamond."

In 1473, two years after he ascended the throne at the age of forty, Ercole married Leonora of Aragon, the daughter of King Ferrante of Naples, who was at the time a very powerful sovereign. The bride was naturally regal, endowed with common sense and queenly courage; she was a sensitive, warm woman in whose company even the chilly nature of her husband thawed.

Into this noble house and into a court traditionally cultivated and schooled in all the humanistic sciences, Isabella and Beatrice d'Este were born. From birth, their destinies seem both divergent and parallel. Isabella, born in May 1474, was welcomed with enthusiasm by parents, court, and populace, who saw in the blonde, softly rounded, comely infant girl, the male heir to come. Beatrice was born in June 1475, and her arrival aroused no joy whatever. For her, there were no celebrations, royal or popular, and no love except perhaps the humiliated tenderness of a mother beginning to feel marked by being "the mother of females." Both infants were given the names of queens, Isabella after her grandmother, the Queen of Naples, and Beatrice for her aunt, who was wife to Matthias Corvinus, King of Hungary. Fortunately, a year later, a son was born; Alfonso was received with noisy festivities by all Ferrara. The next year another son, Ferrante, arrived. The girl infants had been redeemed.

Ferrante was born in September 1477, in the

Neapolitan palace of the grandfather whose name he took. That year, the King married for the second time, taking the delicate, elegant Giovanna of Aragon as his wife. Summoned to pay her respects to her father and stepmother, Leonora went to Naples, with the two girls and the unborn Ferrante. The King of Naples, a dissipated man endowed with ambiguous charms and a taste for the grandiose, took an immediate fancy to Beatrice. He recognized in her the long face and heavy cheeks, the jet-black hair and eyes, and the sulky, heavy-lidded glance of the Aragon. His marriage was duly celebrated, and Leonora's second son was born shortly thereafter, whereupon she was recalled in haste to Ferrara by Duke Ercole, who smelled war in the air. She took only Isabella with her, leaving Beatrice and Ferrante in Naples, where they stayed for eight years. The little Este children played with their cousins, including Isabella of Aragon, betrothed to Gian Galeazzo Sforza, who would one day clash with Beatrice.

In her grandfather's court in Naples, Beatrice learned that pride is vital and splendid, that every gesture of King and nobles was governed by an etiquette formed equally of pomp and fantasy and that power must be deserved. Accordingly, she began to develop the patience that would serve her well when she returned to her secondary position in Ferrara. There was no doubt that the witty Isabella reigned in the Este palace; everyone adored her. No one had ever seen such an intense and vivacious feminine intelligence so smoothly adept in arranging matters to her own liking. Even Leonora was beguiled into calling her "my dearest and sweetest of daughters." Perhaps Isabella was not as beautiful as they say: She was not very tall and her features were not perfect, but she had a clear, rosy-cheeked complexion and an elegant bearing. And her intelligence was exceptional. Her teachers were stunned when she smoothly and rapidly translated a selection from Virgil's Bucolics or a letter of Cicero; she mastered Greek and Latin grammar, committed Terence and Virgil to memory, learned to perform songs and madrigals on the lute, was first in perfecting the steps of a new dance, embroidered faultlessly, and held her own in conversations with ambassadors.

The year 1480 was a year of engagements in the Este house, and it brought Isabella the worst bit of bad luck that she was to suffer in her life. In April, a marriage contract was signed between her and Francesco Gonzaga, heir of the neighboring Marquis of Mantua. Scarcely a month later, an ambassador arrived from Milan to ask for Isabella's hand on behalf of Ludovico Sforza. Il Moro, as he was called, was the guardian of his young nephew, the Duke of Milan, but in actuality, Ludovico was master of both his nephew and half of Italy. Since Duke Ercole would never offend his friend and ally the Marquis of Mantua by reneging on prior agreements, he took advantage of Il Moro's suit to marry off both his daughters. Let Isabella go to the Marquis of Mantua, and let Beatrice, who was the equal of her sister - legitimate, healthy, intelligent, and cultivated - go to Il Moro. (Alfonso d'Este, his eldest son, was already engaged to Anna Sforza, the Duke of Milan's sister.) Ludovico was not enthusiastic, and he accepted this engagement with perceptible disappointment.

Happily, a fresh and unusual relationship developed between Isabella and Francesco. The girl's innocent and touching charm surprised and beguiled her fiancé, a vigorous and already experienced fifteen-year-old youth, and made him fall in love with her. But between Beatrice and Ludovico there was nothing of this sort. Il Moro, the first man in all Italy, and one of the richest, scarcely remembered the dark-haired girl, twenty-five years younger than he, who awaited him in Ferrara. On the contrary, he was flaunting his passion for the beautiful, exquisitely mannered Cecilia Gallerani, the unofficial queen of Milan.

In February of 1490, ten years after her engagement, sixteen-year-old Isabella went to the castle in Mantua, transported in the triumphal carriage designed by Ercole de' Roberti with her elegant trousseau. She was followed by her father, mother, sister, her three brothers, a band of Este relatives, and the acclamations of 17,000 spectators. Isabella was going to a youthful court, since her delightful parents-in-law, Federigo and Margherita, who so warmly wanted her in their family, had died young. Her husband was twenty-five, his two brothers twenty-one and sixteen. Her new eighteen-year-old sister-in-law was Elisabetta Gonzaga, the wife of Guidobaldo, Duke of Urbino.

That February, the gloomiest, foggiest month of the year in Mantua, was a period of acquisition for Isabella, confirmed by a whole series of new possessions beginning with her husband. She came into both title and power, rising to the demands of her role with a sparkling glance and lightness of step that lent wings to her sixteen years. Isabella realized that her marriage allied two reigning political families, and she responded to her husband's passion like a woman who appreciates being warmly involved in marriage without being swept away or losing her own identity. Her young husband, one of the ugliest and most fascinating men in Italy, was a brave soldier, the complete gentleman, a graceful and entertaining conversationalist, a lover of gentle sensuality - and so delightfully ingenuous as to have his humanists compose poems that he sent to his literary-minded wife as his own. He, too, was overcome with admiration for Isabella, but this admiration, which grew greater by day, was destined to alter in kind. Francesco Gonzaga scarcely realized it, but he began to lose confidence in this wife who while obedient to his smallest wish, always seemed to protect her own independence. Yet she was so loyal, so adroit in sensing whatever could benefit the little Mantuan state and the Gonzaga family, that it was difficult to reproach her. The new Marchioness of Mantua was clearly the pride of the city, and her praises were sung throughout Italy.

In Ferrara, Beatrice was awaiting her husband. She should have married immediately after her sister, but Ludovico II Moro was bound to Cecilia Gallerani and was unconcerned about joining his betrothed. But Ercole d'Este was not a man to accept even a small affront, and he allowed his irritation to reach Ludovico's ear. Il Moro, knowing that he needed Ferrara to protect Lombardy against its centuries-old enemy, the Republic of Venice, and pressured by the marriage pact between his niece Anna and the Este heir apparent, finally made a decision. He threw the gates of the Lombard palaces wide, opened the coffers of his treasury, and set in motion the mighty machinery of the Milanese court, teeming with artists, poets, mathematicians, scholars, and a spirited nobility well disposed toward any courtly enterprise. The wedding date was set for January 1491 at the castle in Pavia. Messengers began arriving in Ferrara from Milan, bearing gifts, like the famous necklace of pearls strung with flowerets of gold and embellished with splendid drops of rubies, pearls, and emeralds; the masters of ceremonies came to arrange for the bride's journey - and to recommend that Beatrice bring many embroidered and jeweled gowns; artists came, like Gian Cristoforo Romano, sculptor and engraver, accomplished lute player, and a man of wide literary attainments, who did the bust of Beatrice that is now preserved in the Louvre.

With an intent, childish frown, Beatrice prepared herself for her unknown future and scarcely noticed the fearsome and memorable trip, as the ice-encrusted bucentaurs passed between the snowy banks of the canals. They finally arrived in a Pavia blanketed in snow, but inside the castle everything exuded warmth, wealth, and ease. Ludovico led his bride and her entourage through the princely dwelling, judged the most sumptuous in the world. At the last, he showed them its greatest treasure, the library begun by Gian Galeazzo Visconti, rich in illuminated volumes and Greek and Latin manuscripts that Sforza had had copied in the most remote sanctuaries where they were preserved. In the face of all this splendor, Beatrice appeared reserved, which everyone interpreted as timidity. In any case, she had no time to recover her self-possession after the January 17 wedding, for the next morning Il Moro left for Milan, to arrange for the celebrations on which a legion of artists, captained by Leonardo da Vinci and Bramante from Urbino, were assigned to work. Yet how could one forget that Cecilia Gallerani was living there in the castle?

Eventually, the entire company moved on to Milan, and the spectacle - the imaginatively staged tournaments, elegant dances, theatricals, masquerades, concerts of rare music, and fantasies of every kind – were extraordinary. In a magnificent show in which she was the heroine, the bride was surrounded by energy, grandeur, verve, intelligence, and beauty. She could, it seemed, even be sure of her husband once she realized that her youth attracted him and led him to fondle her, and charmed him into kissing her before everyone. Her olive-toned, girlish face flushed with happiness, and everything she did expressed her joy in having been called to so full a life. Before her startled mother and sister, Beatrice let go; this was her moment, and it was as if she cut herself off from all else in a drive to seize it.

Once back in Mantua, Isabella kept informed of what was going on in Milan. The daily accounts told of a whirl of amusements, including a morning Beatrice, Galeazzo di Sanseverino, and Diodato the jester set out in a carriage, singing three-part songs. They fished, they lunched, they played ball and fished again, and returned home in the evening deliciously exhausted. Beatrice quickly won the upper hand over her husband, and though she did not succeed in dislodging Cecilia Gallerani from the castle, she did manage to break off, officially at least, that lady's relationship with Il Moro. In 1491, Cecilia married Count Bergamini, shortly after she gave birth to a son by Ludovico.

Beatrice never tired of thinking up masquerades, jokes, or expeditions, with herself and her ladies dressed like commoners and spoiling for a squabble. His wife's exploits were irresistibly amusing to Il Moro, who laughed and applauded the girl. In Milan, Beatrice had found her cousin again - that Isabella of Aragon with whom she had played at the court in Naples some years before. From the day Beatrice arrived, she conceded first place in the city to Isabella, acknowledging the unchallengeable primacy of her position as wife of the actual Duke, Gian Galeazzo Sforza. However, Isabella of Aragon's spirit, courage, and exquisite refinement were insufficient to support her husband, given his weaknesses. The young Duke of Milan appeared to combine the vices of his Visconti and Sforza forebears, and the resulting syphilis destroyed both his physical and intellectual capacities. Isabella calmly assessed her present and her future. The desire for power she had recognized in Gian Galeazzo's uncle and guardian was now increased by Beatrice's youthful passions, and the moment was propitious for the ambitious couple. The French King, Charles VIII, was planning to invade the kingdom of Naples; the Borgia Pope, Alexander VI, was unable to dissuade him; and Il Moro favored the foreigners' coming, calculating that he could be free once and for all of the Aragons, who were the natural protectors of

Isabella and her children. Without a thought for her doting grandfather, King Ferrante, Beatrice ardently abetted her husband. When Beatrice's first son Massimiliano was born in January 1493 and royal celebrations were held in his honor, the unfortunate Duchess Isabella of Aragon wept.

But her protests accomplished nothing. Late in 1494, Charles VIII was received with a whirlwind of festivities by Ludovico and Beatrice, who dazzled the King, even though his French followers maliciously evaluated her and observed that "the husk is worth more than the kernel." At Pavia, the tragic discussion between Isabella of Aragon and the French King took place, in which Isabella fell to her knees before him in tears. With a vague promise of protection for the Sforza children, Charles VIII left. While the French King was on his way to conquer Naples, the ailing Gian Galeazzo succumbed to tuberculosis, and Ludovico quickly had himself proclaimed master of Milan by his fellow citizens. Shortly thereafter, Emperor Maximilian granted to Il Moro and his heirs the title to the dukedom, disregarding Gian Galeazzo's son. Beatrice, now crowned Duchess of Milan, was applauded and glorified by all, overshadowing the downfall of her sister, Isabella of Aragon.

But the Italian states quickly realized that the French King was not a guest to be taken into the house so casually, and they hastened to repair the damage done. Even Milan joined the established league of Venice, Mantua, the Pope, and other principalities, for Il Moro had come to see that foreign invasions were most dangerous for him, since Charles made no secret of his wish to annex the duchy of Milan, which he claimed by right of inheritance. The armies gathered, and to avoid being captured in the kingdom he had just conquered, Charles VIII withdrew rapidly up the peninsula, and at Fornovo di Taro met the allied armies in a battle from which he managed to escape and to return to France. Italy rejoiced in her recovered liberty, and in Mantua, Isabella rejoiced to see her husband, Marquis Francesco Gonzaga, captain general of the league, the hero of Italy's liberation.

As the characters of the Este sisters became more differentiated, a rivalry unfolded. It was in no sense petty, for both were women of noble spirit and bound by family loyalties, but it was perceptible, nevertheless. Beatrice's accent on luxury was loud. Everyone found her eighty-four new dresses, heavily embroidered with gold thread, jewels, and pearls, excessive; they hung in a great room that, as her mother, Leonora, observed resembled a "sacristy hung with all the canonicals." Too many rooms were too full of silver, ivories, precious glass, paintings, perfumes, lutes, clavichords, in quantities sufficient to "fill all the shops." Her inconsiderate way of treating people about her, her cruel little games (she used to terrify ladies in waiting by pretending to set her horses upon them at an unbridled gallop), were her way of vindicating her humiliated adolescence. When Isabella realized that the festivities and gifts that awaited her in Milan were intended to oppress her, she found excuses to accept no further invitations. The immense wealth and magnificence of the Sforza court allowed Beatrice to surround herself with men like Bramante and Leonardo; she made her presence felt even in politics, and could engage in well-informed arguments with heads of state.

Another source of bitterness for Isabella was their relative maternal status. In the Sforza household were two sons, Ercole and Francesco; in the Gonzaga household there were two daughters, Eleonora and Margherita. When Beatrice sent her congratulations on the birth of Eleonora, there was a hint of self-satisfaction in her including the greetings of her little son to the newborn girl. Isabella was so infuriated that when she bore her second daughter, she insisted that the infant be removed from the sumptuous cradle which had been prepared for a boy. But Beatrice's life story hung by the thread of fortune that created it. Around 1495, Il Moro fell in love with a lady of the court, Lucrezia Crivelli and refused to give her up. With her feelings and pride wounded, Beatrice, pregnant for the third time, pretended to see nothing and hid her pain. On January 2, 1497, she held a ball in her apartments, with the whole court present. Toward evening she was taken ill and was carried to her bedchamber; at two o'clock that morning, she gave birth to a stillborn son, and within an hour and a half, she died.

The chronicles of Italy were filled with accounts of Ludovico's grief, his repentant self-reproaches, his passionate lamentings, of the funeral at Santa Maria delle Grazie in the midst of thousands of flaming torches and wax tapers and of the final appearance of Beatrice robed in gold upon her bier. The suddenness of the misfortune had moved everyone, and her twenty-two years, consumed with intensity and fervor had, it seemed, upheld not only the fortunes of the Sforza family but also the destiny of the duchy. From the moment she died, the future of Milan began to cloud; the French invasions soon followed, with the fall of the Sforza and the imprisonment of Ludovico, who died in exile in the castle of Loches.

Isabella's sorrow was genuine but controlled. Having shed her tears, she kept in close touch with her brother-in-law, feeling for II Moro - powerful and superstitious, fanciful and realistic, indecisive and stubborn as he was - the attraction that strong, clear-headed women feel for men who are weak and full of contradictions. She recovered quickly from her grief, for she had to ward off the perils presented by the French flanking her to the north, Cesare Borgia threatening from the south, papal interventions, and the bitter hostility of the Venetians. With disdainful patience, she endured a family tie with the Borgia when, in 1501, Lucrezia married her brother Alfonso d'Este, the widower of Anna Sforza, and came to reign in Ferrara as its Duchess.

To Cesare Borgia she sent masks, perfumes, and compliments to hold him at bay; at the same time, she rejoiced when the troops of Faenza successfully withstood the Borgia forces. Her concept of domestic policy was that the people take the prince's cause as their own by making their cause his. This was the traditional Este idea of good government, and Isabella translated it into a series of sustained, sensitive political moves. All Mantua acknowledged the efficacy of Isabella's policies during her regency in 1509, a period when the League of Cambrai united Europe in an alliance against the excessive power of Venice. Unfortunately, Francesco Gonzaga, commander for the league, was taken prisoner while he was sleeping, much to the anger and disgust of his allies. Though the little Mantuan state faced a grave danger then, Isabella demonstrated her courage by calling the people together, offering her young son for the public's acclamation, and forbidding the garrisons of the fortresses bordering Venice to open their gates even were the Venetians to lead Marquis Francesco to the foot of the glacis and murder him before their eyes.

And so Francesco Gonzaga, languishing and ill in Venetian prisons, waited to be liberated, while, in Mantua, Isabella played her skillful hand. Caught in a vise between venomous foes and suspicious friends, she succeeded in keeping the Mantuan frontier free not only of enemy assaults but also of allied garrisons. But because she had governed too well and ably, she found in 1512, when the war ended, that she had lost the love of her husband. Shortly after his return from prison, Francesco Gonzaga wrote her in these words: "We are ashamed that it is our fate to have as wife a woman who is always ruled by her head." Not intimidated, Isabella replied with icy pride: "Your Excellency is indebted to me as never husband was to wife; nor must Your Excellency think that, even did you love and honor me more than any person in the world, you could repay my good faith." Day after day, she watched as her husband became increasingly alienated. When she sensed that she had fallen from power, she protested not in words but in action. She traveled, and one of her destinations was Rome.

Isabella arrived in Rome like a reigning sovereign who was securely established in her own kingdom. No one suspected her real situation. In the splendid papal court of Leo X, surrounded by continuous acclamation, amid the banquets and theatricals and the penetrating, brilliant talk, no one guessed her true isolation. She was buoyed by her taste for experimentation, and the thought of her children helped her - the sons, at least, who must be guided toward great futures. (She cared little about her daughters - at least at this time. When two of them, Ippolita and Paola, entered a convent, she did not weep, but declared herself content, since this son-in-law would cause her no trouble.) Her sons, Federigo, Ercole, and Ferrante, were educated and watched over with daily, unremitting attention. The first was destined to the throne, the second to the Church, the third to the army. But Federigo was clearly her favorite; her affection for him was the consummate expression of her maternal love, her pride, and even a kind of hope in the future. This explains how she managed to separate from the husband who had stripped her of all authority, for she knew that in Federigo she had a future, and in that she planned her own vindication. When Francesco Gongaza died in 1519, Isabella's tears paid tribute only to the memories of her youth. Since her son was far away in France, the one urgent and essential thing for her to do was to rule.

It was 1519, Isabella was forty-four, and to reign was natural. "She trusts no one and will know the motive of everyone," observed the Mantuans, who were content to have power exercised by a woman of her matriarchal nobility.

Federigo, the nineteen-year-old Marquis, was at first overwhelmed by his mother and lived in a state of admiring subjugation, with little more than the occasional restiveness of an unruly colt. She governed well; she maintained a difficult equilibrium among the great powers that divided Italy, and she was the first to foresee that Charles V would prevail over the French King, Francis I. But Federigo presently discovered that his life was partitioned into two roles: the submissive son and an independent, effective man. It was only natural that the second seemed the good and true self, even more so since he had the support of a young and extremely beautiful woman. The young Marquis was so in love with Isabella Boschetti, called La bella Boschetta, that he refused to marry to ensure the continuity of the dynasty. The young woman fueled Federigo's idea of his total independence, and he responded by surrounding her with costly and magnificent gifts, courtiers, artists, and literary figures, while he slyly and imperceptibly eliminated his mother from direct participation in the government. He asked her advice, but privately, Isabella was relegated to the role of an elderly woman.

No moment in her life had been as serious as this, and once again, she bided her time, waiting for her son's mistress to fall from favor. Bitterly, Isabella was coming to recognize that her beloved Federigo was a weak man - and worse. "The Marquis of Mantua is not good for much," Guicciardini wrote with terse accuracy in 1527, when Federigo and the Duke of Urbino opened the way by their betrayal for the German mercenaries to march south to sack the city of Rome.

Isabella d'Este had returned to Rome in 1525 and shared in the final days of the tempered, cultivated, Christian paganism that would be shattered by the brutal impact of the Lutheran gangs from Frundsberg. Rome had received her gloriously in the time of Leo X, and now, under another Medici, Clement VII, it welcomed her again. Again Isabella stood firm in her loyalty to Mantua and to the Gonzaga who had so often betrayed her. Thanks to her modulated tactics, she succeeded in securing the red hat for her second son, Ercole, only a few days before the dreadful pillage of the city began. Meanwhile, Federigo was writing her from Mantua. He had seen the imperial hordes first hand and found them crude, fanatical, blasphemous, and innately hostile to the soil and civilization of Italy. He begged his mother to return to Mantua, but his pleas suggested a strengthening of her position that might restore her to an ascendancy over her son far above La Boschetta. And then the terrible day, May 6, 1527, arrived. From within Palazzo Colonna, where she was securely housed, she heard the mercenaries howling through the streets, bent on robbing, killing, and torturing. Isabella remained steadfast; she took in gentlewomen, princes, ambassadors, priests, and friars who were seeking shelter; she encouraged them, shared her meager food with them, and with them trembled and hoped. Only when they were out of danger did she leave the ravaged city and make her way northward to Mantua. Inspired by her courage, the populace was for her and against La Boschetta. Gradually, La Boschetta had to give in, retreat, and remove herself, allowing Federigo to marry Princess Margherita Paleologa - the wife chosen for him by Isabella.

Margherita was gentle, sensible, and in love. She had just the right amount of native shrewdness, and as her dowry, she brought the entire region of Monferrato. She bore her husband numerous sons, gave him constant, discreet support, and got along well with her mother-in-law, who placed full confidence in her. Federigo's political future was a limited one, subject as it was to the will of Charles V, but within his large and splendid court, he was active, buying painting and sculpture, building extensively with Giulio Romano, quarreling with Pietro Aretino. He behaved courteously and affectionately toward the mother to whom he owed so much, but he persisted in keeping her isolated. Her spirit was truly tried, but her response was a gesture generous to the point of scorn: In effect, she offered to be his accomplice against her own interests, helping him to conceal her humiliation so that no one could suspect him of an unworthy action.

The futures of the other sons had been secured. Ferrante, the future Viceroy of Milan, would become a good general. Ercole would be a great cardinal, a major figure at the Council of Trent, and would come very near to wearing the triple crown. When his elder brother died at barely forty years of age, leaving an infant heir, Ercole would assume the regency of the duchy of Mantua and perform his duties with the prudence, the severity, and the awareness of his mother.

Although no one needed Isabella now, as she moved into her sixtieth year, she was stronger and more animated than ever, always ready and eager to go to the heart of a problem. Every respect and consideration were paid her, and her court was crowded with literary figures, courtiers, and beautiful and witty young women whom she formed and trained in her own school, allowing them freedom but insisting that they be virtuous. In her new apartments on the ground floor of the ducal palace, she collected the noblest and finest creations that her age was producing. The famous rooms, the Studiolo and the Grotta with the celebrated door by Tullio Lombardo, were the talk of all the courts of Italy. Poems, songs, travel memoirs, writings of every description, flowed into Mantua from all over to satisfy her ever lively curiosity. Nor did the luxuries diminish - the gowns, jewels, perfumes, cosmetics, adornments, and extraordinary objects like the doll "dressed inside and out exactly like her [Isabella]," which Francis I requested and received to send to his wife in France. But, above all this, Isabella's inner life was fortified by a secret. This secret was called Solarolo.

Solarolo was a tiny possession in Romagna that belonged to her. This was all Isabella needed. She received secretaries as if they were ministers; she directed and adjudicated and enforced her own methods of management with affectionate ease, fulfilling her nature and finally giving expression to the passion for ruling that could have made her a magnificent queen. As she listened to her secretaries' reports, with the maps of Solarolo spread before her and surrounded by her collections of paintings, marbles, ancient and modern bronzes, her crystal and her alabaster and her ornate clocks, she was expressing her personality fully.

Most rare Phoenix, the humanists called her, reviving the worn image to honor her - but more than that, a most rare woman. Yet why does posterity remember her? In both her marriage and her maternity, she was sorely disappointed; emotionally, she led a wintry life. She has survived thanks to her individuality, to the self-awareness that she sustained with force and conviction fashioned by her mind: the effective alliance of idea and action, and it characterized Isabella's life until her death on February 13, 1539. It is impossible to say whether Beatrice would have developed in the same way, had she lived to the same age. But both these princesses had understood one thing - the necessity of living according to an inner order while responding to the external world.

8
THE SPREAD OF THE RENAISSANCE

In the autumn of 1511, Erasmus, the most distinguished scholar of Northern Europe, took up his lodgings again in Queens' College, Cambridge - a cold, bleak room that overlooked the marshes. He was poor, frightened of the plague that raged about the University, and lonely. He had been swept to England by the tide of the Italian Renaissance, not for the first, but for the third time. For five wearisome years, Erasmus moldered in Cambridge until he could no longer stand the poverty and the ignorance and set off on his journeys again, to the Netherlands, to Switzerland, to Germany, always carrying the memory of those years in Italy when he had discovered himself. The new learning had filled him with such hope that not even the hardships of his personal life could eradicate it. In 1517, he could still write, "Immortal God, what a world I see dawning! Why can I not grow young again?" Erasmus was not unique. In London, the gifted yet wayward Florentine sculptor Pietro Torrigiano was modeling, under the soaring Gothic arches of Westminster Abbey, the first Renaissance tombs of Northern Europe, built to immortalize Henry VII and his wife, Elizabeth of York. For decades, the currents created by such cataclysmic events as the invasion of Italy by the French kings as well as the excitement of the new learning had been drawing men like Erasmus and Torrigiano into or out of Italy. And that sense of wonder, of a new world and a new dawn of the spirit, touched less sensitive men than Erasmus. When Edward IV conferred the Garter, the highest order of English chivalry, on the Duke of Urbino, the court of Windsor witnessed the embassy of Castiglione who came to receive it for his master. Henry VII respected Italian scholarship so deeply that he asked Polydore Vergil to write what became the first serious and dispassionate study of England's history. Indeed, Erasmus's presence in England was due entirely to a devoted band of humanists in Padua, Florence, and Rome, who had studied Greek and sought to understand the old, as well as the new philosophies. Their attitude was deeply Christian, and they struggled to perfect their theology through an exacting analysis of the early Fathers. The band of humanists, with

Lord Mountjoy as its patron and John Fisher as its chaplain, were intimately connected with the English royal family. What was true of England was also true of the Netherlands, of Germany, and of Spain.

As the Renaissance spread beyond the Alps, it was curbed in Italy. In 1495, Charles VIII invaded Naples and unleashed thirty years of carnage. Battle after battle in the Lombard plain eroded wealth, disrupted trade, and escalated taxes, destroying conditions conducive to art and learning. Furthermore, the riches of the New World poured into Spain, the Netherlands, France, and England, but not into Italy, and with the wealth, the art followed. And then came Martin Luther, who in 1517 hammered his Protestant theses to the church door of Wittenberg. To hold off the Reformation, the Papacy needed a stronger hand, and with it, brought the luxurious and wanton times of the Borgia and Medici to an end, and replaced the self-indulgence of Renaissance Rome with a militant asceticism. The venerable Michelangelo became a relic of the age of heroes, a symbol of a time that had passed.

By 1500, Italy's hypnotic influence drew the artists of the outer world to its city-states. Although the Flemish painters felt little or no sense of inferiority when confronted with the brilliance of the Italian achievement, the same was not true of the French and German artists, who had been entranced by the books of engravings of Italian pictures that began to circulate after 1470. Albrecht Dürer, a young apprentice at Nuremberg, somehow acquired engravings of Pollaiuolo and Mantegna. He had already begun, albeit in a tentative, schoolboyish, and rather shocked manner, to draw from the nude, but these engravings released his spirit from the harsh, moral, and cruelly realistic treatment of naked women that had become traditional in Gothic Germany. Still, the secret of the Italian painters seemed to elude him, and he believed that the formula for painting the human figure, like some ancient mystery, was kept hidden by Italian artists. Once in Italy, he sought the magic formula and improved his technique, but the Gothic tradition held him in thrall. Yet without his Italian experiences and his preoccupation with Italian art, his achievement would not have been as distinguished. Scores of artists over the next 400 years came to Italy on a pilgrimage to discover the source of their art. The painting of El Greco is indelibly stamped with the years that he spent in Venice. The way he draws, the glittering light that runs along the edge of his figures, derives from Tintoretto, as his color does from Titian. The two greatest French artists of the seventeenth century - Nicolas Poussin and Claude Lorrain - spent most of their working lives in Rome. Titian's color, atmosphere, even his figures - entranced

Poussin. Again and again, artists paint the same themes - sometimes even copy the same pictures - that the artists of the Renaissance first conceived and executed. Anyone who aspired to greatness in painting needed to make the long journey to Italy. Some went in great comfort under the patronage of the rich, others went on foot and in poverty, painting for their bread. Until the twentieth century, the traditions created by the Italian Renaissance were those in which all Western European artists worked.

During their invasions of Italy, the French kings and their courtiers were delighted by what they saw in Milan and Venice. On the other hand, the austere and more classical buildings of Florence left them unmoved. At first, Italian influences on the new luxurious hunting lodges the French nobility were building along the Loire combined the basic plan of a traditional medieval castle with the sophisticated elevation and comfort of an Italian palace. For a time this marriage of the old and the new satisfied Western Europe, but in the end, no matter how much inspiration might twist and turn within its national traditions, it was drawn back, time and time again, to the purity of classical achievement. In the visual arts, the achievements of the Italian Renaissance permeated Europe like an indelible stain. They had the dreams and aspirations and realities of a world in which men wished to live.

The arts of the Renaissance were not the only achievements that took root throughout the countries of the Western world. Changes that occurred in Italy generations earlier were happening in Western Europe in the sixteenth century, with the result that a similar society grew up with similar needs. Like Italy, it was mercantile and urban, ambivalent toward the old feudal nobilities; it longed for their grace, their courtliness, and their sense of privileged destiny, yet hated their special rights, their selfish independence that cut so savagely across the needs of society as a whole to the detriment of trade and profit. The new men longed for professional government, for a powerful person who could secure order and infuse civilization into a barbarous and anarchic society. For this political knowledge, they looked to Italy: There the wisdom of the classical world had been sifted and refined and adjusted to modern necessities. Even more importantly, the University of Padua could teach them the secrets of Roman government through the study of its laws. The Italians had made a profession of diplomacy in fifteenth-century Europe that had come to be regarded as essential to good government as statistical analysis is in the twentieth. Men in London, Paris, Brussels, and Madrid and in the towns and states of Germany thought they could only manage their new societies if they had studied in Italy. Most of Henry VIII's ministers of state - Thomas Wolsey, Thomas More, and Thomas Cromwell - were fascinated by the new learning and encouraged scholarship whenever they could. Wolsey endowed Christ Church, Oxford, in order to establish the study of the new humanities in England. Thomas More became the life-long friend of Erasmus. Cromwell lent his rare and precious Italian books to his friends and encouraged young men such as Thomas Starkey, who had spent years studying civil law at Padua. This interest in Italian learning had its practical aspects, but it captivated them all - even Cromwell, that hammer of the monasteries - at a deeper level.

This new learning seemed to hold the secrets of life itself for most of them and, for the more sensitive, some of the secrets of eternity. More and his friends were deeply religious men. So were Lefèvre d'Étaples and his colleagues in Paris, as were Ulrich von Hutten and Johann Reuchlin in Germany. They reverenced Italian scholarship, for it took them, via a knowledge of Greek, to the purest texts of the New Testament. Here, they felt, they would find a faith cleansed from the impurities created by centuries of comment and explanation. By applying the new skills which the Italian humanists had perfected, they hoped to lay bare Christianity in its purest and most historical form and thereby strengthen the Church. Before Renaissance influence had touched Northwestern Europe, there had been a strong revival of religious mysticism, put into literary and devotional form by Thomas à Kempis in his Imitation of Christ. This mysticism stressed the importance of the individual's direct relation with God, and, correspondingly, lessened the importance of the priesthood and the Church. The search for historical truth became linked with this religious search for truth and became the seeding ground of Protestantism.

No one typifies the link between Italian humanism and reformed Christianity more than Erasmus, who prepared the ground for Luther. A sensitive, illegitimate son of a priest, half tricked into monastic life, Erasmus concentrated on friendship with scholars of like tastes. As a man of formidable intellect and exquisite literary gifts, his reputation was built not only by personal contact and letters, but also by the invention of the printing press. His sharp satire - The Praise of Folly - exploited the sensationalism only the press can give, and his Latin translation of the Greek Testament rapidly established his reputation as a scholar. For Erasmus, the institutions of the Church were encrusted with silliness, stupidity, and barbarity, and Christian faith could never regain its pristine clarity until this dross was cleared away. Yet he was no revolutionary Protestant, and he quickly retreated from the direction Luther, with his furious denunciations and rash actions, seemed to be dragging him. He refused to listen to Albrecht Dürer's plea: "O Erasmus of Rotterdam, where wilt thou tarry? . . . Hear, Christian knight, ride forth with the Lord Jesus... defend the right, obtain the martyr's crown!" Scared of the new age he had once welcomed with joy, he preferred to die in his bed. But for Dürer, the reformation of religion was an inspiration deeper than any experience of his life, even more so than his artistic experience in Italy.

By their sharp attack on contemporary religious practices, the scholars and critics had undermined the institutions of the Church. They mocked priests, bred resentment against papal taxation, and held the popes up to the ridicule many deserved. Although some drew back, others prepared to go forward with Luther, feeling that he was leading them to the rebirth of Christianity as Christ preached it. So the spirit of the Italian Renaissance, once it crossed the Alps, was diverted into new channels, plunging from the broad, sunlit meadows of secular delights into the dark ravines of religion.

Yet in the early part of the sixteenth century, this political and religious twist to Italian influence was largely confined to England, the Netherlands, and Germany. In France, there were some men who were deeply concerned with theology, deeply distrustful of scholasticism, and ardent for pure religion, but they were not typical of French society. French society was more sophisticated, more secure, readier to pursue the language of personal expression that lies at the heart of the Italian Renaissance. Much of Italian civilization had entranced Philippe de Comines and other noble Frenchman, but it was Francis I who really fell in love with all things Italian even though the greatest humiliation of his career - his defeat by the Emperor Charles V - took place at Pavia. He was the first prince outside Italy to collect paintings and sculpture by the great Italian masters. He persuaded Leonardo da Vinci to spend his last years at Amboise, close to his great hunting lodges, and did everything he could to entice Michelangelo to live in France. Benvenuto Cellini was more successful. Francis tolerated his extravagance and forgave his bad temper in exchange for the embellishments with which he adorned his châteaux.

Francis I was not merely a collector. He wanted his court to outshine in literature and in manners, as well as in art, and he flung his cloak of patronage on everyone who might bring distinction to his country. He was aided by his sister, Marguerite of Navarre, one of the most outstanding women of the Renaissance. She wrote the Heptameron, a bawdy collection of stories, a mystical tract called The Mirror of the Sinful Soul, and a number of outstanding spiritual hymns. She corresponded with Erasmus, befriended Protestants, was accused as a heretic by the Sorbonne, and patronized François Rabelais. Her court contained a world of letters as complex and strange as her temperament. Indeed, many of the contradictions in her own self-expression reflected the contradictions of French artistic and intellectual society as it struggled to assimilate the achievements of Italy. For Italian humanists, discovery lay in the art and history of their ancestors or their country's ancestors, the Greeks. With Frenchmen and with Englishmen, discovery also meant new worlds that knew neither Christianity nor Christian government nor Christian morality. To men such as Rabelais, Michel de Montaigne, Christopher Marlowe, Shakespeare, or Francis Bacon, insecurity, anxiety, and elation mingled haphazardly and fused into art. Reverence for the past, a yearning for tradition, alternated with the intoxicating sense of human capacity, the uniqueness of experience, and the splendor and freshness of the world.

In Rabelais, the greatest writer of the French Renaissance, this conflict was apparent both in his restless, troubled life and in his writings. Like Erasmus, he was a rebel monk who hated the ignorance and immorality of monastic life and sought truth in the world. "Abandon yourself," he wrote, "to Nature's truths, and let nothing in this world be unknown to you." Rabelais's pursuits led him to study alchemy, astrology, and the mysterious exoticism which seemed to offer new truth in the intellectual chaos of sixteenth-century Europe. His work Gargantua and Pantagruel is as odd and as moving as his quest for self-knowledge. Gargantua, Pantagruel, and Grangousier, the chief characters of his extraordinary fantasy, are gross representatives of the instinctive life, yet full of satire and wisdom, capable of nobility and understanding. Above all, they seek life and truth. The turmoil and confusion of real life is stilled by the contemplation of realized ideals; men and women achieve the noble life. The book is written in a fabulous style, by a man drunk with words. This mixture of barbarity and civility, of satire and sincerity, entranced the French court. The Church might be scandalized, the Protestants outraged, but Pantagruelism became the fashion of the aristocracy. It was original, in tune with the medley and confusion of contemporary life, and, above all, it was French.

As soon as a literary renaissance began to flourish in France or in England or in Spain, a strong nationalist sentiment infused it, and the delight that writers and artists took in the Italian achievement led not only to emulation but to envy. In 1549, Joachim du Bellay, in his pamphlet La Defense et illustration de la langue française, exhorted Frenchmen to challenge the triumphs of antiquity in their own language, and the court circle that patronized Rabelais took his words as a battle cry. Du Bellay and his friend Pierre de Ronsard and their group, La Pléiade, too, were preoccupied with the loneliness of men and their dependence on love and affection to save them from unbearable solitude. In Marguerite of Navarre, Ronsard, Rabelais, du Bellay, and the rest, the court of Francis I possessed a galaxy of talent that would have been a credit to any Italian court. Owing enormous debt to the Italian Renaissance, they nevertheless achieved a style, an idiom, and a theme that were distinctly French.

The same was true of the literature written in England shortly afterward. Plots, characters, and entire plays were lifted wholesale from Italian authors. Yet there was no plagiarism: Everything was Anglicized. Like Rabelais, the Elizabethans grew drunk on the discovery of their language. At the same time, they were even less confined by tradition than the French, and their sense of achievement was far sharper, for the English were closer to barbarity and anarchy than their neighbors across the Channel. The Wars of the Roses had ripped apart the fabric of English life. The violent class turmoil of the early Tudor period that followed, which had led men of affairs to seek guidance in politics and diplomacy in Italy, had begun to settle into a new pattern in which gentlemen - but not noblemen - predominated. The break with the Church, combined with increasing knowledge of the worlds beyond Europe, intensified this sense of a new age. Yet the dissolution of the past created anxiety, insecurity, a sense of isolation, and a longing to return to the familiar. The dramatists who held up a looking glass to this society in conflict discovered that the violence and passion of their age was more acceptable to their audiences if they were cast in

Italy, in ancient Rome, or in their own historic past. The crimes in the Duchess of Malfi or the White Devil possessed a further dimension of evil and horror if set in the criminal splendor of an Italian court where incest, riot, poison, and murder were, everyone believed, commonplaces of life. As well as stimulating the poetic imagination, however, Italy and its Renaissance still possessed a serious purpose for Englishmen. Long after politicians had given up expecting to find the secrets of their craft there, and long after dramatists had exhausted the plots of its authors, Italy continued to exert the deepest influence.

As important as the influence of the Italian Renaissance was on art and literature and learning, it was greater still in education. This education possessed two aspects - one for the narrow circle of intellectually creative men, the other for the world at large. How far the intellectual skepticism of the Renaissance, with its search for truth in reality rather than in dogma and authority, stimulated the growth of a rational attitude to the world is difficult to know. Certainly without the greater stimuli of the discovery of the world beyond Europe and the achievements of science in the seventeenth century, it might easily have come to naught. However, to belittle the importance of those first cracks made in fifteenth-century Italy in the all-embracing dome of dogma is to falsify history. Ideologies would continue to rage in human hearts and haunt their destiny, but never again could there be two opposed worlds of Christians and heretics.

Italy, with Flanders, had been the first country in Europe to grow rich on commerce, to build a middle class that could challenge the economic, political, and social power of the aristocracy. These merchants, bankers, craftsmen, found their first security in the economic life they knew and controlled, so they centered their political and social life around their economic activity and ignored as far as they could the structure of the world surrounding them. But the pressure of their wealth and the needs of their professions forced them into contact (and at times into conflict) with the aristocracy, whose sources of wealth, invigorated by the rise of commerce, remained large enough to maintain their privileged place in society. In the end, a link was formed between the aristocracy and the middle class: They remained distinct but joined by common paths, and this mingling wrought a profound change in social customs, in manners, in education, and in the images that seemed socially valuable. In its search for standards, Italy could look where the Flemish could not - into its highly sophisticated past, to the days of Rome and Greece when life had also been urban, rich, and aristocratic, yet commercially minded. Although antiquity could provide some ingredients, it could not provide all, and the merchants' hunger to belong drove them to accept many of the concepts of feudal aristocracy.

By 1530 or so, however, the Italian ideal of a gentleman was neither classical nor feudal, neither noble nor bourgeois, neither rural nor urban, but a fusion of all of these. This image acquired such intensity because Western Europe had begun to undergo the same sort of violent social revolution that Italy had undergone between 1300 and 1450. In the sixteenth century, the commercial wealth that poured into Cadiz, Lisbon, Bordeaux, Nantes, London, Antwerp, and Hamburg raced through the veins of rural society, erupting, creating, destroying. The new men of this age - socially insecure - had to learn to be gentlemen, to move easily in the aristocratic world which they could not or would not eradicate. They adopted Italian clothes and Italian manners and educated their children according to Italian precepts. A knowledge of Latin and Greek became a necessity, and a gentleman also required "breeding" - those aristocratic airs, that easy nonchalance, that assumption of privileged position lightly borne. A taste in the visual arts was as essential a part of breeding as sitting a horse. As Europe assimilated its immense wealth, and society became more ordered, the image of a gentleman became more tenacious. It represented the triumph of the aristocracy at the expense of the middle class, whose own merits came to be regarded as either boorish or comic, from which the young not only wished to escape but were encouraged to do. This is why the possession of land achieved such sanctity in Western Europe - it was the way to salvation, the route by which a merchant's children might become gentlemen and gentlewomen. Excluded from true social power, hypnotized by the snobbery and sophistication of aristocratic life to which the Italian Renaissance had given such vivid definition, the merchant classes of Europe lost much of their dynamic and creative energy, and it took nearly two centuries of frustration before they challenged the aristocratic foundations of European society.

During this period from the Reformation to the French Revolution, the spirit of the Italian Renaissance pervaded Europe. It taught the rough and very raw provincial aristocracies of the West how to move easily through a world of bourgeois delights, without being contaminated by it. While it intensified snobbery, further defined social classes, and checked the scientific imagination by focusing on character rather than aptitude, it taught the new men of Europe that the purpose of art and the call of learning, were essential parts of the use of wealth. Its central theme - the uniqueness of personal experience, the idea of men and women caught in the jaws of time - gave rise to the world's greatest art and literature. The spirit of the Italian Renaissance broods over these centuries, which link the age of feudalism to modern times, and makes them a part of itself.

Chairwoman, CEO, and Publisher
Donna Carpenter LeBaron

Chief Financial Officer
Cindy Butler Sammons

Managing Editors
Molly Jones and C. David Sammons

Art Director
Matthew Pollock

Senior Editors
Hank Gilman, Ronald Henkoff, Ruth Hlavacek, Paul Keegan, Larry Martz, Ken Otterbourg

Associate Editors
Betty Bruner, Sherrie Moran, Val Pendergrast, Susan Peyton

President Emeritus
Helen Rees

Chairwoman Emeritus
Juanita C. Sammons

Printed in Great Britain
by Amazon